If Salt Has
Memory

To all those who write
to combat oppression

If Salt Has Memory
Jewish Writing in Exile

Edited by
Jennifer Langer

Five Leaves Publications
www.fiveleaves.co.uk

If Salt Has Memory
Edited by Jennifer Langer

Published in 2008 by Five Leaves Publications,
PO Box 8786, Nottingham NG1 9AW
info@fiveleaves.co.uk
www.fiveleaves.co.uk

ISBN: 978 1 905512 36 2

Cover image: traditional
Jewish-Ethopian embroidery,
artist unknown

The title "If Salt Has Memory" is taken, with thanks,
from Mois Benarroch's poem "Again in front of the sea".

Five Leaves acknowledges financial assistance
from Arts Council England

Five Leaves is a member of Inpress, representing independent
publishers (www.inpressbooks.co.uk)

Design and typesetting by Four Sheets Design and Print
Printed in Great Britain

And the bits and pieces of the dreams/will they get
    back together some day?
Together again/bits and pieces?
Are they telling us to weave them into the fabric
    of the dream?
Are they telling us to dream better?

From Note XII*
Juan Gelman

---

*from Unthinkable Tenderness, edited and translated
by Joan Lindgren (University of California Press, 1997)

Contents

Introduction

This is an anthology of literature by contemporary Jewish writers in exile who were forced to flee or felt compelled to leave their countries of origin. This seemingly straightforward statement is fraught with ambiguity and complexity in relation to the words "Jewish", "exile" and even "countries of origin".The countries of origin of the exiled writers are Argentina, Bosnia, Chile, Croatia, Cuba, Egypt, Ethiopia, Hungary, Iran, Iraq, Israel, Libya, Mexico, Morocco, Poland, Serbia, Slovakia, South Africa, Tunisia, Turkey, Uruguay, Yemen and Zimbabwe and their countries of exile are Australia, Canada, England, France, Germany, Israel, Mexico and the USA. Some writers are well-known in the UK while others are published in their countries of origin or areas sharing the same language and, although established writers, may not be widely translated into English. It delights me to bring the work of these writers to the attention of the reader.

Identity is a problematic issue frequently involving the intersection of identities, with Albert Memmi, for example, asserting three — Jewish, Tunisian and French. It is evident that Jewish identity itself is a complex area. Jewishness can include all or some of religious, racial, ethnic, cultural, linguistic, historical or national identities permeated by the internalised collective cultural memory of wandering and dislocation. In addition, a tension in terms of identity and belonging is evident in the work of some Jewish writers. A memory of loss and the historical experience of persecution are paradigms for Jewish identity. I did not ask the writers to identify the nature of their Jewishness or stipulate that the work had to contain "Jewish" content or references because I felt that it was sufficient that the writer had identified him/herself as Jewish, whatever the nature of that identity. One writer declined to contribute as she did not perceive herself as a

"Jewish" writer and commented that she tended to resist ethnic and other classifications. Nevertheless, Jewish identity is frequently not a matter of choice but is imposed by the "outsider". In fact, not all the collection is set in a Jewish context or contains Jewish aspects. This included work by some of the writers living in Israel because, presumably, their Jewishness is an intrinsic part of their Israeli nationality and does not have to be examined and analysed given that they live in a Jewish state. Likewise, David Albahari's almost existentialist, post-modernist short story in this anthology does not contain so-called Jewish content although his novels, *Bait* and *Götz and Meyer* do have a Jewish focus. The latter is set over the course of a few months in 1942 when the Nazis systematically exterminated the majority of Serbia's Jews using carbon monoxide and specially designed trucks. In the novel *Bait* the narrator is listening to a series of tapes he recorded of his mother who had died several years before in Serbia. He reflects on her life and their relationship, attempting to come to terms with his Jewishness and his own new life in a foreign culture. Ariel Dorfman's poetry focuses on the links with his country, news of comrades arrested and in hiding and on guilt and powerlessness in exile. Bart Wolffe is desperately concerned about the plight of the people of Zimbabwe, and the suppression of free speech and human rights. He also writes about the pain of internal and external exile. Naim Kattan's short story focuses on a relationship with a Chinese neighbour in Montreal.

My original assumption was that all the writers would have fled because of persecution and danger to their lives. However, this had to be challenged as the anthology progressed because of the complexity and diversity of reasons for leaving the country of origin. Many of the writers were persecuted because of their Jewish identity in the context of the oppression of Jewish communities in a range of countries such as Yemen, Iraq, Iran, Libya, Morocco and Ethiopia. In most cases this was stimulated and in others

10

exacerbated by events connected with Israel such as the 1948 War of Independence, the founding of the State of Israel or the Six Days War alongside the rise in Arab nationalism.

Other writers were persecuted, not because of their Jewish identity, but because of their left-wing, socialist, trade unionist views — writers and political activists from Latin America such as Juan Gelman and Alicia Partnoy from Argentina, and Ariel Dorfman exiled from Chile since the military coup in 1973. I have included Mauricio Rosencof's work in the anthology although he still lives in Uruguay because he has compared his thirteen year imprisonment, eleven of which were in solitary confinement (for being leader of the Tupamaros) to exile and, when released, living in a new political climate because of regime change. During the military rule in Argentina there were more than 3000 Jewish victims. Alicia Partnoy 'detained' in the "Little School" in Buenos Aires makes the point that although one of the guards had discovered her Jewishness, she realised this was the first time the subject had been raised. "I heard you're a Jew, is that right?" "Yes sir." "Okay. If you don't behave we're going to make soap out of you, understand?" However, the narrator is sceptical about this. "Chiche's warning didn't frighten me, maybe because I'm convinced that at the Little School there isn't sufficient technology to make soap out of anybody. Perhaps I didn't take him seriously because I already knew I could be killed at any moment." Her mother, Raquel Partnoy makes the crucial point that generally if the victim was a Jew the cruelty of the soldiers and the torturers was intensified. In addition, there is evidence that in many cases Jews were detained solely because of their origin, due to the Nazi and anti-Semitic ideology of the perpetrators. In some detention camps the guards displayed swastikas and painted them on the prisoners' backs.

Bosnians, such as the philosopher and writer, Predrag Finci, left because of the 1992-1995 war which included the siege of Sarajevo causing immense suffering for all the inhabitants. The Sarajevo Jewish organisation 'La Bene-volencija' was instrumental in helping members of all communities regardless of ethnic and religious back-ground and organised convoys to help thousands of people to escape. The poet George Szirtes, then a child, and the writer and journalist, Matyas Sarkozi, were amongst the quarter of a million who left Hungary in 1956 when the Hungarian Revolution was suppressed by Soviet troops. Gillian Slovo was sent to exile in England with her grand-mother and sisters because of the danger to the family given that her parents, Ruth First and Joe Slovo, were eminent, targeted anti-apartheid activists. Bart Wolffe, the Zimbabwean playwright and journalist, left Zimbabwe recently because of the total lack of freedom of expression under Mugabe so that continuing as an artist was intoler-able and dangerous. The banning of all independent newspapers and the jamming of radio stations such as SW Radio Africa from London by the ruling ZANU PF cur-tailed his freedom to continue to make a living as a writer and free thinker. Ruth Knafo-Setton left Morocco because her parents were concerned about disturbing trends in the growing Arab nationalist movement and wanted to give their children a future of possibility and freedom.

Other writers left their countries of origin because of multiple factors, which in some cases included anti-Semitism. This was experienced by Ilan Stavans in Mexico and took many forms being perpetrated by the political establishment including the president and his staff, the left-wing intelligentsia, the Church, folklore, and the masses. Vesna Domany Hardy from Croatia left because at the beginning of the seventies nationalisms "started rising their ugly heads". In one such instance she was told by a colleague that as a Jew she had no right to teach the Croatian language in Croatia and that "she should pack up and go to her Judea". The factor that unsettled her most was that her colleagues kept silent without protesting. This led to the realisation that despite her disapproval of the then authorities in many aspects, the alternative to them was "the murderous knife". She therefore made the decision to leave, not wanting to risk her child/children living in a country where "one's origins would perpetually be questioned, and would always serve as a reason for persecution". David Albahari left Belgrade for Canada because he needed space to write as an individual unfettered by a nationalist agenda. He abstains from speaking out and taking sides on controversial political issues, a decision he made in the former Yugoslavia where under the communist system writers were seen as dangerous enemies of the state. He has said "Art is what we go back to when everything is over." Moris Farhi fled from Turkey, aged nineteen, because of anti-Semitism, some of which was imagined projections from the Varlik Tax years, and from the oppressive political climate where freedom of expression was suppressed. However, he retrospectively constructs this as running away from himself. Ruth Behar, who fled with her parents from Cuba to the USA, explains "My parents decided to leave in 1961, after the rest of our family and most of the Jewish community left, when properties and businesses were expropriated by the government. Although my parents owned nothing, they chose to leave because their world crumbled all around them." Benjamin Black considered Israel his home but felt forced to flee because he was a pacifist who had evaded conscription and would be imprisoned in Israel. The pain of living in exile is palpable in his writing. Shelley Weiner states that leaving South Africa was a combination of revulsion for the apartheid system and a need to find a place for herself.

The focus of the anthology is not that of the Holocaust, but inevitably the collective memory of this dark past continues to affect the work of writers from a range of countries. Matyas Sarkozi writes about a childhood experience during the German occupation, and the impact and traces of the Holocaust are ever present in the work of Henryk Grynberg who left Poland in 1967 because of the

Gomulka purges, and of Ladislav Grosman who left Czechoslovakia following the Soviet occupation in 1968. There is also the nexus of the effects of the Holocaust and recent oppressions. In his paper "Versions and Perversions of the Holocaust in Latin America" (2001), Ilan Stavans states that the the two major events that have coloured his life are that of repression as a Jew, and that of repression as a Latin American. Mauricio Rosencof's text "The Letters that Never Came" links the cruelty of the Holocaust to that of the Uruguayan military and the resistance of Hitler's victims to his own. Predrag Finci evokes collective memories connecting the contemporary Jewish community's escape from Sarajevo to the Jewish community fleeing during the Second World War. During the German occupation of Tunisia, Albert Memmi was interned in a labour camp from which he later escaped. Tunisia was the only Arab country to come under direct German occupation during World War II. However in his autobiography, *Farewell Babylon*, Naim Kattan describes the *Farhoud*, the 1941 pogrom against the Iraqi Jewish community, which involved Nazi-sympathetic Iraqi army elements against the pro-British Prime Minister, Nuri Said Pasha.

Many of the writers fled to Israel but can Israel be considered as exile given that Israel is considered the Jewish Homeland for the ingathering of the exiles? The notion of a Jewish state was proposed by Herzl and had its origins in the Polish and Russian Ashkenzi communites who were the victims of anti-Jewish actions in these countries. It could be suggested that the Sephardi and Mizrahi communities' stance towards Israel diverged from that of the Ashkenazi groups with the former's connection being more of a religious one.

The poetry of the Moroccan born poets, Erez Bitton and Mois Benarroch and the prose of Samir Naqqash, suggest the complexity of their space as Israelis and as Mizrahim perceived as "the other". Interestingly, Nancy Berg's book on Israeli writers from Iraq is entitled *Exile from Exile* because, in her view "The move to Israel from Iraq is an end to the national state of exile and the beginning of a personal exile from one's homeland. The imposition of the national paradigm on the individual experience results in ambivalence and confusion." Once in Israel, Iraqi writers and others had to confront settlement and identity issues and struggles as well as culture shock, given the hierarchy privileging Ashkenazi status, culture and history so that to a certain extent, the notion of the ingathering of the exiles was subverted for these writers. Although Iraqi Jewish writers have made a major contribution to Israeli literature, until recently the Ashkenazi literary establishment was not interested in Mizrahi literature. *The Transit Camp* (1964) by Shimon Ballas, *Equal and More Equal* (1974) by Sami Michael and Eli Amir's novel, *Scapegoat* (1984), and others, constitute the subgenre *sifrut hama'abarah* — literature of the transit camp. Living in *Ma'abarot* was the demeaning, demoralising experience of Iraqi Jews when they first arrived in Israel.

Avraham Adgah articulates the desperation of Ethiopian Jews to reach Israel, given that they possessed a religious, mythical yearning. However on arrival they experienced trauma because of the imposed separation of family members and over time felt alienated and "exiled" in spite of Israel's efforts to integrate them into a modern Israeli lifestyle. Ethiopian Jews have experienced discrimination and racism although some young Israeli Ethiopians are developing a new sub-culture of Afro-Israeli identity. The community grievances include a perceived national disinterest in preserving Ethiopian-Jewish culture and history and in familiarising Israelis with it — although the Ethiopian festival of *Sigd*, commemorating the giving of the Torah and ancient communal gatherings in Jerusalem, is now beginning to be celebrated by some non-Ethiopian Israelis. There is also bitter resentment of the collective aspersions cast on Ethiopian immigrants because of the original denial by rabbis of their Jewishness and because donations to Israel's national blood bank were routinely thrown away because of government concerns about possible transmission of AIDS.

Language can be another issue for writers who left their countries for exile. David Albahari writes in Serbian but lives in Canada where two of his thirteen books have been translated into English. His stories are now set in Canada. He has however, strong ties with the former community of writers in Belgrade where he is a well-known literary figure and where he continues to be published. Samir Naqqash, the novelist, continued to write in Arabic unlike other Iraqi Jewish writers who transferred to Hebrew. For him writing in Hebrew equated the denial of his roots and his past as he rejected the adoption of a different identity and a new society. The use of Arabic served as a link to his past and his childhood, while maintaining his self-identity. In *Keys to the Garden*, Naqqash said in an interview with Ammiel Alcalay "… I cannot come to terms with this society… I reside here, but I don't feel within my spirit that I live here."

It is not surprising that the narrative of many exiled writers focuses on the representation of memory with writing having a particular role in the creation and maintenance of individual and collective memory. The exile lives in a space between the alien host land and the familiar homeland, a realm of the imaginary. Memory in the life of the exile maintains a tenuous balance between homesickness and amnesia about the past. For exiled writers personal and cultural memory becomes a creative means of exorcising the trauma of loss of homeland.

Both nostalgia, mourning for loss of the past, and trauma are articulated through the literature.

Nostalgia derived from the Greek *nostos* for return home and *algia* for pain, is evident in much of the work included with nostalgia representing an idealised past. In Freud's work on nostalgia, melancholia, and forgetting, he argues that melancholics and nostalgics suffer from the irreparable gulf between past and present. However, I would suggest that nostalgia is a response to the pain of exile and helps the exile negotiate his or her identity in exile. André Aciman deduces that he can never be whole in exile in spite of being indifferent to his place of origin because "Part of me… never came with me. It never took the ship. It simply got left behind." A poem by Juan Gelman is entitled "My Beloved Buenos Aires" but nostalgia is complex and can be lived vicariously as in Henryk Grynberg's story about his "uncle": "Perhaps he imagined that I was returning in his place. To the place of his youth. And that I would be him there. A guard, guarding memory." However, at the end of his short story "Imaginary Childhood", Shimon Ballas expresses his doubts about representations of childhood memory in the form of nostalgia: "They are stories, a faded shadow, or a polished reflection of an imaginary experience. I do not put great trust in childhood stories, just as I do not put great trust in dream stories."

The present situation i.e. the identity of the exile, influences the construction of the past in the present and the subject can be seen to identify with what s/he has lost while in so doing creating loss as an irretrievable identity. While Mauricio Rosencof is held in isolation under the military junta in Uruguay, he takes refuge in the world of memory, composing another letter that never came — a letter to his father that embodies his own quest for identity. Gillian Slovo also uses the construct of memory in an attempt to define her individual identity. The narratives are defined by non-linear processes of remembering and forgetting, characterised by repetition, rearrangement, revision and rejection. New memories are thus constantly constructed, deconstructed and reconstructed by narrative strategies incorporating representations of time and space.

Cultural mystical roots are important for writers such as Ruth Knafo Setton and Erez Bitton who focus on Moroccan Jewish folklore, saints and mystics, particularly Suleika. *The Road to Fez*, a novel by Knafo Setton is a love story interwoven with that of Suleika, a 19th century

Jewish martyr revered by both Arabs and Jews. Knafo Setton has explained that she was attracted to Suleika because in the Fez Jewish cemetery she saw Muslim and Jewish women weeping and praying at her tomb, lighting candles, and offering her couscous and lucky *hamsas*. In saint hierarchy, she is too minor (too female) to have her own *hiloula* (anniversary of the death of famous rabbis and scholars often celebrated by popular pilgrimages and rejoicing). Prayers to Suleika are devoted to areas such as pregnancy, birth, miscarriage, illness in the family and menstrual cramps. Although she was executed in 1834, at the age of seventeen, for refusing to renounce her faith, contemporary women sense her *baraka*, the mystical ability to transcend borders imposed by humans.

The traumatic pain of exile is articulated in a range of narratives. Bart Wolffe has written: "When I first left Zimbabwe, I realised that it was necessary to 'go blind' into the no-man's land of the future, leaving everything I cherished without even feeling. Feeling would have prohibited me from making the journey. I threw myself into survival mode but the backlash came some months later when I found myself weeping and powerless in Golders Green, actually Temple Fortune, where I was staying. Not a single tree nor bird spoke my language. These touchstones, my talismans of identity, simply did not exist any longer. As Uspensky, the Russian expressed, when a man loses his references, he goes insane. I became voiceless, despite trying to maintain a journal, keep a diary, that is, as a means to tracing something of who and what I was. It was rape. Change at a personal level is no easy thing, despite change being often the call of art."

Traumatic memory is articulated in some of the work. However, memory is affected by the trauma which is a psychological wound that may have been repressed in the unconscious although a deferred reaction might have occurred. Trauma may cause narrative to be fractured and disjointed. Juan Gelman's unbearable pain at the loss of his son and daughter-in-law amongst "the disappeared" of

18

Argentina is reflected in his poetry. Other narratives describe perilous, traumatic journeys to exile, including Avraham Adgah-Israel who travelled from his Ethiopian village to reach Israel and Gina Waldman who escaped from Libya with her family.

Some fear is attributable to the writer inhabiting a conflicted space where Jews were a minority group in the country of origin. Farideh Goldin articulates the fear of Jews in Iran when Muslims commemorated the death of Imam Ali on special days each year. In his diary *All Waiting to be Hanged*, Max Sawdayee writes about the horrors of everyday life in Baghdad under the Ba'ath regime. Roya Hakakian states that Jews were forced to leave Iran because of the 1979 revolution and a fundamentalist anti-western Islamic regime intolerant of those who did not share its ideology. "Jahuds go home" was the graffiti written on the wall opposite Hakakian's home in revolutionary Tehran in 1978.

Albert Memmi, the Tunisian born Jewish writer exiled in France, contests the claim made by many Jews from Arab lands that they lived in idyllic harmony with their neighbours under Arab rule and asserts that fear of Arab Muslims in the country of origin was part of the Arab Jew's historical experience. Nevertheless he states that to a great extent, Jews and Arabs shared languages, traditions and cultures. Historically, Jews were classified as *dhimmis*, that is, a person living in a Muslim state who was a member of an officially tolerated religion. *Dhimmis* had to pay *jizyah*, a poll tax and were subject to restrictions with the extent of these imposed limitations varying according to country. Roya Hakakian states that Iran was not an anti-Semitic nation given that there had been two thousand years of a history of co-existence between Jews and their Persian neighbours. "Our neighbours prayed for our safe passage, and marked our departure by throwing water behind us for good luck." The impression gained is that in a range of countries Jewish and Muslim communities generally had

19

good relationships on a personal level in spite of sporadic pogroms. This is expressed by Erez Bitton in "Moroccan Wedding":

"Arabs and Jews, Come in! Slowly our hearts expand and our souls rejoice."

However, in a public context and sometimes in a personal context, relations deteriorated after the founding of the State of Israel.

Writers who left their country at a young age excavate and retrieve memory that they themselves did not experience — the fragments and narratives of their relatives — in order to reconstruct identity so that it inevitably becomes a hybrid, more complex identity. For poet Ronny Someck, whose parents emigrated to Israel in 1953 when he was two, a seminal moment in his artistic development occurred in 1991, as he watched bombs falling on Baghdad on television during the first Gulf War. He later wrote "Baghdad February 1991", a poem reflecting on his infancy in Iraq and he has tried to imagine and relive the Baghdad past in several of his poems. Only his grandfather followed Baghdad life styles. Someck has commented "He spoke broken Hebrew and 'took' me to the café near the River Tigris where they played the music of Egyptian singer Um Kulthum and served black coffee. As for me Baghdad turned into a metaphor, into a place that existed only in my grandfather's house." Roya Hakakian, George Szirtes and Erez Bitton have all been compelled to search for their roots and histories although they left their countries of origin as children.

In the text, "From the Other Bank" by André Aciman, the issue of space and exile for Jews is examined and problematised. "*Neither this nor that*. You are, as one who has experienced exile or displacement, just provisionally here, provisionally somewhere, provisionally someone. ...Jews have no permanent address. They have nomadic roots. They have many homelands. It is exile that is their home." Many of the writers have complex roots and identities and their parents or grandparents may have fled from or left a previous country for the country of origin. Juan Gelman from Argentina, now in exile in Mexico, has Ukrainian ancestry and spoke Russian and Yiddish at home. Gelman once stated that "the only real Jewish writers are those who wrote or write in Yiddish or Hebrew." However since he is unable to write in these languages, he wrote his poetic work "Dibaxu" in Ladino thus creating the linguistic possibility of a "return to origins". He therefore destabilises fixed notions of identity. Shelley Weiner's Lithuanian parents dispossessed and incarcerated by the Nazis, survived and managed to find a relative who brought them to South Africa in 1948. Mauricio Rosencof's roots are Polish. In his memoir *The Letters that Never Came* (which moved me to tears), the reader discovers that the remainder of the family still lived in Poland and "The Letters that Never Came" are those that ceased arriving in Uruguay from Poland because the family had been deported to concentration camps by the Nazis. Alicia Partnoy's grandparents were Russian-Jewish immigrants who escaped Czarist persecution and settled in Argentina in 1913, shortly before World War I. These roots frequently impact on the writers' work.

Some of the literature by women exiled writers addresses issues of gender oppression and the traditional roles women were expected to play in the Jewish context and also in the wider Muslim context, in terms of the lack of women's power outside their assigned roles. This is articulated by Bracha Serri, Farideh Goldin, Roya Hakakian, Gina Nahai and Ruth Knafo Setton. Autobiographical narrative is deployed by some of the women writers with the notion of autobiography perceived as resistance to dominant narratives which are usually male. In some Middle Eastern countries, Jewish women could be perceived as doubly oppressed outsiders — as Jews and as women. In addition, within the Jewish community women existed in a world defined and dominated by men as Gina Nahai explains "I saw a hierarchy of pain *within* the Jewish Iranian society itself — generations of women gripped by an eternal sense of loss that transcended class and family". In her novel *Moonlight on the Avenue of Faith* written in the genre of magical realism, the women of the family are the main focus, with the intergenerational legacies transmitted through a matriarchal genealogy in the form of Shusha the Beautiful's tear jar. Nahai's narrative gives a voice to her female ancestors whose lives were lived in the ghettos shrouded by chadors. I would suggest that Gina Nahai writes in the genre of magical realism in order that the women can be liberated by magic from the cycle of repeated patterns of oppression. In addition this genre also acts as a "veil", a layer to protect her from writing openly which was not customary in Iranian literature, particularly for women.

This anthology is a contribution to the corpus of literature of exile as well as to literature by Jewish writers. I was tempted to include work by Hélène Cixous and Jacques Derrida, both from Algeria, but felt that this anthology would not do justice to the enormous range and depth of work they have produced. However, I could not resist including a quote from "My Algeriance" by Cixous: "Neither France, nor Germany, nor Algeria. No regrets. It is good fortune. Freedom, an inconvenient, intolerable freedom, a freedom that obliges one to let go, to rise above, to beat one's wings. To weave a flying carpet. I felt perfectly at home, nowhere."

Through the diverse work in the anthology, we see the immense complexity and diversity of roots and origins with ambivalence articulated in the relationship with the ever elusive homeland. In addition, a number of writers engage with the painful processes of adapting to exile and of confronting the alienation experienced in the new host country.

I should like to express my sincere thanks to all the writers whose literary work is so enriching both emotionally and cognitively.

Jennifer Langer

References

Alcalay, Ammiel, *Keys to the Garden: New Israeli Writing*, 1996, City Lights Books

Berg, **Nancy**, *Exile from Exile: Israeli Writers from Iraq*, 1996, State University of New York Press

Cixous, Hélène, "My Algeriance", *Stigmata: Escaping Texts*, 1998, Routledge

Partnoy, Alicia, *The Little School*, 1985, Cleis Press

André Aciman

From the Other Bank

One day I asked my grandmother, who spoke more languages than five generations of my descendants ever will, what language she spoke at home. We spoke Spanish, she said. A misnomer — because what she called Spanish is really Judeo-Spanish, generally referred to now as Ladino. In Constantinople, where she was born, she spoke Turkish with street vendors, Greek with the maid and cook, Yiddish with her nanny — and she went to an Italian nun's school, where she mastered something I will never master in any language: the correct use of the imperfect subjunctive. Indirectly she also got to learn her catechism — I call it "her catechism" because she had literally incorporated all of it, the way every good Catholic is supposed to learn his or her religion. She never forgot it.

When I finally got to ask her one day with whom, then, did she speak French, her answer was: at home. *Chez nous. À la maison.* But how could she be speaking French *chez nous* when her mother did not know more than 100 words of French and her father didn't know a single one?! Where was *chez nous*?

Facts of course are immaterial. There was simply a *perception* that they spoke French, that French was natural. That French existed *à la maison*. And that perception alone made all the difference in the world.

How my grandmother learned French is not a secret — it is a mystery. She picked it up. But she picked it up not the way she picked up Greek, in the kitchen, or for that matter Turkish, in the street. There was something ceremonial in French, something which did not exist in Greek, Turkish, Spanish, or Italian. She spoke it with her sisters or relatives not because the *mot juste* is a French institution — the *mot juste* as far they were concerned would have existed in Spanish, not French — but because, if they spoke French, they wanted those within earshot to *know* they were speaking French. The nearest example is the Russian romance with French. You spoke French to give an impression. You spoke French to give yourself an impression.

My grandparents spoke two languages with their children: an affective language, the language of the heart — Spanish; and the language of substance (the language of the mind, Descartes would be pleased to know) — French.

Had they plotted the course of their lives the way their life trajectory was probably intended, they would have at some point gone to French university or chosen to live their lives in France or established life-long economic links to France. By my parents' generation, everyone had relatives in France; and this would have seemed quite natural: at home, they spoke French first and foremost; they went to French schools; they counted in French; they thought in French; quarreled in French; corresponded in French; made love in French.

That I speak French, or, greater irony, that I ended up teaching French literature; or that the language I speak with my children is not English, which I know best, but French; or the fact that many who, like me, came from Alexandria, Egypt and today live in the U.S. send their children to a French *lycée*; all this merely says — to quote Nietzsche, a German philosopher, quoting Stendhal, a French writer who opted to live in Italy by adopting a German pen name — that French represented a promise of bliss, *une promesse de bonheur*. All this not because I, and many like me, love France — which I do — but because speaking French is what one does when one is with family.

To put it differently, for my ancestors French was a ticket out — out of the Ottoman Empire, out of poverty, out of the ways of the Third World. And into the West, the modern West. They spoke French; ergo, they were Westerners.

What I wanted to show in my 1994 book, *Out of Egypt*, when I stressed the inordinate importance placed by older members of my family on such things as correct table manners, proper posture, proper etiquette, or proper grammar, was not just that most members of my family wanted to give the impression they had always moved in educated affluent circles; but also that they were not like their immediate neighbours in the Middle East, that they were not even like other (Middle Eastern) Jews; they were French-speaking Jews. They already had a foot out the door of the Middle East and in the door somewhere else, which they hoped — dreamed — would be France.

But they were not French.

Most of them had never seen France, some would become French and never see France, some would never even find the France they came looking for. For the real France, of course, had absolutely nothing to do with the land each Jew in Turkey or later in Alexandria had become an imaginary citizen of: a sort of fairy-tale France made up of Jean Cocteau, Jean Gabin, and Maurice Chevalier, a France they didn't find when they eventually got to France, but one they would manage to "remember" many years later because it continued to linger in their imagination, the way unfulfilled dreams may endure for years and finally seem real in retrospect.

These in fact were Jews who always sought a ticket out. It wasn't that they didn't like where they lived, or that they didn't want to plant roots, or that they loved France so much — or any other country, for that matter — but that they loved having the option to leave. They were transient Jews, diaspora Jews. Everything they owned was conveyable, transportable. Many Sephardic families even claim to have retained the keys to their ancestral houses in Toledo, which they were forced to leave over five centuries ago.

You're tempted to think that the key is nothing but a mere symbol of the house; actually, it's what you're able to carry with you while you're escaping that matters more in the end. You can lose everything. It's remembering that counts. For if there's one thing I hate, it's extinction — not just the extinction of people, but the extinction of time, the extinction of memory.

They came to Egypt as settlers, but they were settlers with exit visas, in Egypt, in Turkey (where they had lived before Egypt), in Greece, in Spain, in Portugal, all the way back to the day when one Jew, crossing the Red Sea, waved hello to another Jew on his way to Egypt. It is in their history, in their genes! In fact, the word for Hebrew is originally *ibhri*, meaning "he who came from across (the river)." You refer to yourself not as a person from a place; but from a place across from that place. You are — and always are — from somewhere else.

The problem with being a settler with an exit visa is that you're never quite out of where you're in, nor are you firmly in when you're thinking of getting out of the place you're in! I've phrased the previous sentence as cumbersomely as possible to give a flavour of the paradox with which ambivalent people live, people I classify under the genus of *homo duplex*.

None of this is very new to Sephardic Jews. Sephardic Jews have a tradition of being Marranos, Jews who were forced to convert or who converted for political gain. Though they were Christians outside, inside they continued, despite all sorts of dangers, to practice Judaism in secret, sometimes a warped sort of Judaism called crypto-Judaism. The other name for them is *alborayco*, which comes from al-Burak, Mohammed's steed, which was neither horse nor mule, neither male nor female. As a Christian priest tells my father in my book: "Poor Jews, you're citizens nowhere and traitors everywhere, even to yourselves. And don't make that face, your own prophets said it, not me."

An *alborayco* is in fact neither fish nor fowl, neither here nor there. Neither in nor out.

Neither this nor that. You are, as one who has experienced exile or displacement, just provisionally here, provisionally

27

somewhere, provisionally someone. Which is almost the same thing as being a permanent alien, except that you are not permanently a permanent alien. A permanent alien who becomes naturalised essentially acquires something new, something better. But I am talking about individuals who are permanently provisional guests. A provisional guest is neither staying nor leaving; he is — to use a mood I find more congenial — conditionally here. He could leave at any moment, but, then, he might stay longer than anyone expected.

Jews have no permanent address. They have nomadic roots. They have many homelands. It is exile that is their home.

I speak about provisional beings because my ancestors were already provisional dwellers in Spain, in Turkey, and in Egypt. You did not live out of a suitcase, but you definitely kept your suitcases. Even after being in the US for fifteen years, when it became sort of obvious we weren't going anywhere else, my parents still kept a few suitcases which took up an enormous amount of space in one of the closets. Some, I remember now, bore the characteristic stickers of famous pre-World War One resort hotels in the south of France. The suitcases were sturdy and had been passed down through generations of relatives.

Had I asked, their answer would have been: "You just never know." I never asked because I knew and totally accepted their answer. We knew of only one way to be: provisional. It did not make us bad citizens in Egypt; Egyptian Jews were probably the wealthiest Mediterranean Jews outside of France and many were philanthropically inclined. Some also built palatial homes. But as all this was going on, none was averse to considering a second home elsewhere, investments elsewhere. Other citizenships.

Being provisional does not mean that you are quick to pick up danger signals. A provisional being, as irony would have it, is the last to pick up and go. He spends so much time worrying about the worst, so much time rehearsing the pain as a way of inuring himself to it, that, when the worst comes around he is immune to it, he doesn't *see* it. He has been practising fire drills too often to think disaster is really waiting around the corner. Surely the building won't burn down.

Alexandria has the longest hours in the world, my grandmother says in my book. But, as a reviewer in the *Times* of London was very quick to note, "time was running out."

We simply waited, the way Jews did elsewhere when it was already too late to wait for miracles. My book is about people who were smart enough to know what lay in store for them, but indolent enough to wish they were panicking too fast, that things could never get worse, because they had already gotten pretty bad. Edward Lutwak calls this the "logic of passivity." It is the passivity of people who are cunning in small things because they are totally dysfunctional in the big ones. It is the passivity of people who, in the end, have lost things too many times. Exile may hurt, but it doesn't stun any longer. "We saw it coming," we said, or to use an American expression, "We had it coming. We're used to it. We almost deserved it." In hindsight, of course, every disaster should have been entirely predictable. We have rehearsed our leave-taking so often, that, when it comes time to leave, we think it's just a more credible rehearsal.

* * *

Let us reverse the rituals of rehearsal and say: if I never went back to Egypt in thirty years, it's not that I didn't want to, but that I was rehearsing my return *back* to Egypt with the same obsessive abandon with which my family had been rehearsing its departure *from* Egypt.

As a writer, I needed to do so not only to remember and unload all my memories onto paper, to purge my mind of mnemonic deadweight, but also to twiddle with the past, to redeem it, to return to it on paper, or perhaps only to

29

rehearse that return, the way some of us would like to return to an old country, or to an old flame, provided we do so in our own minds only. Sometimes we may write to remember, when in fact we merely wish to forget, to be rid of things memory finds tiresome and has long since ceased to love. Sometimes we remember because memory is the ultimate metaphor for displacement.

I want to explore here not why I wrote *Out of Egypt*, or what were the physical and historical conditions of living there at the time that I did. I want instead to understand exile, loss, the passage of time, memory. In fact, the word exile is inappropriate: you cannot be an exile from a place that does not exist. I don't want to go back to a place that expelled me, or get back what was taken from me. I want nothing of Egypt.

Not true. I want something.

I want to understand how a Jew living provisionally in Egypt and learning to accept provisional status as a way of life remembers Egypt. What is it that I think of when I look back at Alexandria? And how does looking back, which I do every day, as I am sure everyone looks back on something every day, define my way of being as a human being? What is *my way of being as a human being* when I look back and ask myself *how can I long to go back to a place from which I longed to get out*? Or let me ask the question a bit differently: how much of me as a human being is not invested in this question?

The answer is frightening. No part of me is not invested in a place for which I feel the utmost indifference. In fact, part of me is still there. Part of me, as someone said to me a few months ago, never came with me. It never took the ship. It simply got left behind.

I don't know what this means. But it made an impression on me. And the more I think of it, the more it rings true: part of me *didn't* come with me. The French philosopher Merleau-Ponty was fond of evoking the phenomenon of amputees who feel excruciating pain in a limb that no longer exists. Memory can sometimes bring to the senses things that the senses should realistically no longer be able to feel. But suddenly, by virtue of this confluence of sensations, for a few moments, it is as though we were whole again. Or, to use an American idiom that is frightfully and uncannily appropriate in this context, we have come home. Some of us *come home that way* several times every day.

Some of us mistake this sense of coming home as the answer to a longing to go back.

It is a longing to be whole. Except that for me, "going back to Egypt," "thinking back on Egypt," is somehow embroiled in the whole notion of being whole again, the way some people think that having their childhood back might make them whole again.

Let me extend the metaphor, if only to try to clarify my own thoughts: it is as though what we left behind was precisely an amputated limb, something was cut away there, and was not allowed to travel with us — an arm or a kidnapped child, a baby brother. Except that the arm did not wither, just as the child did not die.

I am here, across the Atlantic, and this arm is there, beyond Gibraltar, all the way across to Europe and then south in a tiny city where no one I know lives any longer. Can I go back and find that arm and put it back where it belongs?

And then comes the terrible thought. Not that the arm wouldn't fit. I've known that already. What is scary is the thought that what I am is not a body minus an arm. I am just the arm doing the work of the entire body. The body stayed behind. The arm is all that got away. The real me stayed behind. What took the ship was nothing more than a symbol of me.

My life never started.

No wonder I spend so much time thinking of the past. No wonder everything feels so provisional. Most of me is not even with me now.

But I am piling up metaphors. Of course there is no arm, no body parts, here nor there. But this is how it feels imagistically. It is simply my way of imagining what my life is all about when what I call life is also an attempt to take into account the life I would have lived had I stayed behind and never left.

Or I am trying to picture something more narcissistic yet: imagining the me who stayed behind in Alexandria imagining what life would be like in New York City. My double is not just a parallel self. To use the language of Emily Brontë or of Djuna Barnes, he is more me than I am myself.

This is my way of picturing two beings: one who stayed behind, and another who got out. Once in a while the two meet. The one who loved Alexandria and loved the people, the smells, the beach, reaches out and almost touches the hand of the other me who lived in several countries, did all kinds of jobs, plotted his errancy in many places, if only to give himself the impression he was going places.

I could go on, and I am sure those who understand what I am talking about have their own storehouse of metaphors for the occasion. The point of it all is that both these men inhabit one body. I mentioned *homo duplex* earlier: let me repeat it again. *Homo duplex* is not just a man who is simultaneously in one door and out the other, or one who is rehearsing a return while in exile or rehearsing his departure when at home. It is a man who is *out here* and *back there* at the same time.

One part of me wants to go back. The other knows there is no going back. One wants to remember; the other doesn't trust memories; one longs for the beach; the other is happy to write about it. One still loves Alexandria; the other remembers hating it.

Let me put these two selves in perspective.

A bit more than a year ago my wife and I were invited to dinner at someone's home in Brooklyn. Ironically for the subject at hand, our host was the Commissioner for the Department of Homeless Services at the time. We were sitting on her terrace. It was a wonderful dinner — music, food, wine, guests, conversation. As it got darker, I looked over the horizon, and there was a magnificent view of the Manhattan skyline just after sunset on a midsummer evening. And it occurred to me that here was something strange indeed, one of the oldest nagging riddles in the annals of real estate: would I rather live in Brooklyn and have the luxury of such a breathtaking view of Manhattan, or would I rather *be* in beckoning, awe-inspiring Manhattan looking over to Brooklyn, where, as it was said in *Saturday Night Fever*, everyone dreams of being in Manhattan?

Brooklyn and Manhattan, in case you forgot, belong to the same city.

And then I did what we all do when we're standing on the Empire State Building, or overflying Manhattan, or sitting high on a rooftop, as I was that evening in Brooklyn. I strained my eyes and asked: Can I see my home from here? Which is another way of saying: Can I see myself from here?

When my parents met, they were both living on *rue Memphis*, in Alexandria, across the street from each other. The rivalries between my grandmothers were such that I soon learned to hide from one the fact that I had visited the other. I would sit on the balcony of one grandmother, trying to hide from the very window across the street where only a few hours earlier I had been told to avoid showing my face for fear of being spotted from the balcony across the way.

"*J'habite en face de chez vous*," I live across the street from you, would say one grandmother, meaning: don't play with me, I know where you live and what world you belong to; I know all about you, I know when you fight with your husband, what you fight about, and who hurls the most insults at whom. "*J'habite en face de chez vous*."

But let me alter my grandmother's words ever so slightly: from "*J'habite en face de chez vous*," let me make it: *J'habite en face de chez moi* — I live across the street from me.

I am in one place and me is in another. But we live across the street. No strange notion to descendants of the

Marranos. We are of one faith, but we practice another. I am in two places at the same time, but I am in both places provisionally. My mother tongue is French and yet I am writing in English. I speak to France from the English shore. I belong to two countries, but I care for none. I am the onlooker and the onlooked. I dream in French, but I quibble here in English.

English is the language through which I search for French roots that are, as I have tried to show, not even French. I love French but I prefer to write in English about the French that I love.

I am writing about me today but I'm talking to the young man I was once, the better to grasp the person I am today. I invent ways of going out of myself, the better to come home. To use Joyce's words: I fret in the shadow of English. But I fret in the shadow of time.

I am, let me hazard a word, elliptical: I have two centres. But like an ellipse I am not whole. I am even an elliptical Jew. A provisional, uncertain Jew. I am a Jew who loves Judaism provided it's from the opposite shore. Provided others practice it. I am a Jew who longs to be in a world where everyone is Jewish, where I can let down my guard and, like left-handed people who have been forced to do things with their right, use my left hand as freely as I wish. But I am a Jew who's spent so much time defining himself in relation to gentiles that I wouldn't know how to live, much less who to be, in a world in which everyone was Jewish.

* * *

When I wanted to buy my son, who is American, a history book, I did something that seemed so natural, it almost scared me: I bought him a book called *Ma première histoire de France*.

When I told him of the battle of Agincourt or Fontennoy or Waterloo, it occurred to me that I had never really decided whose side I was on, the French or the British.

My son said, of course we're on the French side. Why? I asked. *Parce que nous sommes français!*

I find this particularly uncanny because nearly the same scene occurs in my book when my grandmother tells my great-uncle, her brother, that she wants me to become a diplomat. Of what country, he asked me. Of France, I replied. You are not French, he said. You are Turkish...

I am not Turkish. But I am, and the adjective is not inappropriate, Alexandrian. But then again, the Alexandria I speak of no longer exists.

When a friend from Alexandria tried to impress me once by claiming he was totally settled in the U.S. and would never think of living anywhere else, I asked him, "Well, would you want to be buried in America then?" He balked. Most of us are very fussy about where they'll bury us. We want to be buried in a place that reflects who we are, that completes us, that gives meaning to the whole traffic jam of our life, even if, as we also know, it makes no difference whatsoever. A nomad, a true exile, may say he doesn't care where they bury him, but it's not that he doesn't care. He doesn't know.

And that, in the end, is what I'm writing about. Not about death and burials, but about people who are in search of a capital. I don't even mean a physical capital; something that helps us know who we are; something that *reminds* us of who we are, that makes us whole again.

In the immediate world of my childhood, that capital was not Istanbul, not Cairo, not Jerusalem. To claim it was Jerusalem, the way a displaced Holocaust survivor might ultimately have to confess, would be hypocritical. We were staunch Zionists, but Israel was for other Jews, for real Jews. Our capital was, we thought, Paris — *le petit Paris*, as we were so proud to remind ourselves.

Our images of a better life were projected onto Paris, but an imaginary Paris. On a good, rainy day when the sky was grey and you roamed and shopped about downtown Alexandria, the particular flavour of bliss derived in good part from the inward feeling that you had been to Paris.

35

For it almost felt like being in Paris.

We ticked to French time, the way in a larger sense we all have our watches set to Greenwich time, the way I still do when I come back from France and refuse to readjust my watch; I keep it synchronised to French time, not because by so doing I reject the dullness of my humdrum, day-to-day life and give myself the illusion I'm still on vacation, but because any time now, imminently, I might have to return to France, my real homeland!

We saw French movies, we read French magazines, we spoke French everywhere, our mothers rushed to have their tailors cut clothes according to the latest fashions in France, and when someone, on rare occasions, came from France bearing gifts, even those small, anti-acid white Vichy candies (which one can buy in any Paris subway station) had heaven written all over them. "*Ça vient de France!*" we would say as if we were talking of manna that had fallen from heaven.

And there were indeed magical days, and I wanted to capture one in my book: a day when I came home from school early because my teacher was sick, and my grandmother told me to go downtown with her. She bought me several French ties, took me to a French restaurant, and bought me French books. It doesn't matter that on that day we were being followed by the secret police and that she had nevertheless succeeded in smuggling a cache of gold coins abroad. What matters is that when you spent a day doing so many French things, and almost forgot you were in Nasser's Egypt, you felt whole, you felt as though you had come home!

Still, think of the paradox: when I was in Egypt, I got spiritual gratification when I felt I was walking on Parisian sidewalks. What gives me gratification today is when I feel I am almost on the Corniche in Alexandria.

In fact, and just to make things yet more complicated, during my last few days in Egypt, I began to miss Egypt, but I couldn't wait to leave Egypt. It was even then that I decided I would write a book about leaving Egypt. At the end of the book, in fact, I stand along the Corniche looking out at the Mediterranean, thinking *over there is France*, but I know that once in France I'll look back to this very evening and long to be here in Egypt. Not to be back here. But to be here longing for France.

When I think of Alexandria it's not just Alexandria I think of. When I think of Alexandria I think of a place from where I would imagine being somewhere else. To think of Alexandria without thinking of myself in Alexandria thinking of Paris is to miss the point.

When I remember Alexandria I must ponder what it means to remember wishing you were somewhere else.

What I am alluding to is not just memory, or the memory of memory, the personal catalogue of memories which we revisit and remember having revisited, the obituary of memories. What I am alluding to is this ambivalence, which is not new. We were ambivalent then; we are ambivalent now. It is just that the terms of our ambivalence have been reversed.

That makes no difference. What remains constant is the fact that we always inhabit at least two time zones.

* * *

I have often been asked whether it was emotionally difficult to write about a place I loved so much. Until speaking to readers of my book, I had no idea that I conveyed any love at all for Alexandria. How could people have misread me so much? The point is that for me, to quote Lawrence Durrell, Alexandria is the capital of memory. It represents the act of memory. But it's not the places or the things I remember that are beautiful or that I love, but the act of memory itself. To think of Alexandria is to deal in memory. Most people are convinced that I love Alexandria. Actually, what I love is remembering Alexandria. Mention the word Alexandria to me and it's not the city I think of, but the book I must write about Alexandria; not the streets, or the odours, or the names of the tramway stops, but the process of culling all these things together. It is the posture I must take when I begin to summon the pictures — not the pictures that I summon. I may enjoy seeing Alexandria again, but it's remembrance I love. Because it is me I long for, me I'm looking for, me I keep missing, me I keep re-inventing.

I have always been fascinated by cities that have rivers running through them. Because there is a right bank and a left bank. And the break between them is almost absolute. Part of you is here, part there, and between, to use another phrase from Nietzsche, there is at best a very narrow footbridge connecting you to yourself.

In fact, you are — and the word is more than a mere metaphor — an exile from yourself as well as being an exile from everything else.

Each part of me is a city — each facing the other, with a long body of water between us, and at night we look out, the way you look out towards New Jersey across the Hudson, or towards Manhattan across the East River, or towards the Right Bank or the Left Bank in Paris, or from one bank of the Hellespont to the other, and you think back at this other self, this other life that is being lived right now as you're living yours. This other life that could be.

The negative and the positive, as in photography. The negative and the positive, not staring each other down from great distances, but missing each other's gaze, the way we miss our own gaze when, in the mirror, we try to catch our eyes looking at something else.

One of the reasons why almost every chapter in my book ends in the present is that I wanted to show what happens to people who are taken out of their world. In fact, what I really wanted to show is how all the members of my family have in some form tried to adapt to the West but are happiest when they can slip back to those days when they would imagine an imagined West. When they could shut out the world of Italy or France or the U.S. around them, seal their windows as they did during the 1956 war (when

38

part of my family couldn't wait to see the people bombing us win the war), and for a few absurd moments, make believe they are all in Egypt again, that everyone is very rich again, that we're together again in one city, one street, one home, one room, that everything is back to where it should be, that everything is back in its place... if only we knew where that place was.

To please me one day in Paris my pseudo-aristocratic Turkish aunt, who wouldn't be caught dead saying a word of Arabic, cooked falafel for me. She said she loved the odour. I did not remind her that, years ago, when I came home eating a falafel sandwich one afternoon after school, she had bluntly said: "*Ça, pas chez nous,*" this, not in our house.

The problem of course is that neither here nor back there did we have the foggiest notion of what *chez nous* meant.

We were not *chez nous*. Never have been. Here or there. That is the meaning of exile. I wrote my book because I wanted to go to the beach, because I wanted to walk down the old streets, because I wanted things to be the way they were, even if I knew that most of the time when we were "over there" we couldn't wait to be elsewhere. I did, therefore, what all Jews could do, being a people of the book. If I couldn't take *my* Alexandria wherever I went in the world, then at least I could have a pocket version of it.

I wrote a book. I even arranged for a cover with a patch of blue on it so that, when in doubt, I could look at it and say there's beach water, and beach sand, and beach salt inside here. Ironically, the cover on the British edition, which is the cover that conveys the beach best, has a picture, not of Alexandria, but of *La Baie des Anges*, in France. Somehow it made perfect sense that way. It made me feel that my entire life had taken place in the dreamed-up France of Alexandria.

* * *

When I returned to Alexandria in 1995, I had expected deterioration, not massive overcrowding. I knew how memory works. I knew that memory always makes the streets narrower than they were, that buildings shrink, that time warps everything. Had I gone back to a place I had reinvented? Not even!

Here I was, on the very evening of my arrival, walking on the same sidewalks I had described in the last chapter of my book, remembering not what had happened on that street thirty years earlier, but writing that passage in a small coffee shop off 105th Street in Manhattan.

I knew there was something missing. I began to think that to be back in Egypt, without the figure of an adult, my mother, holding my hand, was all wrong. What did I care for such great weather if my mother wasn't there to urge me to go to the beach the next morning? What meaning if my father wasn't waiting in his car for me outside the movie house along the same sidewalk which I was walking on now?

Here I was walking the streets on my first night, streets I knew from memory. If only I could step out of my body and look at myself finally being back after thirty years. And then I realised that I had in fact stepped out of my body: but it was as though someone else were looking at this city and reporting it to me, as if I were blind. Nothing hit home. I couldn't come home. I had used it all up in my book. Unlike so many people who go back and get emotional, I felt nothing.

And then it hit me: maybe this is what happens when you come home. You hardly notice that things don't feel odd at all.

This is also why we prefer to long for the things we want for fear of finding they don't make much difference once we have them.

It was only later that day, when it was clear to me that I must have drunk some Egyptian water and wasn't feeling well, that I walked into a pharmacy and asked for some medicine. On my way out, from between two buildings, I caught sight of the Corniche and beyond it the sea. And it clicked. I saw myself on West End Avenue looking down 106th Street towards the Hudson saying, as I had said a week earlier: next week, this time, I'll be in Alexandria. I knew this would happen. I became homesick for a place that could never be my home but from which I had learned to recreate Alexandria the way, in exile, the rabbis were forced to recreate the Book from scratch, the way prisoners learn to love the free world from the pictures they paint on their cell walls. It is the wall they worship now, not the world.

The falafel hole-in-the-wall on Broadway and 104th, the beguiling lure of sunlight on Madison and 75th on a glaring summer day reminding me of something I still can't quite place, the view of the West Side across from the reservoir in Central Park reminding me so much of Alexandria when you'd be coming back from school on a school bus along the beach, all of these had suddenly become more important to me than the city I had always thought I could never forget. The city had shifted elsewhere. And I felt like North African Camus who, in his very early writings, was able to rediscover his entire world, childhood, and beloved city in the fig trees of Italy, on the sidewalks of Paris, or, uncannily enough, on twilit evenings on Riverside Drive in Manhattan from whose "uninterrupted flow of smoothly running cars there suddenly rises a song that recalls the sound of breaking waves."

Avraham Adgah

The Journey to Jerusalem

Translated from Hebrew and edited by
Riva Rubin & Dafna Gold Melchior

"The day will come when we will reach Jerusalem."

This was the fervent hope of Ethiopian Jewry during an exile that lasted thousands of years. The City of Jerusalem had always been a remote, very mysterious legend which inspired tales of superhuman bravery that were the elixir of life for the Jews in their hard day-to-day existence in Ethiopia.

The departure from the villages was conducted on three levels: information gathering, finding escape routes and evading encounters with army border patrols. The organising stage involved the clandestine sale of property and fateful decisions regarding the selection of those who would be included in the night treks, which were made difficult and dangerous by the topography, the rain forests, the dangers from beasts of prey and above all, the long, devious route. In addition, they were fearful and intensely uncertain about their fate, even if they overcame the many obstacles and reached Sudan. The Tigri Jews were aware that they faced indescribable danger and were likely to lose their lives long before they reached Sudan.The departure of a family group created an immediate snowball reaction in the village. People left without gathering the harvest, without returning the cattle from pasture, without selling property, without conducting planned weddings. It was no longer possible to stay behind. Anyone who delayed leaving found himself suffering at the hands of neighbours who had once been good friends, but now had turned into beasts of prey, robbers and looters. What had been, ceased to exist. There was no point in staying.

Meanwhile, favourable news began to come from those who had reached Sudan; reports of good reception by the various refugee relief institutions, and the Mossad. But the journey from the village to the Sudanese border was strewn with battles between various enemies and death by a stray bullet was a distinct possibility. An increasing number of people lived by looting and robbery and the community's armed guides were forced to fight short battles that created panic among the women and children and even loss of life. The border was closed at crossing points on several occasions and the Jews had to retreat and reorganise. It goes without saying that the dangers on the return journey were the same as those on the way out.

The departure of the Tigri Jews stirred the imagination of the Gondar community. The two districts were separated by between 200 and 600 kilometres, but in spite of the distance and real difficulties of transport, the two communities had had harmonious relations for scores of generations, resulting in bonds of kinship. The Gondar Jews regarded the action of the Tigri community as heroic and instructive, but more than this, the departure of family members created an emotional void. In all, the situation was like a dam bursting and releasing a fierce, unstoppable torrent. Throughout this period of uncertainty, the Jews of Gondar were preoccupied with the fate of those who had set out for Sudan. There were questions, hopes, fears, but no answers, no information. Rumours of all kinds were rife, beginning with those among us who said that the walkers had become slaves in Sudan, others held that they had been killed in military skirmishes, while still others were convinced that the walkers had already reached the land of the forefathers with no losses. Meanwhile, the day to day situation in Ethiopia was deteriorating without an end in sight. Military courts appeared everywhere like mushrooms after the rain, making themselves felt by everyone — high school and university students, members of the free professions, and others.

43

At the time, I was in high school. My friends and I, like our peers in other village districts, understood that the flight to Sudan, the opening of the way and passing on correct information to families was the task we had to undertake. We acted accordingly. We lost interest in our studies. The gist of conversation at our daily meetings was how to find suitable opportunities for escape. These whispered conversations were held in code for fear of discovery, which would mean certain death. In the eyes of the regime, escape or attempted escape was treachery against communism and its leader. There was only one punishment for the escapee and that was a bullet in the head, after which the corpse was flung onto the main avenue of the city, as a lesson and warning to all. Whenever such a thing happened, tender children were led past a parent's corpse to impress them with the power of the tyrannical ruler. Mothers and fathers would pass by the corpse of a child without uttering a cry of grief at their loss, because anybody expressing pain or sorrow received the same punishment.

Some other villagers and I, having come to the Provincial Capital to acquire an education, rented an apartment for the duration of our studies, returning to our families in the villages once or twice a month to replenish our supplies and pass on information. Our worried families would have preferred to have us close to them, even if this was at the expense of our studies, but without permission from the authorities, nobody was allowed to leave the educational framework. Those who took the decision into their own hands were subject to severe punishment, together with their families. Life in the city also became hard; severe limitations were imposed on us, demanding extra caution. Curfew was from six in the evening till first light and curfew breakers were shot by snipers. Gatherings were prohibited, loitering and discussing current events was prohibited. If a group numbered more than two, they were taken in by civil detectives for interrogation at the nearest police station. Students who lived near the school returned

44

home every day after lessons to help with the fieldwork. They were free to organise, prepare themselves, train and act. In the large high school population, we Jews who came from the villages made sure that we got to know one another. We used a few Hebrew words as a recognition code. The fact that we came from different villages helped us to gather fairly reliable information.

When we gradually came to the conclusion that it was necessary to act, we had to find clear answers to questions concerning who would leave first, accompanied by whom, according to what plan, and so on, before we made a move. Those of us who lived away from our villages were more easily able to plan an escape without arousing the suspicions of our worried families. We had little specific information and no experience, but we knew that after leaving the village we had to run full speed in order to get out of populated areas. Once in the hilly district, it was possible to hide in the caves. We knew that the estimated walking time to the border depended on the composition of the group and could take at least a month. Therefore, we had to equip ourselves with food and suitable clothing for the period, as well as find a guide good enough to navigate and manoeuvre past obstacles. We had no way of knowing if the tales of cannibals on the way were true and if there were beasts of prey. We also did not know how to communicate with the different tribes we would encounter and, above all, we did not know if the uncertainty would be over once we reached Sudan, or if we would be fumbling in the dark then, too. With all this, we had to consider the fate of the families we would leave behind.

We had to confront the fear that as soon as we left the area, the authorities would take a member of the family, throw him into prison and torture him to discover our destination. As mentioned, the rulers regarded escapees as potential enemies. Arresting the head of a family was an accepted, efficient method to break the will of those planning to escape, or their families. Neither our return nor pleas for mercy were any use. Boys and girls were executed on the basis of treason, but not before being tortured to reveal the names of scores of their companions on the way. It was difficult to keep the preparations secret. There were signs by which the anxious families could tell that we were planning something. The energy, the gathering in yards, the mysterious elements that had developed in our way of life, did not leave much room for doubt about our plans. For example, I remember that I began to ask for more pocket money and began hoarding necessities, like medicines and clothing that would help me to be unobtrusive. Meanwhile, we heard rumours of the capture of many Jewish students who had set out from another district. It was said that they were thrown into prison, where the torturers awaited them with whips to lash them into revealing the preparations for escape. Ironically, the few who withstood the torture were actually those who remained true to themselves and their comrades, like a friend of mine who was suspected of hostile activities and of conveying information and equipment to the enemy, and was taken to prison. He was immediately blindfolded, shackled hand and foot and tortured. When he was released, he told me that as soon as he was arrested his torturer suspended him upside down from the ceiling and beat the soles of his feet until they bled. From the beginning, he said, he kept silent. The torturer went wild and shouted that he would kill him if he didn't reveal who his partners were. When he still did not answer, the fury of the torture increased. At this stage, the beaten part of his body lost all sensation and his toes began to separate from one another. When the method failed to produce results in his case, another means of torture was introduced. He was prevented from sleeping. Food and water were withheld, he was prevented from performing his bodily functions; chains were inserted into his mouth and tightened to force him to cooperate. Victims often began to "sing" after the first blow, but in the case of my friend, the torturers were surprised that they were unable to extract even one shred of information. Therefore, after a full year of torture and

46

humiliation, he was released, physically and mentally exhausted and severely disabled.

Like any other Jew living in the Diaspora, some of my friends were non-Jews. One of these friends had all the advantages needed for their escape to Sudan, including sound reasons in favour of leaving Ethiopia. Both his older brothers, one a college student and the other a graduate, had left with the outbreak of the revolution. Their father had served under the deposed Emperor as the local ruler of a district and he and his family were targeted by the new regime. The two brothers had reached Sudan by a secret route and from there had gone to the USA, where they were soon granted American citizenship as political refugees. They were in constant touch with their brother, my friend, promising that if he managed to reach Sudan they would immediately bring him to join them. Since our early childhood, there had been no secrets between us and now we openly discussed the possibility of escaping together. It seemed to me that our friendship had an added value, or advantage, because he would be able to assist me when it was time to leave, since his father had colleagues along the escape route. In the end, in spite of everything, I decided to wait for him to take the initiative and tell me if he wished to go. I was curious to find out if he regarded me as a suitable partner. I found out soon enough, after one of our most difficult shared moments, when we saw a friend of ours lying dead in the town square. Muttering something about escape, sounding uncertain at first, my companion then revealed his well-ordered table of escape routes, his network of people and the fact that they could get him out of Sudan as soon as he arrived there. As for me, I was in no hurry to confide in him, but a weight lifted from my heart as I heard what he had to say. Instead of jumping for joy, I cautiously went to get the advice of an older, Jewish, friend. He examined what had been said, word for word, then asked me to imitate the tone in which the key sentences had been spoken. After thoroughly checking and clarifying all aspects, he

47

advised me to say that I wanted to take part in the escape, but he warned me to be careful about the amount of information I would share.

I met my friend the next day and raised the subject again. We promised each other not to reveal the secret to anyone who might ruin our plans. But, apparently, growing up together, eating from the same plate is not always enough to ensure the survival of friendship, because he disappeared for three days before we had completed our plans.

It turned out that during those three days he had tried to leave with another group of friends. Before they got very far, maybe because they had taken the mission too lightly, they were turned in by villagers eager to prove their loyalty to the regime. To earn points at the expense of the "traitors", the villagers tied their hands behind their backs and led them to the door of the prison. The local ruler was immediately invited to view "the lambs for the slaughter". He congratulated and praised the villagers. My friend and the others immediately disappeared behind the prison's high walls. What awaited them there can not be described.

From then on, I had no time to sit and dream of possible escape routes, but had to run for my life. I knew that as soon as my friend entered the prison, particularly when the torturer dealt him the first blow from his club, he would "sing" my name. My Jewish friend, seeing my distress, helped me to calm down and hide my worry. On his part, he began to organise my escape without wasting any time. On the fourth day of my friend's imprisonment, as the sun was setting just before curfew, my older friend and I strode towards the suburbs, crossed the little river that separated the city from the villages and sat down, watching as the electric lights flickered on in the city. Incidentally, the man in charge of the generator serving the city was my uncle, who emigrated later. We waited until dark, then moved in the direction of the familiar area of caves and forests near our village. The only threat was from the dogs we passed on the way. After tramping in the dark for five hours, we approached our village and had to face one of the first difficult tests on our way to escape. We had to decide whether to enter the village and inform our parents, even getting their blessing and perhaps some supplies, or exploit the darkness and go on our way.

Both choices were risky and difficult. If we went into the village, we could not be sure the parents would agree with us and bless our journey. After all, they knew the inherent dangers to us as well as to themselves; they could be hauled off to prison. If we did not go in, our parents would be driven crazy just by the thought of what had become of us and, in any case, the authorities might come and arrest them. We held a brief consultation and decided that instead of going in and making a fuss, we should write a few words to one of the younger brothers, who would pass on the message to our parents. Therefore, we crept into the silent village where only the dogs were awake and barking from the moment they sensed us. We called them by name and they approached, wagging their tails in recognition. They were the only ones we parted from formally, patting them and saying a few words. I remember having tears in my eyes. After these few comforting moments with the dogs, we left a short letter addressed to my younger brother, who was always my confidant. When he found the letter, he broke the news gently to my parents, telling them that we were on our way to the Sudanese border and that if all went well they would hear from us and if not, they could go into mourning.

That dark night, to the accompaniment of barking dogs, we sprinted southwards towards the plain below the villages. To add to our physical and mental pain, the skies opened and we were drenched in the downpour. The resultant mud further slowed our progress. In spite of this ordeal, neither of us considered stopping. On the contrary, we wanted to hurry as much as possible to take advantage of the darkness and get past the settled areas. My companion was my senior by five years and therefore more mature in considering things from all angles to reach solutions relevant to given situations. That first, dark night of our escape, we encountered animals that might have been nocturnal predators and froze in our footsteps until the animals passed, or until we realised that what had scared us was only a pile of rocks or a bush. As the eventful, frightening night was drawing to a close, just before the farmers emerged into their fields of grain, we looked for a place to hide.

It was an ordinary day for the monkeys awakening to the daylight. It was a joyful day for the birds shaking off the remains of the night's raindrops. It was the month when farmers organised themselves to begin tilling the soil. It was a morning when we dashed around until we found a cave where we could hide during the day. We wrung out our soaked clothes, peeled the drying mud from our feet and removed the traces of our frantic search for cover, which turned out to be a monkey cave. There was no point in thinking about food or drink, but we made sure of resting all day. We guarded against unpleasant surprises by sleeping in shifts. We had decided to head for an area that was not under military control. We knew that we could cover the distance over two nights with good navigation and a lot of luck. But, unfortunately, it took us three nights. During all that time, we had nothing to eat but a few berries and some ripening fruit. It was obvious to us that we could not carry on in this way. As soon as we entered the enclave beyond the reach of military rule, where the villagers did not need to prove their loyalty, I suggested that we approach one of the villages and ask for food. He explained that while it was true that the villagers were not under military rule, our situation would be worse if they discovered that we were students. The villagers claimed that the students were enemies of the deposed emperor, unbelievers and to blame for everything that had happened.

Since I was feeling very weak after the three-day hike and lack of food, I decided that it was better to fall into the hands of the villagers than to die walking. Having no choice, we decided to enter the village and get food, even if we had to buy it. Very politely and pathetically, we asked for something hot to eat. As it happened, this village was sympathetic to the rebels and had experience in dealing with army deserters. To our surprise, we were very warmly received. It was the first time in 72 hours that we had been close to a tray of hot food. As soon as it was served, I fell on the food without shame. I was afraid some-one would come and take it away before I had eaten my fill. I hope I didn't leave a bad impression, but I think our benefactors understood our circumstances. After the meal, came the questions. We entered the spirit of things and joined them in cursing the new regime that had brought absolute ruin, but we were careful not to reveal that not only were we Jews, but students as well. Having estab-lished that we shared their opinions, we cautiously broached the subject of Sudan as a centre of anti-regime activity. We told them that we were on our way to join oth-ers who were undergoing military and other training there. We added that we had no idea of how to reach Sudan. There were spontaneous cries of encouragement from our listeners. They urged us to stay with them for a week and suggested we leave with a group of their own youngsters, who would be pleased to have extra support on their way to the Sudanese border. Their task was to lead some cows there for slaughter in exchange for cooking salt, which was very scarce at the time owing to the many civil wars that disrupted the supply routes from the north. We knew about the trade between the villagers and the Sudanese, but the week's delay was critical at the time. I was afraid to stay that long in the village, among people we didn't know and in a society with a different and unfamil-iar code of behaviour. Also, we were afraid that they might be trying to prolong our stay until they could turn us in, after all. However, despite all this, we decided to stay.

We began to prepare ourselves for anything that might arise while we were in the village. For example, what would happen if they woke us up on Sunday morning and asked us to go to church with them. We decided to reply that since our attendance would arouse curiosity, our hosts might get involved in complicated explanations... We also thought of our response in case they asked us to help them at work in the fields. I was particularly concerned about this, because I had no experience in that kind of work. Anyway, our response would be the same as the first. And what if they offered us meat? All the religions in Ethiopia expressed themselves distinctly regarding the eating of meat. Jews, Christians and Moslems all strictly forbade eating meat slaughtered according to the rituals of another religion. We decided to cope with this differently: one of us would say that he was under doctor's orders to abstain from meat and the other would politely decline, saying that he had just eaten elsewhere, at one of the other houses. If they insisted, we would eat and discreetly throw up, as soon as possible.

One way or another, the week passed very quickly. All preparations for departure were completed the day before and the guides made sure we all knew the correct behaviour for predictable situations. If we encountered an armed patrol, everyone would make a dash for the forest and hide there. If we encountered robbers, we would adopt the tactics of the traders, who never surrendered, but resisted to the extent of opening fire. If the robbers gained the upper hand, the traders would return to their village and reorganise. This would mean that we would either have to return with them, or continue on our own. If we reached the border crossing only to find that it was closed for political or other reasons, we would have to decide whether to sit and wait till the border re-opened, or go back the way we came. If we found ourselves in a situation that combined all the above, matters would be out of our control and we would obviously have to stay close to the trackers and those with previous experience.

As it happened, five of my schoolmates from a village fifty kilometres away from mine also set out when we did, but they arrived in Sudan six weeks after we did. We discovered that when they reached the other side of the enclave and asked for directions, they were not treated as well as we were. It was the height of the season for work in the fields and when the villagers saw the five agitated escapees, four boys and a girl, they locked up the girl and sent the boys to work in the fields, after stripping them of everything they had. They provided them with food and drink, but treated them as slave labourers for a whole month. After exploiting them to the full, they showed them the path to Sudan and let them go. It is superfluous to add that they had endured horrifying experiences. We were the lucky ones.

Before we left, the donkeys were loaded with dry bread, sugar, coffee and other dry foods. The cows to be traded were herded together at the beginning of the path, footwear was firmly tied, weapons were cleaned and ammunition was slung around the hips for swift loading in case of need. We set out at about ten o'clock at night: five donkeys, ten cows, five traders and us, the escapees. The tracker, with his special sense, was in the lead, followed by the cattle, the herders and us. We went by night, to be safe, but this principle was also known to those waiting in the narrow passes to loot, rape and kill. The trail led through stunningly beautiful rain forests. The ascents and descents tired us more quickly than usual and we breathed with difficulty. It required special fitness to match people who had already made the journey a number of times and to cope with the topographical difficulties, but in such situations one draws on inner strengths whose source is beyond my comprehension. The ancient trees and bushes along the way create illusory figures in the dark, requiring skilled, bold guides to find a path through them. Any deviation from the few dirt tracks leading towards the border could end badly. For 200 kilometres, we saw no villages, no agricultural areas. The wild animals we saw this time were real, such as lions and leopards. There were also human predators lying in ambush to rob us. Luckily, they left us alone when they saw that we had an armed escort.

A week of waiting in the village and a few nights of marching together were enough to make us understand that not everyone who marches with you is a friend. There were those who opened up and helped and those who regarded us with suspicion. My friend and I came to the conclusion that during the daytime rest periods after the forced night march, we had to take turns to sleep; one really sleeping and the other pretending to do so in order to prevent trouble. Our fears increased when, during one of the rest periods, I overheard a trader loudly boasting to his companion that he was prepared to rob us and return to the village, rather than march all the way in the hope of selling a few cows. He said that he knew we had a lot of money and persuaded his friend to cooperate with him. My friend had gone into the bushes to relieve himself and he heard even more of their conversation than I did, including the details of their planned assault on us. I was already imagining weapons pointed at me while someone demanded my money or my life, but I controlled myself, trying to keep cool at least until my friend and I could discuss this new development. My first thought was that my miserable life was coming to an end, I was about to die, my body would be left as food for the vultures and nobody would ever know what had become of me. My friend pretended to be asleep, so as not to arouse the suspicions of the two, who had finished discussing their campaign. But he tossed and turned until he gave up and suggested that I should sleep. Naturally, after such an exhausting walk I would have slept like a baby, but this time my eyes refused to remain shut. Whenever I was overcome by the need to sleep, I would remember the trader's menacing words.

The next day passed slowly and we did our best to act naturally until it grew dark and it was time to prepare for another march. We found a few moments on our own and my friend said we had to act before things became more complicated. From then on, we were confronting a new situation. There was no point in dragging on for another day and night. We would have to separate from the group.

However, this was not so simple. Not all of them knew about the plot, but there was nobody we could rely on in the moment of truth. Although we had been on the march with them for a week, we were strangers and, as such, helpless. We considered making use of the darkness to drop behind and run off in any direction. But since everyone was alert at night, we couldn't simply disappear. Further, one of the honest traders would notice our absence and look for us out of genuine concern. Therefore, we thought it would be best to escape during the day. This theory had to be tested, so we disappeared for an hour or two at a time, either together or one by one. Nobody showed any concern about these short absences, confirming our belief that the best time to leave was during the day.

Two days later, we took our clothes and our money and fled in the direction we guessed would take us to Sudan. We ran as fast as we could, in order to put some distance between the traders and ourselves. They would be angry when they discovered that we had made a run for it, particularly the two who were plotting to rob us. We went without rest by day or night, walking for two whole days, deviating from the path every so often in case we were being followed. We lived off fruit growing near the trail. My friend noticed a beautiful tree in a little valley and went towards it to pick some fruit. When he was close, he saw a black snake coiled on a branch, sunning itself. He shook the tree and the snake was flung over his head, landing in the branches of a neighbouring tree. It was one of the snakes we had been warned about before we left home, one of the most venomous and aggressive species, whose bite caused immediate paralysis of the brain. I stood frozen with fear. My friend had shown great strength of character and I wondered what I would have done in his place, confronted with one of the worst scenarios described to us.

After two days of running, my feet were full of big, painful blisters. I could barely take a step and cried bitterly, cursing my parents, my companion, my situation and my cruel destiny. The blisters began to break, the skin began to peel. This created a new situation demanding new planning. It was obvious that I could not continue the march. I tried to crawl, but the road would be endless that way. I tore my undershirt and bound my feet, but then I could not put on my shoes. My friend carried me, but I was afraid that he would also collapse and neither of us would remain alive. In the end, we decided that I would wrap both feet in grass and we would sit under a large tree that showed signs of being a resting place for travellers. We assumed that traders coming to rest early in the morning after an exhausting night would discover us and demand to know what we were doing there. Having no alternative, we prepared ourselves for the worst. I sat down, looking pitiful. I wasn't trying to fool anyone, I was really disabled, in a state of general weakness and total helplessness. It made no difference who arrived first, casual travellers, robbers, or the group we were running from. Whatever the case, I would try to explain why I was on the run and if they did not believe me, I would simply offer them every-thing I had in exchange for their help in reaching the border. Indeed, early in the morning a group of traders arrived at the tree. As soon as their leader saw me, he thought I was hiding something. Therefore, they carried out the standard drill for such occasions: they bounded into the bushes, aimed their weapons and began to inter-rogate us. In weak and trembling voices, we told them that we were unarmed and had no aggressive intentions. I explained that the way I was sitting was due to my injured feet and nothing else.

According to the lore of the forest, one must not believe anyone, nor be taken in by apparently unfortunate people. Eventually, when they seemed to understand that this was not a diversionary tactic, they sent an elderly man to have a look at me. Covered by their weapons, he examined my ruined feet and reported his findings to the others, who gathered around to see the truth for themselves. We tact-fully asked them not to go off and leave us lying there. We discovered, after having walked in the area for two nights that one could walk there during the day, depending on prevailing conditions and the skill of the guide. The latter was supposed to be able to recognise significant signs. For example, if a certain bird emits a warning cry, it means that suspicious characters are lurking on the way, or that there is going to be an unpleasant encounter. If a donkey brays on the right hand side of the road, it is a sign that the way is clear and all wishes will be granted. When we promised to obey every instruction, they allowed us to join them in the march planned for the same night. Out of sheer happiness, I managed to overcome the inhuman pain in the soles of my feet, but the next day, as they were loading the donkeys I asked brokenly if I could hire a donkey. This was a terrible mistake on my part, since I had indicated that I had the money to pay for the ride. Clearly, I was "a person of means" and therefore a target. They quickly consented, offering me one of the donkeys. Although this obliging behaviour struck me as a bit strange, I failed to realise the power of the word "money". Quite naturally, I was happy to be able to load myself on the donkey's back and let it do the walking for both of us.

It was common for guides to rob the escapees they were escorting. For this reason, there was an intricate system for concealing money in all sorts of places and we had also been careful to keep our money safe. The large bills were sewn into the seams and folds of our clothing, while the small change was kept in our pockets. The donkey I was riding showed no signs of fatigue and ran to join the other donkeys. In this way, we proceeded for three nights in the direction of the border. Seventeen days had passed since we left the village and we were anticipating the end of the journey. Suddenly, for no good reason, the traders began to quarrel among themselves. The quarrel broke out because one of them refused to rob us. It reached a point where the man aimed his gun and said, "They're two poor kids who want freedom. I won't let you harm them!" Another one ran at me and said, "Get off the donkey and

hand over your money! If you refuse you'll end up dead."
Apparently the quarrel had been going on for days, ever
since I asked if I could hire a donkey. But my friend and I
weren't alert enough to see what was happening. To prevent bloodshed, I got off the donkey at once and my friend
and I emptied our pockets. The man who was so keen on
getting our money was disappointed and demanded more.
I explained that we had no more and pleaded for mercy.
Furiously, he threw me to the ground, stamped on my
neck and told me to shut up and do as he said. Within seconds, our defender aimed at the attacker and told him to
leave us alone, return the money and let us go on our way.
The furious robber then took his foot off my neck and
leaped to a firing position. The first man aimed and shot
him in the forehead. He died instantly. The others, who
had been standing on the side till then, could not remain
calm any longer and crowded around, taking sides. I'll
never know if there had been a previous quarrel between
the two men, I don't know if our defender's motives were
pure, but the undeniable fact is that one man murdered
another, who happened also to be a relative of his, because
of his behaviour towards us. When I arrived in Israel I
tried to find out what had become of him, but without success.

One way or another, after the murder everyone treated
us strictly according to tradition. And tradition held that
we were open targets in a blood feud. The shooter
remained in firing position in case the one he had shot
revived, or one of the others tried to attack him. He gave
us brief instructions as to how to continue, pointing and
saying, "Carry on in this direction for three or four days
and you'll get to the border." In addition to giving us directions, he equipped us with a kilogram of sugar, explaining
that it had the advantage of making one feel full without
creating thirst. As we were leaving, he added, "Don't ask
for help! If you ask for help, it means that you're new in
the area and open to robbery and other trouble! Go now,
and don't worry. As for me — that dog deserved what he

58

got!" My pounding heart was noticeable in the rise and fall of my ribs under the shirt. How strange that we two innocent youths should be caught up in a fight to the death between two men whose common intention had been to conduct some trade and return home safely. Again, we resumed our wild dash towards the unknown. We rested every three or four hours, poured a little sugar into our cupped hands and licked it to suppress our hunger and thirst. I had stopped complaining about my bleeding, painful feet, I thought of nothing but staying alive. I wanted to run fast and far, I wanted to save myself, I wanted at long last to reach the Sudanese border. After running for two days, we began to see signs that the border was near.

The border between Ethiopia and Sudan is unmarked. There are no checkpoints and no fences between the two countries for thousands of kilometres. In fact, the River Bahar is a natural border. The absence of barriers and the geographical conditions encouraged Sudanese nomads to cross into Ethiopia and raise cattle without being disturbed. This was also convenient for Ethiopians wishing to escape. There was a weekly Ethiopian military patrol, which passed quickly and without the soldiers dismounting from the trucks. It was a show of force more than anything else. Apart from occasional wars, the border between the two countries was very quiet and very open.

A huge herd of cattle covering a vast area indicated to us that the border was close. While this was a good sign, it also had its bad aspect. For historical reasons, relations between that particular tribe of cattle breeders and Ethiopians were complicated. They had no liking for Ethiopians and the Ethiopians returned the sentiment, nicknaming them "The Cannibals". About two centuries ago, the Sudanese were defeated in a bloody war with Ethiopia and since then some Sudanese tribes believe that they and seven generations after them would go to Paradise if they killed an Ethiopian and brought his head to the village chief. As someone who grew up in the shadow of this threat, I knew that the cattle breeders were fanatical in their beliefs and their feeling that justice was on their side. That is why we hastily took cover to allow the herd to pass. Mounted on camels, the cannibal shepherd and his companion had, respectively, a huge knife and a light rifle. They had almost gone by without noticing us, when the cattle picked up our scent and began to mill around the bushes where we were hiding. Fortunately, the shepherds didn't notice us and led the cattle away. When the danger was over and before a new one would arise, we came out of hiding and hurried to continue our run for the border.

At last, we were standing with wide smiles on our faces, looking at the river that lay between us and Sudan. We crossed quickly and without incident and turned ourselves in to the Sudanese border guards based in Bahar, the town named after the river. Transport from the town to the heart of Sudan, an immense distance, was by means of cattle trucks. These came neither regularly nor often and when they did come, they would not move until they were tightly packed. Therefore, we had to wait where we were until others like us turned up. Some groups of boys and girls arrived during our waiting period, all of them weak and debilitated by the hardship of the journey. The way had not been smooth for any of them. We sat in the holding camp, waiting for more and more to arrive. When they came, we received every new group with open and reassuring arms. Soon after they arrived, they would flood us with their stories. Some had left with their parents' blessing, some had stories like ours to tell.

One of these stories remains engraved on my memory. A group of three girls and eight boys had set out. They came across robbers whose interest was not in finding money, but in raping the girls. The guide, who had sworn an oath to the families, tried to bargain with the robbers, offering them money or goods if they would agree not to molest the girls. The robbers refused. In order to save her friends and prevent bloodshed, the oldest girl offered to subject herself to the agony of being raped. But the guide refused to allow this. He regarded such a solution as a personal surrender and breach of faith on his part. After a brief negotiation, during with the robbers understood that there was no way to force the guide to agree, they decided to use scare tactics and opened fire on the group with automatic weapons. This was the first time the youngsters had come under fire; they panicked and their screams echoed throughout the forest. The rapists deliberately provoked this reaction, because they knew that while everyone was running around and screaming in panic, they could snatch one or two of the girls and have their way. This hope proved false, because the guide had trained them for such a possibility and, despite their shouting and screaming, everybody stayed focused and together. The robbers were infuriated. They aimed at the guide and shot him in his left hand. He took cover and although he was losing a lot of blood, he returned fire and wounded one of the robbers. The encounter turned into a real battle. The shooting increased the youngsters' panic, they finally forgot what they had been taught and scattered in all directions. The guide was wounded a second time and died on the spot. Only six of the group, two girls and four boys, reached the camp. We later found out that this story was by no means unique. Of the others, the four boys turned back and one girl was left behind in a village, unable to cope with the hardships of the return journey. The village strong man immediately claimed her for a wife, although he was married and a father. He continued to take pride in his deed in spite of village gossip. In retrospect, it turned out to be a good thing that he took her under his protection, because in other similar cases, girls were taken as sex slaves and mercilessly raped. One of those who reached the camp was the group leader. He found it hard to come to terms with what had happened to them. He slept little and ate only to stay alive and finally refused to get onto the truck that had come for us, deciding to go back to his home village instead.

Recently, I heard that he became a daring and devoted guide, helping a great many people to complete the journey safely.

Life in Sudan

I had been in Sudan for six months and, as a veteran, was able to observe certain changes in the characteristics of new arrivals. At first, most of the Jewish migrants had been boys and girls, but now whole families were coming, including little children, old people walking with the aid of sticks and invalids carried on stretchers.

Those responsible for receiving the migrants were unable to cope with so many people in such a short time. All the huts that had served as living quarters in the beginning were now full and the refugees had to be housed in tents, which spread over muddy, polluted, uncultivated land. There were no access roads to the tents. There was no way to dispose of refuse, nor were there any toilet facilities. These crowded, unsanitary conditions naturally led to the rapid spread of disease.

Migrants entering over the eastern border of Sudan were concentrated in a number of refugee camps located in the outlying areas of the country. Most of the migrants wandered from one camp to another, some in search of a way to penetrate deeper into Sudan and others moved by the authorities, who wanted to relieve the crowded conditions in some of the camps. The majority were located in, or passed through, the Amara Kuba refugee camp.

When I arrived, the situation had allowed us to reach the big towns, but when the flow of migrants became unexpectedly strong, the authorities began to control them making it impossible to simply get up and travel around without an official permit. To prevent illegal passage, plainclothes policemen checked the travel passes. Anyone without such a permit was taken from the truck to a refugee camp. Often, the head of a family was separated from his family and sent to prison or to a remote refugee camp. The refugees called this *"Lejina"*, that is, banishment and severe punishment to deter anyone from repeating the offence. Further, from the moment the head of a family was taken, the members of the family were unwilling to endanger themselves and remained stuck until someone rescued them.

Unluckily for us, the winter of 1983 was long and rainy. Nevertheless, in spite of the deluge and the danger of overflowing rivers, rockfalls and landslides, people continued to arrive at the Sudanese refugee camps to crowd into tents. Because of the bad sanitation, dysentery and malaria were rife and many people perished. It was not easy to get medical care and even when this was available, people did not seek it. Death struck without mercy. International aid was given to all refugees in Sudan, but owing to conditions in the field, and the difficulty of visiting every family, some individuals and even whole groups were overlooked by the international refugee relief agencies. Needless to say, those who did not receive the allowance were among the first to die.

The Jewish groups received an additional, generous allowance from the Mossad, according to the size of the family. This allowance was distributed in strict secrecy by dedicated young members of the community, who passed from tent to tent with a list of families. This operational secrecy was necessary for fear of Sudanese reaction and to prevent infiltration by non-Jews attempting to get to Israel. The Red Cross was the biggest international relief organisation providing basic means of subsistence: tents for shelter, medical aid for those who reached the points where equipment was available, and flour to fight starvation. But the flour was also the major cause of death for many people. During the packing and shipping process, it was stored in bad conditions of heat and damp and, as a result, when it was distributed it was unfit for consumption. However, the near-starving people who received it, having no choice, tried to remove the worms and in other ways make it edible. Naturally, the children were the first to eat it and consequently were the first victims. In addition to these sorrows, the field hospital set up near the camps lacked adequate medical equipment to treat the hundreds of sick that thronged to it. All over the world people turn to hospitals to be cured, but here, most who came for help died, including those who had walked in, only to be carried out on stretchers.

In retrospect, this raises some questions. The voices of the dead cry out. I am not accusing anyone of evil-doing, or of practicing euthanasia, but the facts are material for thought. Treatments were not recorded, hordes of people died, leaving the questions unasked and unanswered. Then as now, they hover like a dark cloud over Camp Amara Kuba.

The mass deaths led to many problems. The burial of our dead has always been a difficult and complicated problem because of the ritual strictness concerning uncleanliness and purification. In a foreign country, this problem was much more complicated. The Sudanese, who are mainly Moslems, bury their dead in cemeteries so rigidly restricted that even casual visits by the curious must be authorised. The many migrants from Ethiopia who were of the Christian faith built their own churches and buried their dead in the churchyard. Only the Jews, wanting to conceal their religion in a hostile country, were left without a reasonable solution. Circumstances forced us to bury our dead at night, in secret, close to the Christian churches hoping God would forgive us. Often, when the church workers discovered the unmarked fresh graves, they offered a reward to anyone who would find those who were defiling their sacred places. Fingers were pointed at us, but we restrained ourselves and managed to hold out. When the number of dead rose and the problem of burial became more acute every day, the heads of the community gathered and decided that it was impossible to continue to bury in the Christian areas and that we had to bury in our own quarter. According to the laws concerning defilement and purification, anyone coming into contact with a corpse became unclean. This was cause for deep sorrow. The new system of burials lasted only a few days, because it could not keep pace with the rate of death: some fifteen people died every day in the Amara Kuba camp. In three months, about two thousand men, women and children were buried. There were more than 4,000 victims from the time the Jews began to stream out of Ethiopia until the end of their long journey. Each one an entire world lost, each life a tragic story. Incidentally, someone in the community has begun collecting the names of those who died in this refugee camp in particular and in Sudan in general. I hope that this important undertaking will receive a wide response. The new burials close to the houses caused terrible pollution. Some could not be buried in the yards and were buried inside the houses. When the community leaders realised that this endangered those who were still able to stand on their own two feet, they decided to go back to burying them near the Christian churches, but without a religious ceremony. It was quite clear to the Christian religious leaders that there was a large community of Jews concealing their religious identity and when they came to ask for permission to bury their dead in the churchyards, they did not object. However, they insisted that the Jews be buried with Christian rites. This condition was unacceptable to most of the Jewish religious leaders, but with reality striking them in the face, they had to agree to the humiliating and sad terms. Death left them no choice. Nevertheless, they evaded the ceremony whenever they could.

It is important to mention some outstanding figures who led the community, even in those difficult times. The greatest was Rabbi (*Kes*) Yahis Madhinah, who educated his sons to follow in his footsteps. He had a powerful religious and spiritual influence and participated in the joyful and sad moments of many Jewish families. His blessing was sought by those on the eve of their escape to Sudan and, in the end, he himself became convinced that he would reach the Holy Land, Jerusalem, via Sudan. He was almost eighty when he and his large family uprooted themselves from the village and eventually arrived in Sudan. There, in sorrow, he fasted, wept and prayed for the wellbeing of the community. Feeling that his strength was failing he requested, more correctly, ordered his children not to bury him with Christian rites. Despite the great danger of clashing with the Christian element, he was given a Jewish burial, near the church. His grave, which had been isolated, was gradually surrounded by scores of new Jewish graves.

People who were in the camp during the "time of death" relate that the funerals went on day and night at such a pace that sometimes corpses had to be left until the following day. In retrospect, it seems to me that it was easier to die than to stay alive. Death did not differentiate between weak and strong, old and young, it struck the way the burning sun strikes and withers flowers. The funerals were hasty and devoid of emotion. It was sadder than words can tell. Some of those I have met while writing this book say that they still cry over what they went through at the time. Entire families vanished as though they had never existed. I personally know people who lost a wife and children, a husband and children, as well as children who lost parents, parents who were left childless, and so on. One of those I interviewed said, "I saw a child crying next to his parents' corpses, trying to rouse them to help him. He couldn't understand that they were dead, that they couldn't answer him, so he nagged and wheedled, because that is how nature makes us act towards parents. I looked at him," he went on, "and it broke my heart; I couldn't help him in any way, because I could hardly move. The little I did was to drag myself to the nearest doorway and ask the people there to separate the child from his dead parents. I never saw him again. I don't know where he belonged nor what became of him…"

It is hard to describe that life in the shadow of death, certainly not in a few words. There was a feeling of general weakness, of helplessness. The language was different, the food was different, the climate was different. People were at the mercy of decisions made by others who did not understand their feelings. A person would sit, bursting to speak, but something would stop him, because he didn't know what the reaction would be. A person was shoved in the food line, often the food he had received by so much effort was knocked out of his hands, but he dared not pick it up because he was afraid he would be trampled by the crowd. Days and nights passed in this way, with no hope on the horizon. Sometimes one was whipped mercilessly, like an animal. One's self respect was trampled out of existence. Under such conditions one loses control over one's own destiny and, mainly, over the destiny of those who rely on him to keep their heads above death. Sometimes a man would return to his family beaten and wounded and hides it from his wife and children in order not to break their spirit.

Every day like that was made even more unbearable by the sense of being hopelessly trapped. Escape to the centre of the country became a matter of life and death. A group of youngsters dared to look for illegal ways out, since it was difficult to find anyone willing to provide the necessary legal documents. They investigated escape routes and methods suitable for smuggling large groups of refugees, on foot, to the big city. It soon became obvious that only the strong would be able to participate. In addition, the Sudanese were keeping a watchful eye on possible escape routes. Paradoxically, the Sudanese proved to be fairly compassionate, especially if the price was right. Clerks of all ranks were accustomed to accepting money in return for doing a personal favour and the amount of money was not always the major issue. You gave what you could and doors suddenly opened. The agents working to get Jews out of Ethiopia used this system to ensure a quiet exit. Young men who had learned the local language, ventured to directly request transit permits in exchange for money and these were soon provided. Most found their way to the city and from there, by various routes, to Israel.

The great urge to reach the big city was accompanied by high hopes fed by rumours of the wonders and miracles that happened there. Further, the death rate in the big city was low compared to the outlying districts, though it is hard to pinpoint the reason for this. Perhaps modern medical care was more available; perhaps the allowances were paid more efficiently; perhaps it was because they no longer lived in tents, but in weatherproof structures; perhaps the food they ate was freshly bought in the markets and perhaps it was possible to find less polluted water to drink. In spite of these advantages, life in the city had many drawbacks. Local crooks, aware of the extent of their bewilderment and confusion, exploited the newcomers to the full. They began to deal in exit permits from the outlying districts, generally promising much and delivering little; they took the monthly allowances of families and disappeared. They assumed the names of these innocents to cheat them out of the allowance due to them. The great efforts by some of the operatives to prevent such exploitation had no effect. Instead, the crooks studied their methods and learned how to throw them off their trail. In many cases, this cat-and-mouse chase used up a lot of energy and diverted attention from the main issue.

Gedarif was the common goal. Everybody emigrating by way of Sudan passed through the city at some stage or other. From Gedarif they went to Khartoum, the capital of Sudan, and from there by various routes to Israel. At a certain stage, it was possible to go directly from the outlying areas of the city to Israel.

Masses of Christian migrants came to Gedarif to organise themselves for a military attack on the Ethiopian government. Almost all the Christian fighters were young, a factor that caused a severe problem for the Jews, who were there with large families that included young girls who became sexual targets for the Christians. The issue was partly solved by what was called a "Sudanese marriage". This was a technical arrangement by which the girl was handed over to the Jewish bridegroom after checking seven generations back to make sure the couple were not blood relatives and after verifying that the fellow would treat her with consideration. Many such marriages were immediately annulled by the immigration officials in Israel, in view of the tender age of one or both of the partners, or because the girls learned that they would not be able to study in the framework of the Youth Immigration organisation, if they remained married. When a marriage was annulled for either of these reasons, the parents lost face to a certain extent, because they shared some commitment to the marriage. In a few cases, the marriage was legally renewed when the couple maintained a warm relationship during their studies and army service. Although the girl gained the protection of her new family after the wedding, it was a sad situation compared to the joyful preparations that would have been made for at least a year in advance in the home village. There, it would start with the courtship that was conducted by both sets of parents after a careful search for a suitable match. The ceremony itself would be planned for the hot summer months so that all branches of the scattered family could attend. Nothing was spared in providing a generous, dignified wedding feast, even if the families were poor. The wedding lasted for at least ten days, during which everyone ate, drank, laughed and exchanged vital information. However, in Sudan, that cursed country, none of the above had any value because the rhythm of life was so different and so dependent on factors beyond our control.

The causes of death in the remote refugee camps as well as in the big city were hunger, thirst and violence. Migrants from all the districts were collected in one big refugee camp under abrasive, stressful conditions. It did not take much for knives or axes to flash and for people, usually the weak, to die. There were organised gangs, areas were divided into protection zones and border

69

disputes often erupted in knife fights. The gangs would enter houses as they pleased, at night or in broad daylight, to demand money or possessions. I experienced such an attack.

Like other youngsters who had escaped from Ethiopia on their own, I was taken in by a family. Late one night, we were gathered in front of the fire, all in good spirits because we had received our monthly allowance that day. Suddenly, the flimsy stick door was knocked down and two men burst in, waving long knives and choppers. "The money!" they yelled. Stammering with fear, we handed over everything we had. That was goodbye to our monthly allowance, but we were unhurt. There was nothing unusual about the incident; night after night someone we knew would suffer the same trauma. Our efforts to defend ourselves had no effect.

Our lives were further complicated by the superstition and prejudice against us prevalent among those of different faiths. The number of incoming refugees was balanced by the number of those leaving for Israel. The Christians, who kept an eye on events in the Jewish community, didn't understand why a number of people, individuals or groups regularly vanished to be replaced by new faces. The veteran Christian migrants began to be curious about this exchange that took place under cover of darkness. Some wanted to know who was responsible for the support of these strange people who did not go out to work in the fields, but always had food and drink. They spread a rumour that *falashas* were living among them. These, the Christians said, "look like anyone else, but at night they change shape, as they used to do in the villages." The Christians firmly believed that Jews had the singular ability to assume the form of animals by night, particularly hyenas, in order to prey on their little children. They also believed Jews could cause a baby's death by the evil eye.

In spite of everything, the Jews did their best to observe a Jewish way of life, even in Sudan. They observed the Sabbath as a day of rest, which also set them apart. At the same time, due to environmental pressure, abuse or threats, some families tried to prove that they were not Jews and assumed Christian or Moslem names, or used such expressions as "Christ our Saviour". Others attended church on Sundays, faking participation for the sake of being left in peace until they could leave for Israel.

Each departure made life harder for those who remained behind. These were often threatened, beaten and cursed and those who anticipated what lay in store for them, moved to different neighbourhoods by night. The children paid the highest price. They had been made to leave their natural, nurturing village, to wander for months on foot till they came to a strange country, where they were housed in refugee camps. Here they reached a point of despair that they would remember all their lives. Instead of playing like children in other countries, these little ones became partners to fateful decisions. They were the ones who stood in line for food, water and flour. The smallest of them had to be counted every few minutes to make sure they didn't get lost either by the wayside, or in the undergrowth, or among the tents in the refugee camps. Children who had grown up in a village where they knew every face, encountered crowds of unfamiliar, some-times unsympathetic, people. Not a few tried to run away. They didn't care what would happen to them, all they wanted was to sit in the familiar yard with the cows, sheep, goats and other domestic animals they missed. The adults also prayed for an end to the hard times and a return to earlier days. They talked about it, but the chil-dren remembered, longed and expressed their feelings by withdrawal, fear and melancholy glances.

Despite the dreadful suffering of Ethiopian Jewry on the way to Sudan and in the refugee camps and despite the day by day humiliation, they tried to sustain their morale, their hope, their dream that the day would come when the sun would not rise in vain, but would bring the joyful news that their dream was coming true. They would reach Jerusalem; they would live to achieve the dream of their ancestors.

Sadly, the sense of alienation and isolation that began in Sudan was prolonged and intensified in Israel when families were thoughtlessly separated on arrival by being placed in absorption centres far from each other. Many of the wounds from their experiences in Sudan reopened.

David Albahari

My Husband
Translated from the Serbian by the author

Today is Friday. Every day since Monday my husband, when he comes back from work, remains seated in his car, parked in front of our house. He doesn't move at all. He just sits there, and only sometimes does he bend his neck and touch the edge of the steering wheel with his forehead.

He sits longer and longer. On Monday he got out of the car after fifteen minutes; on Wednesday he stayed in the car for almost an hour. The streetlights are on now, and he, the dark silhouette, is still sitting.

On the first day, when he came into the house, I touched his cheek with my palm. He didn't look up. I did not touch him again after that, did not ask him anything. I was patient. When we went to bed, I lifted my nightgown all the way up to my chin, moved closer to him, and put my legs around him. He slipped his hand between my thighs, like he always did, but I knew that his fingers were in some other place.

Last week, in one of the houses on our street, a dead woman was discovered. Her neighbour called the police because the cats in the house of the dead woman, who at that time was not thought of as being dead, did not stop meowing. When the door was broken down, the cats ran outside. The woman was discovered in her bedroom, on the floor, by the bed.

I remembered that yesterday. I thought that there was some connection between her death and my husband's behaviour, but I quickly gave up trying to find out what it was. It is not easy to think of somebody's death, even though neither my husband nor I knew what that woman looked like.

The cats stay in her yard. Sometimes they go behind our house, tear our garbage bags, pull out the scraps of food.

I don't know what time it is anymore. My husband is still sitting in the car, partially lit by the street lamp. If he doesn't get out soon, I'll have to fetch him a blanket. When we moved here, the apple tree in front of our house was in full bloom, but now it's autumn, branches are bare, nights are cold, clouds gather up in the sky.

I think of our neighbours. They have certainly noticed what was going on in front of our house. They always notice everything, anyway. In the evening they sit in darkness, by day they hide behind their curtains, and they never stop watching out of their windows. I don't know what they expect to see. In the morning, before nine, the postman walks down the street. At noon, on Tuesday and Friday, a young man, Chinese, puts fliers into mailboxes. At four in the afternoon, probably after school, an older man and a girl with a tiny knapsack on her back enter one of the houses. On Saturday morning, or perhaps on Sunday, Jehovah's Witnesses come. Nothing else happens.

Now they're watching my husband, hanging onto the steering wheel like a drowning person.

Once he did dream that he was drowning. In his dream he swam too far from the bank, he told me, and couldn't get back. He dropped his arms and began to sink. While he was sinking, the surrounding landscape slowly began to disappear from his sight, as if a giant eraser was erasing the view. The bank of the river disappeared, the willows and poplars followed, then the tower on the hill, and only the blue sky remained. Soon, instead of it, the blueness of water appeared. The bubbles of air danced in front of his eyes, rushing to get out. After that he saw nothing. He felt terrible fear and woke up.

I tried to comfort him. I held him and whispered sweet nothings into his ear. Let it all go to the dogs and cats, I said rocking him gently. One, two, three, stronger than fear are we.

When that woman was discovered, a black cat was sitting on her chest. She sat there throughout the investigation, and jumped off her only when paramedics

74

put the dead woman on their stretcher. After that I suppose the cat also went outside.

By the middle of September the tree was full of apples. We ate three or four every day, I made apple pie, cooked them, baked them. I packed two plastic bags full of apples, and left one in front of our neighbour's door. The other one I left in front of our door, for the postman.

On Wednesday, he told me that sometimes, while driving to work, he could hear birds singing. When he stopped at traffic lights, he would bend down to look through his window, but couldn't see anything, only the wasteland of the empty sky.

I don't know why I think of all these things now. My legs hurt from standing, but if I sit in the armchair, I won't be able to see the street; if I sit on the sofa, my back will be turned to it; if I lie down, I'll fall asleep.

Yesterday, on Thursday, he stayed in the car for two hours. I stood just like this, by the window, like who knows how many neighbours, and waited. The food on the table grew cold: chicken legs and peas, green salad, chocolate pudding. In the end I threw everything away.

Today I didn't cook.

This morning, while we drank coffee, I asked him if he wanted to tell me something, anything. Now is the right moment, I said, afterwards it'll be too late. My husband put the newspaper down, took off his glasses, rubbed his eyes. Too late for what? he asked. I didn't know. I said: For everything. My husband put his glasses back on and looked at me. He hadn't looked at me for a long time, I thought, and even tried to smile. My husband kept looking at me. Then my eyes filled with tears and I lowered my head.

We should have taken in a cat. It would have run between my legs now, arched its back, held its tail high.

Nothing is connected to anything, said my husband when I told him about physicists looking for the final, all-inclusive theory. I had read an article on them in the weekly magazine that the postman left in our mailbox

75

every Wednesday. That theory, I said, should connect every phenomenon in the world in an inseparable whole. My husband closed his eyes. Each one of us, he said, walks through this world all by himself. And what about me, I said, where am I? My husband looked at me again. That's something, he said, that I would like to know myself.

I didn't say anything then. I stood up, took the box with cookies and searched for a round one. I put it into my mouth and tried to push my tongue through the hole in its middle. The cookie broke into pieces, became wet in my mouth, and dough stuck to my teeth.

I should have said something, despite that dough. I should have shaken him, grabbed his hair and said: Look! I'm pulling your hair out! You're not alone! Actually, I did not have to move at all. I could've said that without getting up, sitting, there was nothing to prevent me from doing that. Had I said something then, I would not be standing by the window now.

Then he continued to speak. He said: When you reach out with your arm, do you really think you touch somebody? At best, you'll touch somebody's reflection, and it won't be you touching it, it will be your reflection. A reflection touches a reflection, that's our whole life. This world is like a giant mirror with reflections of things happening somewhere else, somewhere beyond us. In the mirror, we are illusions, surrounded by other illusions. I am not there.

I go to get a blanket. I've waited long enough. I'll lift him up, he's so light, and I'll carry him into the house, make a soup for him. I'll tell him that loneliness is something that we choose ourselves, that there is no other way for us to believe, with or without that mirror, it doesn't matter. And I'll hold him tight until he melts into me, until he is not alone anymore.

When I step out, stars surprise me.

Eli Amir

Farewell Baghdad
Extract from the untranslated novel in Hebrew

"Cowards!" shouted Ismail at us.

"Who beat you in Palestine, huh?" yelled Edouard.

"The Ingleez!"

"The Jews!" Edouard boasted.

"*Yallah*, who's game?" called Ismail, disdainfully scanning us as if already chalking up his victory. "Where's your champion?" And seeing Edouard, our leader, hesitate, he added: "Say the *shahada* and I'll lay off."

What a sap, I thought. He really believed that we had only to say "I testify that there is no God besides Allah and that Mohammed is the messenger of Allah" for our Jewishness to disappear like a stain that came out in the wash. Rabbi Bashi had told us in his sermons about the Marranos in Spain who pretended to become Christians but secretly remained Jews for generations — and here this imbecile believed that we could be turned into Muslims in a matter of seconds!

"You want us to say the *shahada*?" asked Edouard.

"Yes."

"Over your dead body!"

"Clear out, this isn't your country!" Ismail shouted. "You're traitors. You don't belong here!"

"We were here long before you Muslims," Edouard called back. "We were born here and we aren't going anywhere."

Yet my father was for clearing out too, and I felt caught in the middle. Why should I have to leave? protested one part of me. Because this isn't yours, answered another. Which was what Ismail, who turned up in our neighbourhood at least once a week to challenge us to a holy war, kept telling us. My father wouldn't let us forget who we were either. "If you're given the choice between

77

conversion and death," he liked to remind us, "the Bible says: choose death!"

I took Ismail's threats seriously. Not long ago I had seen him grab a cat by the tail, twirl it around his head and send it flying against a wall. The thud still sent a shiver down my spine. There were many stories about his exploits, and he was as much of a tyrant with his own gang as with us. The only Jew he had anything to do with, even though she was Edouard's sister, was Amira, who studied in the girls' wing of the Muslim high school that he attended. According to her, he loved Iraqi history and worshipped its heroes. Once, he told her, he had dreamed that the Babylonian king Nebuchadnezzar was returning victorious on horseback from a war, accompanied by thousands of his soldiers who followed him through the gate of the goddess Ishtar. He, Ismail, the monarch's trusted adjutant, rode beside him, and Nebuchadnezzar, fresh from routing the Egyptian pharaoh Necho, led him to the triumphal platform, handed him the ceremonial bow, and proclaimed: "Ismail my son, I crown thee king of Iraq. Thou wilt conquer many nations and even reach Jerusalem."

Ismail's dream was actually reassuring, since it left no room for doubt that he was mad. Suppose I had gone around saying that I dreamed of being king of the Jews and re-establishing the empire of David! "He's no older than you are and you can beat him," my father encouraged us. "Where's your Jewish pride?" Yet when my uncle watched the next belt fight, he saw us whipped by Ismail again. It was then that he decided to gather us all and teach us the art of the slingshot.

The slings took Ismail and his gang by surprise, and they scattered before our sudden volley while we whooped and capered like billy goats. My father waved his turban in the air, treated us to baklava, showed us his old army sword, and said: "They won't be back again, not if I know them."

But they were back the next day in full force, each with a sling of his own, which they knew how to use. This time it was we, licking our wounds, who beat a shameful retreat. My father, nonplussed, raised arms and said with a melancholy nod: "What a world! You can't even trust the *goyim* any more. God only knows what we're in for at the hands of those Ismails. It's they and their ilk that will be running Iraq some day."

My father refused to back down. "You can beat them," he insisted.

One way or another, Ismail was a force to be reckoned with when he appeared in the narrow streets of That-el-Takya, an Islamic bully with an enigmatically arrogant smile. And I especially had to reckon with the admiration of Amira, who liked to sit reading propped on colourful cushions in her window seat overlooking our battlefield, from which she never missed a single skirmish. "He's braver and stronger than any of you," she taunted us, aiming her sharpest barbs at her brother Edouard until he struck back and hit her, which only made her stick out her tongue and jeer harder. Most of her girlfriends were Muslims and she spoke Arabic just like them. Her dream was to win a government scholarship to study engineering in America, from which she would return to build a super-bridge over the Tigris, and she had ceased to view Ismail as an enemy from the day he had rescued her from an Arab boy who tried sticking his hand down her blouse. Our stone and belt fights were a form of gladiatorial combat that she enjoyed watching from her box seat.

I jealously had to admit that Ismail was tall and handsome with large, fiery eyes and a head full of black curls. There was something proud and aloof about him, and he was the only one of his barefoot gang to wear shoes. Sometimes I had the feeling that I had known him all my life, perhaps even in some previous existence. Now, mocking and swearing at us like Goliath, he called to Edouard (who — no doubt fearing a new rival — had unproletarianly vetoed my proposal to enlist the baker's apprentice Sami in our ranks):

"*Ya yahud*, what's your weapon today: belts, slings, stones or knives?"

"Knives, knives!" howled Ismail's gang members.

"Belts!" decreed Edouard, slipping his own from his trousers.

"Cowards!" swaggered Ismail. "I told you the Jews were yellow."

As he took the field, Edouard's tongue slid between his lips, a sure sign that he was nervous. The two belts whistled through the air, our eyes on the bright gleam of their ornamented buckles, even before their owners closed in. Suddenly the belts met and twined around each other. Had Edouard been a bit quicker, or so I imagined doing in his place, he might have jerked Ismail off his feet. But the belts unwound and the tense ballet resumed.

"Lower, Edouard, go for his belly!" I yelled, smacking my fist in my palm while shouting advice along with everyone else. A second later Edouard was on the ground, where he remained lying submissively. As long as you stayed on your feet in a belt fight, it was fair play even to kill you, but the minute you were down, the unwritten rules called for mercy. Ismail stood waiting for his next victim.

"Cowards!" screamed Amira.

"He's your own brother, you bitch," I yelled back. "Why don't you go and mop the floor?"

"You shut up, Kabi," she shouted down at me. "All you've got is a big mouth."

Before I knew what had happened, I was facing Ismail myself. He raised his hand and everyone stepped back and formed a ring around us. What was I doing? It was already too late to explain to him that it was all a mistake. As though I were someone else being watched by me through a fog, I was dimly aware of twirling my belt, lunging forward, dodging and springing back. Yet not even the fear that blurred my senses could keep me from hearing Amira scream "You clown, you!" and from realising that she meant me. Our belts met and with a quick motion Ismail plucked mine away and left me barehanded. A second later his own belt shrieked over my head, its buckle dangerously close to me. I was about to be killed. Had he knocked me down I would have been safe, but now I would have to grovel of my own free will. And in front of Amira too!

Ismail took my measure with his eyes. At first I thought I saw contempt in them, as if I were not even worth a whipping. Yet as he went on staring at me like someone struggling to remember, I again had the feeling of knowing him from somewhere.

"Beat it," he said at last in a toneless voice.

I would rather have been whiplashed than humiliated like that. In a flash my fear yielded to defiance. I had nothing left to lose. As my father used to say: Once you're wet, you needn't fear the rain.

"Hey, zombie!" shouted Amira.

"You tart, I hope you marry a cross-eyed cripple!" I shouted back with a resolution born of despair. Once and for all I would show her I was no coward. I picked up my belt and charged blindly. Ismail's buckle hit me just above the temple, leaving me dazed from the explosion in my head.

"I told you to beat it, *ya Id*." He was standing very close to me.

Despite the flashes of pain running through me, I looked at him in astonishment.

"You Jews are our slaves forever," he cried, as if recovering possession of himself, and signalled to his gang. A moment later it was gone.

I stood there surrounded by my friends, one of whom examined the bruise on my forehead and pressed it to keep down the swelling. It took me a minute to come to my senses. Then I replaced the fingers on my forehead with my own, mumbled that I had to go, and took off after Ismail through the winding streets of the souk.

I knew that he was heading for Razi Street, on the far side of the marketplace, which I reached just in time to see him latch on to the back of a passing carriage and hitch a ride. Although my father had warned me against this form of transportation, no self-respecting boy my age hadn't tried it at least once, and I grabbed hold of the next coach to come along and crouched against its tail end. From both hearsay and a bit of experience I knew that I would be safe if I wasn't noticed by the driver right away. But I was and his whip lashed out at me, once, twice, and yet again, each time missing my head, which was protected by the high overhang of the rear wheel. From time to time I peered out of my shell to check that Ismail was still ahead of me. By now we were in the Muslim quarter of el-Dehidwana, passing shops and coffeehouses and speeding southward away from That-el-Takya.

Oddly, I felt no fear despite breaking my father's injunction. He had never allowed me to stray far from home. Since the day I was old enough to walk on the streets by myself he had placed strict limits on where I went, while at the same time considering it his duty as a Jewish father to acquaint me, as his own father had done for him, with every back alley down which I might flee if trapped by a Muslim mob on my way to school or in the souk. When I was older he took me to Bab-el-Sheikh and taught me to talk and act like a Muslim and to tell one from a Jew. When I was born he gave me the Arab name of Sa'aid to go with my Jewish one of Ya'akov Kabi, which greatly pleased me though no one ever used it; warned me when I grew older never to go to a Muslim neighbourhood by myself; and — as if doubting my obedience — whispered "God speed" every time I set out somewhere.

I might have put up a better fight against Ismail without my father's fears, and yet here I was, flouting all his rules. The coach sped on and I kept my eyes on Ismail, who was staring down at the roadway racing beneath him. Was he thinking about his feud with us? Could Muslims like him really feel threatened by a small minority of us Jews? We looked like them, we were circumcised like them, we spoke their language, we sang their songs and danced their dances — what made us any different? Why were their menacing looks and hawk-like eyes always trailing us, the strangers, the tolerated *dhimmi* looked down on by the lords of the land?

Ismail jumped from his carriage and turned right, and I followed him as he progressed by fits and starts, speeding up and slowing down as if his tempestuous nature were unsuited to an even gait. Single-storey clay houses with narrow windows lined streets that smelled of burning dung, boiled sheep ghee, greasy food, and rank vegetation nourished by sewage. Ismail halted by a butcher's shop and sat down beside a paunchy man who was straddling a small stool and had on the red keffiyah of the mujaheddin, the Palestine volunteers, while I crossed the street and hid behind the big mulberry tree, which seemed to have shrunk. The long hours we two had spent beneath it, eating its berries and staining our clothes with their dark juice!

Suddenly it all fitted together: my mother's stories about the little house in el-Me'azzam — the butcher's shop with its meat hooks — fat Hairiyya with her son Ismail. The rush of memories was like a picture abruptly coming into focus. It had been so long ago: before the *Farhoud*, before Zionism and the State of Israel, before the Muslims and Jews had gone crazy and stopped living peacefully together. This was where I was born, in the little house that I now stood in front of as if ten years had never passed, with its storey and-a-half and its cellar and its flat roof and its three steps leading up to a wooden entrance gate whose rusty hinges, irregularly oiled by my father, had creaked to a continually changing tune that grew spine-tinglingly sweet toward evening when every unexpected knock bore the promise of novelty and surprise. Only its colour had changed. The house itself looked dreary, almost dismal, and much smaller than I remembered it, though it still had the same smell of basil mixed with goat dung. I was dying to enter it, walk down the narrow hallway, mount the steps to my room, stand on my little stool, and look out of the window at the street below — or else, to climb to the roof and peer down at Hairiyya and Mihsin's courtyard in defiance of my mother's prohibition.

Ismail and I were both our parents' first sons, born two days apart, I at the end of the holiday of Sukkot and he in the middle of it. Hairiyya and my mother shared nursing the two of us. *Fidwas ya ibni, ya Id*, she would sing to me, shortening Sa'id to Id, the Arabic word for "holiday". It was Ismail's calling me by that name that had brought it all back to me.

Actually, a moment before placing him, an image of his mother had flashed before me, my face buried in the soft, fat folds of her neck. On her side of the fence was a patch of eggplants, the deep purple of which enthralled me. Once I stole one, and when my mother slapped my wrist and made me return it, Hairiyya laughed with her white teeth and said: "*Fidwa, ya ibni, ya Id*. It's just an eggplant. Take all you want."

Sometimes the two of us, Ismail and I, roamed among the palm trees in the fragrant rose garden near our home, or played hide-and-seek among the oleander bushes, while listening to the drawn-out cooing of the doves. Once we lost our way and Hairiyya and Abu Ismail the butcher went to look for us. "*Ya wiladi, ya Ismail, ya Id, weynkum*?" she had cried. "Where are you, my sons?" She sounded a triumphant trill when she found us and gave us basil water to drink as an antidote to the oleander flowers that we had eaten.

My mother loved our house, which she was always cleaning or scrubbing or painting or polishing. On Fridays I was sent off to Hairiyya's garden while my mother prepared for the Sabbath unhindered, after which I was bathed in the large basin, dressed in a *dishdash*, a white smock like Ismail's, and allowed to watch the lighting of the Sabbath candles that were placed out of my reach on the window sill, their white wicks floating in little pools of oil. Her head covered with an embroidered shawl and her breath causing the yellow flame to flicker, my mother murmured the mysterious blessing in its strange language, gazed heavenward, and prayed — what for I never knew. But the house was full of a great light when she finished and everyone in it felt at peace.

Saturday mornings, when we were forbidden by the Sabbath laws to light the gas burner, Hairiyya came with Ismail to make us tea, boiling milk fresh from her brown cow. Sometimes Ismail spent the day with us, listening with a white skullcap on his head as my father recited the Kiddush and sang Sabbath hymns to the melodies of the Iraqi singer Abd el-Wahab. After dinner we raced to the *jalala*, always quarrelling about who had won and who could swing first. At the end of our last Passover in el-Me'azzam, Hairiyya brought us hot, fragrant bread. It was the first I had seen in eight days and I fell upon it wolfishly in disregard of the manners taught me by my mother.

Summer nights we slept on the roof, where my parents walked about with a funny slouch, fearful of inadvertently glimpsing our Muslim neighbours in a state of undress beyond the low balcony. It was my first realisation that being small had its advantages. I liked sleeping under the sky. Sometimes I was woken at night by the call of the muezzin, from whom I learned that there was a Muslim God as well as a Jewish one. When it ended I would proclaim huskily, as though I too were one of the faithful: "*Sadaka Allah el-azim*. Just is the great God."

And then something — I was not sure what — began to go wrong. My father stopped listening to music on the radio and tuned in to every news bulletin, flitting from station to station. He and Abu Ismail sat talking about distant fighting in countries I knew nothing about. One day we heard on the radio that a great war had broken out. Everyone was afraid. And there were new names that I couldn't pronounce, such as Hitler, Stalin, Churchill and Mussolini.

Afterwards Australian soldiers appeared with big, funny hats and there were whispered rumours about Jews being killed in far-off places I hadn't even known they lived in. My father and Abu Ismail took to arguing. Sometimes they shouted at each other. My father was for Churchill and Abu Ismail was for Hitler. I was sure that was because Hitler had an Iraqi moustache. Life was no longer the same. Neither was el-Me'azzam. Outsiders appeared, beating Jews and throwing stones at them. One old woman was stabbed. I could tell how worried my father was by the way he pushed his dish of saffron rice with the back of his hand and wouldn't eat.

One afternoon a burning torch was tossed into our house. My mother put it out in the nick of time. A few days later a crowd of Muslims gathered outside and yelled: "Jews, get out!" Hairiyya stood by the front gate and screamed: "Have you no shame? The Jews have lived with us forever." For whatever reason, they went away, but though it was the middle of the rainless summer, my father, who was white as a sheet, said to my mother: "Woman, there are storm clouds brewing. We have to leave el-Me'azzam." My mother clawed her cheeks with her nails and cried without a sound. The tight arch of her lips frightened me. The next day Hairiyya and Abu Ismail helped load our belongings on a truck. The two women kissed and hugged tearfully. At the last minute Ismail sat on the *jalala* and wouldn't get up. My mother begged me to let him have it. "It's too big and heavy," she said. "And anyway, we'll be back after the war." I balked and screamed. In the end we took it, leaving Ismail other toys of mine.

This opened a new chapter in our lives. At first we moved to Kahwit el-Kebiri, a Jewish neighbourhood into which thousands of refugees had poured. Its ugly, colourless, shapeless houses were covered with tin sheets and huddled so closely together, roof against roof, that you could see what everyone was doing. All winter the rusty tin rattled scarily, threatening to fly off in the wind. Open sewers ran in the streets, turning to frozen dung heaps in winter and muddy cesspools in summer. Hungry children ran up and down the filthy alleys that teemed with stench, noise and neglect. My mother hated the place and begged to go back to el-Me'azzam. I prayed that my father would agree. "After the war," was his stock reply. But the war dragged on and then came the *Farhoud* with its wounded, raped and dead. The world had gone mad. "Woman, there's no going back," my father said. "Not a Jew is left in the old neighbourhood." He refused even to visit it, and the two of them fought for a long time.

And now the visitor was me. I thought of saying hello to Hairiyya and giving her a big hug. She had nursed me; I was like a son to her. But I was afraid. Perhaps she too had changed.

Ismail rose. He did not go home though. Rather, he started down the street, perhaps on an errand for the maj-jahed. The harsh smell of burning dung was a grim reminder of the Muslim slum I was in. Anything — my face, short trousers, European shirt, leather sandals — could give me away. A donkey brayed loudly as if pro-claiming my presence and I decided to head back, trying in vain to keep my eyes straight ahead of me. All around me — or so I had been taught from childhood to believe, the monstrous fear of them as much a part of me as my native language — was an alien crowd of vengeful killers and loathsome sodomites. What was I doing among them? I could be kidnapped, body-snatched, thrown into the river. "If you're ever alone among Muslims," my father had told me, "don't attract attention, whatever you do. Try to behave as naturally as if you were a born-and-bred Arab." And now, of all times, I had to go to the toilet. Why, all I had to do was pee on some Shi'ite's wall for him to come at me with a knife!

I tried holding it in. Oh God, give me strength, I prayed. The ache in my bladder grew worse. Oh God. A hot trickle ran down my shorts all the way to my knee. The pressure eased, but now my pants had an embarrassing stain. It was hopeless to try to hide it. My one consolation was that no one knew me in this place.

I started to run. Although Razi Street was still far away, I now had a new worry. How would I get home without my pants being seen? Suppose Amira was still in her window seat! And even if I managed to change the shorts in time, I would still have to explain the bump on my forehead, which must already be turning black and blue.

The sun hung low above the horizon on a fiery carpet of scarlet clouds. Like a promised salvation, Razi Street loomed in the distance. With the last of my strength I picked up speed and crossed it; then, my physical confidence suddenly gone, I grabbed at a passing carriage and missed. It had seemed so easy on the way to el-Me'azzam. Only now did I grasp what a crazy thing I had done. To hitch a ride to the heart of Muslim Baghdad! How had I failed to be afraid when now just thinking of it made me shudder?

The fact was — to be honest, I had known it all along — that my courage came from Ismail. Deep down I had felt sure that I need only call him to be rescued from any trouble I got into. Even if he had clipped me with his belt buckle on purpose, it was because I had asked for it, and I had followed him to el-Me'azzam in a kind of ecstasy, which only now yielded to the realisation that, though startled to see me, he had no more room for me in his life. He had granted me the most I could have hoped for and then — strong, solitary, implacable, a leader of men — had walked away and left me forever. And still I had run after him, consumed by the need for his protection! Perhaps my father was right. Iraq had made slaves of us. It was time to clear out.

Shimon Ballas

Imaginary Childhood

Translated by Ammiel Alcalay

I grew up in the Christian Quarter of Baghdad, in two houses, separated only by a narrow alley. We moved out of the first house when I was six; I spent all my school years in the second house from the first grade until the end of high school. The first house was one of three in a cul de sac; it was in the middle and its walls hugged those of the neighbours from either side. On our right, there lived a well-to-do Jewish family whose house was the biggest and most luxurious in the lane. A cone-shaped lantern was made of stained glass and crowned with a serrated tin plate hung in front of it. At nightfall, when I heard the guard's heavy steps, I would rush toward the window to see his shadow in the darkness as he leaned a wooden ladder against the wall and climbed up to light the lantern. The flame from the wick would leap across his burnished, withered face, sending an eerie flash across his dark eyes. Then I would see him come down, hoist the ladder on to his back and disappear down the alley. I eagerly awaited the ritual to continue and when the long whistle shook the night out of its slumber, I would feel chills going down my back. I don't know how old I was at the time, but I do remember that long before we left that house the colourful lantern was replaced by a small electric lamp, turned on at the same time every night by a mysterious hand.

To our left lived an elderly Armenian couple, refugees of the disturbances in Turkey. They had a smoothly polished copper knocker on the front door; late at night, the door would open as the knocker struck. Strange songs drifted out of the house, sad songs accompanied at times by the commotion of men and women's wild laughter. The landlady, a short, ungainly woman, was the uncrowned queen of the lane. The grown-ups respected her and the kids called her Auntie. The kids particularly liked her because she provided refuge for them whenever their parents got angry. She offered them sweets without sparing her admonition, but her rebukes were as sweet and gently to the ear as her treats to the palate. She had a way about her that fascinated me, an air of mystery that surrounded her life. During the summer, she used to sit by the entrance to her house, embroidering lace. When she saw me watching her, she would ask me to come over and sit with her while she told me stories from another world. Her voice was clear, though it wavered a little, a gold tooth gleamed in her mouth and her laughter gushed forth like a gurgling spring. She was a singer for the Turks, and her portrait from those days, in a long, white dress, stood on a square table between two large divans in the courtyard. Her husband, who was quite a bit older than she was, listened to her stories silently, occasionally getting up to pat my head with his cool, bony hand. Odd guests visited the house and spoke to her in their language while I — left to myself — was proud to see her as the centre of attraction, with everyone's eyes fixed only on her and their ears cocked for whatever she might say. When I was asked to go home, I would get up despondently, dragging my feet. Her husband would put a piece of candy in my hand and accompany me to the door before shutting it. I never knew what went on behind that locked door and when I asked my mother, she would reprimand me and tell me to keep quiet.

This aging singer was a remarkable woman. She grew up in a foreign land and took refuge in a foreign land when her people were struck by evil. Later on, I portrayed her in a story called "Aunt Ghawni".

Our house was old, with a heavy black door in a wooden frame that creaked every time I leaned against it to open it. There were two cellars in the house, an upper cellar and a lower cellar. The upper cellar's festive time came during the summer months, when we used to stow ourselves away in there during the hottest part of the day; it was always cool and an invigorating breeze flowed through the vents. As for the lower cellar, I was afraid to get near it. There were many stairs leading down to it, the last of which faded away in the darkness. In the spring, up till mid-summer, it would fill with water and a corps of snakes would emerge and spread every which way throughout the house to find a hiding place. I used to lie down by my mother on a mat spread across the floor as I saw a long line of snakes slither by under a wooden footstool near the wall. In those days I wasn't yet aware of how dangerous snakes were so I could amuse myself by watching this incredible spectacle. Later on I got to know how dangerous they were, when I started to grasp the stories told by the grown-ups. I remember a story my mother used to tell me often when I was a kid. She went into the attic, which served as a stor-age place for old things, and when she moved a wicker basket, a spotted snake leapt at her. Transfixed by fear, the upright snake ferociously hissed at her. In that awful moment, she only remembered one thing, the magic incan-tation she had learned from her parents, and which had come to them from their ancestors: "Home snake, home snake, don't hurt us and we won't hurt you." And indeed, the snake accepted her supplication and backed off, coiling itself up on the floor in a great circle.

The people who moved into the house after us were not afraid of snakes. The father of the family, a carpenter by profession, was a seasoned snake hunter. When he was younger and worked as a carpenter's apprentice, his Muslim employer gave him "snake water" to drink, made by dipping a poisonous snake into a jar of water for twenty-four hours. This water served as a remedy against snake bites and whoever drank it became immune for the rest of their days. He would hold the head of a snake between his fingers, with the snake's body wrapped around his arm like a spring. But he never killed the snakes he caught. He set the snakes that weren't poisonous free in the fields; as for the poisonous ones, he plucked out their fangs. I saw him do it on the roof. He brought a piece of cloth right up to the snake's mouth and when the snake stuck its teeth into it, he snatched the cloth away and pulled out the hollow, venomous fangs.

The second house we moved to was also crawling with snakes. They fed on mice and found shelter amongst the wooden ceiling rafters. We could hear them crawling over our heads with their incessant loathsome hissing. A big, black snake made its home in the kitchen and on hot days it would venture out of its lair in search of water. We learned the magic incantation and we used to chant it like a prayer.

But other, more pleasant strains also resounded in my childhood. These were the ringing bells. There were many churches clustered in our quarter and their bells rang for prayer at a fixed hour of the day. I got to know the sound of the bells and I could recognise each and every one of them. The big bell of the Catholic church made slow, heavy sounds, like the stride of a priest on his way to the sanctuary. Compared to that, the fine modest ringing of the small bell at the Armenian church seemed speedy. On New Year, Easter and other holidays, the bells made the window-panes shake, violating me with a strange feeling of dread and happiness. Sometimes a solitary bell could be heard ringing sadly at an odd hour. It was then that I knew that a funeral procession was making its way to the church. Many funerals passed under our window. The young boys would appear at first, at the twist in the lane, in their white gowns, holding candles; after them strode the priests in their black robes, with one in the middle, conducting the procession; after that, the pallbearers followed and behind them came the family and other mourners. The sound of their prayer hushed as they entered the lane and only picked up again as they reached its end. They proceeded in silence the whole length of the alley and the coffin, whose lid was adorned with a small crucifix, was borne by the men. Passers-by stopped near the walls, Christians crossed themselves while Muslims and Jews observed the procession with their heads bowed.

The trumped-up voices of professional mourners couldn't be heard at Christian funerals. This was strictly the terrain of Jews and Muslims. Sometimes on my way to school I encountered Jewish or Muslim funerals; they seemed quite similar. The coffin was borne along on people's shoulders as the mourners beat their chests and ripped their hair out, and everyone hustled and scurried about in a great frenzy. I was drawn to the magnificent splendour of Christian rituals. I loved their houses of prayer and on the holidays, I would slip in and watch Mass, enveloped by the smoke of the incense, rocking to the waves of the organ.

There was a monastery of the French mission that I often visited. This monastery, which was also a school for girls, gave piano lesson in the afternoon. I passed the monastery several times a day and longed to see the piano that brought forth such sweet melodies into the world. But I was apprehensive about going in because of the stern guard that always sat on a stool by the gate and never let any strangers in. I was surprised when I accompanied our maid one morning to buy milk at the dairy on the outskirts of the neighbourhood, and she stopped to chat with the guard. I pulled at her sleeve and whispered my request into her ear, but she dismissed me with a smile and just kept on talking. I wouldn't let go of her until she agreed to hear what I wanted. The guard smiled and promised that he would let me go in if I came back in the afternoon. I reported to him right after I got out of school.

"Too early," he said, "come later."

When I came back, I found the Mother Superior standing at the door. He had told her about me and she offered me both her hands as she pulled me in. She asked if I studied French at school and when I told her I did, she said, "You're an intelligent boy."

She took me up to the second floor and led me into the spacious room that looked like a regular classroom, except for the black piano standing on a platform near the front, with a nun and a student sitting at it. They stopped playing while we stood in the doorway and the Mother Superior said something that, in my confusion, I couldn't quite understand. Then she led me to a bench and left. The teacher nodded to me before going on with her lesson; I shrank back into myself, anxious and excited. From then on, I visited the monastery almost every day. The Mother Superior always welcomed me with a smile and asked me all kinds of questions. She was a beautiful woman and the white cowl adorning her habit lent her a saintly grace. Everyone, including me, addressed her as *"Ma Mère"*. I was a bashful kid and didn't say much but she wouldn't let me evade her questions. Sometimes, when she had free time, she called me into her small office and gave me a long lecture that I couldn't make heads or tails of.

"You're still young," she would tell me with an apologetic smile, "you'll understand when you grown up." Naturally I did understand many things as I grew up, but I no longer took an interest in the ways of the monastery nor did I seek out the company of the old nun. I was occupied by other things that would determine the course of my life.

Many Jewish families lived in the Christian Quarter and their presence was felt along its lanes and alleyways on holidays and the Sabbath. On Rosh Hashanah, we dressed in white, from head to toe; on Purim, we roamed around with pistols, shooting every which way; and on Passover, we vented our anger at the Gentiles. We didn't really grasp the meaning of why we did certain things; we never knew, and to this day I still do not know, why we flew kites on the Ninth of Av. It was a day of fasting and prayer for the grown-ups but a joyous festival for the kids. Lentils, a dish symbolising destruction and lamentation, were prepared at home, but for us it became a delicacy that we looked forward to with great excitement. More than anything, though, we loved the Ninth of Av because of the kites. There wasn't a Jewish child who didn't fly a kite on the Ninth of Av. Of course it was one of our favourite things to do throughout

94

the summer anyway, but on this special day the kites took on a ceremonial significance. We put them together ourselves, adorning them with colourful tails and we competed to see who could make the most beautiful kite that would sit best in the sky. On summer nights, the skies of Baghdad would fill with kites in an abundance of colours. We would tie the end of the string to a railing or a pole and leave the kite floating all night. On summer nights, Baghdad took its rest on the rooftops, and the rustling of the kites under the stars was a lullaby for the children.

My favourite holiday was Passover. I loved the *seder* night sitting around the long table, the reading of the *haggada*, and drinking the sweet wine that my mother had prepared herself. But, as the holiday drew near, I always felt pangs of anxiety over whether or not my father would be with us in order to conduct the *seder* at our house. My father had a textile shop in southern Iraq and only came home every month or two, when his stock ran low and he had to come back to the capital for new goods. When he came, the house was filled with commotion; he would call to my mother and the maid from the doorway and shout to the porter carrying his luggage that he had better not ruin anything. We would gather around him and he would kiss us, leaving our cheeks sore from the rough stubble of his beard and our nostrils filled with the pungent aroma of tobacco. Pedigree chickens would bolt from his parcels squawking, flapping their wings and leaving their droppings all over the place. The courtyard would fill with trunks and packages and a huge pile of dirty clothes.

But just as our joy was great at his arrival, so was our distress when he was absent at the holidays. In his letters, he would usually announce the day of his arrival, but there were times that he left us waiting until the night of the holiday. As my mother and the maid toiled the whole day over preparations for the holiday meal, I wouldn't budge from the window until the late afternoon. On days like that no miracle took place and I harboured great resentment in my heart against him.

Are the two houses that I grew up in still standing intact? A young Iraqi friend in Paris could not answer my question, but he gave me a map of the city, one of those given out to tourists. I found streets and gardens there, squares and bridges and blocks of apartment buildings on the outskirts.

"I have a different map," I said to him, "a map of alleys twisting and intertwining like an intricate cobweb. I can draw it on paper because I remember every single curve, every single niche, every single arch, every single window and every single side of a house that protrudes in a sharp angle near which men stood and pissed."

"Many quarters have been pulled down," my friend replied promptly, "Yours too, perhaps."

Whether it has been pulled down or not, what is the difference? As far as I'm concerned it will stand forever. The world of childhood is beyond time, located in the imagination rather than reality. It is a complete experience that cannot be apprehended by mere words. We are used to telling stories in a logical way. The language we use is arranged according to fixed rules and it obeys time. Every result has a cause, and causality is the guideline of the sentences we utter. Otherwise no one will understand. How should we retell a dream? How should we relate an experience that is beyond time? Childhood experiences can only be retold at the expense of locking them up in time, of binding them in a tight chain of cause and effect. Such are the childhood stories that we read. They are stories, a faded shadow, or a polished reflection of an imaginary experience. I do not put great trust in childhood stories, just as I do not put great trust in dream stories. I particularly do not believe writers' childhood stories — those whose main strength lies in writing fiction are less trustworthy in telling things as they really were, not to mention the events of childhood.

The house that I grew up in, the quarter, my childhood, are all a wonderful dream, a fantasy, a marvellous vision. No, I cannot apprehend them in words.

Marion Baraitser

Taking Tea in Africa

Miriam tentatively enters her mother Rose's bedroom. Her mother is about to have breakfast served to her in bed, so she sits up against the pillows, her child-like night dress emphasising her crushed bouffant hair and the purple shadows under her small hazel eyes. She lifts and rings the little silver hand bell beside her. Stephena, the live-in maid, arrives from the kitchen in her fresh pink apron and cap, and places the breakfast tray across her madam's lap. It holds a matching bone china teapot, milk jug and two cups, three slices of toast, butter, home made jam, and one glass of freshly squeezed orange juice.

"Stephena," Rose says in clipped tones. "The sugar."

"I remind madam yesterday we need a new packet from the store cupboard."

Rose turns stiffly to look directly at her. "But I gave you one two days ago."

"I am baking for Miss Miriam, *né*?"

Smiling pleasantly, Stephena leaves, returns with a small bowl of sugar that she places neatly on the breakfast tray. Rose places a large white damask serviette across her bosom, drinks the glass of juice, eats two of the slices of buttered brown toast, and pours herself a cup of tea just as she likes it — very hot, not too strong, with a dash of milk, and a spoon of sugar.

Miriam sits in the leather armchair and leans across to help herself to the last piece of toast, balancing the plate awkwardly across her knees. Then she pours herself a cup of tea.

The two women exchange pleasantries.

After breakfast Miriam puts on her bathing costume and wrap while Rose dresses, and Stephena begins to prepare the lunch. Mother and daughter take the lift to the basement car park. The swimming pool is set in the condominium's lush gardens where ibises stalk. The two make their way across the lawn — an elderly groomed woman walking with a silver and ivory handled stick, the sun flashing off her diamond ring, accompanied by her plump, plain daughter.

Miriam presses a bell in the gate, and a man in dark glasses holding a gun and standing in the bullet-proof room above them, releases the locking mechanism. Rose lowers herself into an elegant poolside lounger under an umbrella. The gardener, destined never to swim in the pool, patiently flicks long silver necklaces of water from the hose on to the lawn. Miriam self-consciously slips off her wrap and slides into the water. She is a natural swimmer. She concentrates on angling her mouth for air, beating the warm chlorinated fluid with her legs, smashing the surface with all the force of her arms, as if she were in the sea. She swims until her limbs are heavy with tiredness.

Sunlight glints off a lock of the gate that forms part of the wire fencing round the pool. A dog yowls. The pool janitor undoes the lock. He is a tall black man dressed in an informal uniform, well worn but clean. He carries pool-cleaning equipment across the lawn, his small barefoot son running behind him, the light glinting off the water, dazzling his eyes. The boy turns and takes an orange from his pocket, throws it and catches it like a ball.

Miriam comes out of the pool and lies on her towel in the hot sun at her mother's feet. A radio speaker crackles and relays a news flash about a riot in a nearby suburb, something about looting and police trying to take control. A Beethoven sonata follows. Miriam closes her eyes, transported by the music to the lounge of the family home. She is sitting under the Blüthner grand piano on the hard and unforgiving polished floorboards listening to her mother play Beethoven. She is watching her mother's cut-off feet in flat leather shoes, pump the pedals by some mysterious rhythm that only her mother understands. The terrifying

98

electric storm of Beethoven crushes Miriam as she cowers helpless and miserable, always knowing — because her mother says so — that to play the piano is the only estimable thing in the world to do. Miriam can't even sight-read a music score, so she has no hope in the world to come. The piano is positioned, like Rose, the absent Father and God the Father, at the centre of the universe. The child Miriam presses the round hard piece that made her doll's heart say "love me love me love me."

"I think it's time we went up for lunch, Miriam. You should cover yourself," said her mother, rising from her chair. "So many eyes, you know."

Lunch is served by Stephena on the balcony of her mother's flat, which overlooks a golf course bordered by the green expanses of giant grey eucalyptus trees. Miriam can hear the "pock" of a ball being struck. She looks through her father's old binoculars at the birds in the flowering gums. She is falling, like Alice. Surfaces blur and billow. She is running into the giant grainy surface of a moving image, a gorgeous sudden burst of yellow and black, fluttering in gaudy innocence on a bare branch. "Look. Look. A bird. A lovely bird!" she cries. Stephena is laughing and trying to use the binoculars too.

"I never look with this thing before," she says. "Madam is not looking too much at these birds."

Miriam helps her to focus, to keep her hands steady until Stephena shouts at seeing the bright rippling detail of a long tail, a wing of the Bishop bird.

Her mother is put out. She moves to the lounge, sits down at the Blüthner grand piano and plays Beethoven. Her fingers are stiff now, her red nails scuttering a counterpoint to the notes. Miriam turns the pages for her mother, tears pricking her eyes.

"Lunch. Lunch, Stephena, please."

She waits for Stephena to leave, then leans towards Miriam.

"Do you remember how I got Stephena her pass so she could come from the township and work for me?"

Miriam shakes her head and waits.

"Well, I took Stephena in the car to the officer in charge at the station. 'Do you like honey?' I asked him. (Her mother winks at Miriam as she says the word "honey", forcing Miriam to collude.) 'I like honey very much,' says the Afrikaner policeman. 'Well I happen to have some honey with me,' I say. 'That's good,' he says. 'Show me your honey and your girl can have a pass, no problem.' So I wrote him a cheque and he puts it in his pocket and he stamps her pass."

They can hear that Stephena has put on the radio, softly, in the kitchen. "Play some more," said Miriam, "while we wait for lunch."

So Rose lay in the lounge with the stuffed leather armchairs and small polished tables bearing delicate pieces of carefully chosen china and silver. On the fourth finger of her right hand the magnificent Art Nouveau ring of diamonds and sapphires catches the light from the balcony. Earlier, Rose unlocked the built-in cupboard in the spare room to show Miriam her jewellery. Miriam, on her knees and blinded by the dark, rummaged for the jewellery case, her mother's silver-topped walking-stick whipping past Miriam's right ear. "Left. I said left," said her mother. (Rose has always told Miriam how she knows her left from right, truth from lies, and black from white, and Miriam believed her.) When the box was out in the open, Rose lifted tray after tray of jewels, like Aladdin, selecting for Miriam's admiration a cascade of moonstones, a filigree brooch set with precious stones like a peacock's tail, a gold bracelet as solid as hand-cuffs, chains of smoky pearls. Rose gestured towards the kitchen and mouthed to Miriam.

"Can't wear any of them outside. They'd strangle you to get a necklace from your throat." She pauses and gestures to the undertow of the sound of the radio coming from the kitchen.

"I never let *her* see. Light fingers, you know."

Half way through her life, Rose began playing golf instead of the piano. "You compete against yourself," she explained.

Suddenly Stephena bursts into the lounge.

"Madam. The radio! It says *tsotsis* are coming this way! We must lock up."

At once the jacaranda drops its purple heads, en masse, like a violet blanket falling into the blue swimming pool.

"This is… too terrible!" gasps Rose. "Lock the front door, Stephena!"

"Yes madam. Both locks… the bolt… the chain. They must now break the door down!"

Miriam looks through Rose's binoculars at the lawn and the swimming pool below.

"Miriam… Miriam… What do you see?" whispers her mother.

"Two men… guns… talking to… the janitor. His son… is splashing in to the pool. The janitor… has a gun too, now. He's untying his dog. More men with guns. Drinking from bottles. Dancing on the lawn… in the pool."

"I always knew this would happen," cried Rose in a voice quavering with emotion. "Never trusted that janitor. Give them a finger… After all we've done for this country — They'll ruin us!"

There is the sudden sound of a burst of gunfire.

"What's happening? What's happening now?" cries Rose, trying to rise from her chair.

"The armed guard is firing on them," says Miriam, quietly. "They're falling. There's blood on the grass. Police officers. Truncheons, whips… I can't look any more." Miriam lowers the binoculars and sits down.

Suddenly Rose pushes herself up with her stick and makes her way to the piano. She crashes out the chords of a Beethoven sonata. When she is finished she says "Stephena, don't you think we need a cup of tea?"

"Don't worry," Miriam finds herself saying. "I'll make it."

Stephena pauses, then sits down on one of the stuffed chairs in the lounge.

Rose doesn't say a word, simply stares in astonishment at her maid in her leather armchair.

Then Miriam says softly. "We could make tea for all of us. Together, Mom," she says. "Come into the kitchen."

The three women stand silently in the kitchen and go through the ancient ritual of making tea — boiling hot water, Earl Grey from Fortnum and Masons, not too strong.

As she brings the cup to her lips Miriam remembers the afternoon when she last drank tea with her mother.

She and Rose are walking down Oxford Street. Rose makes a brave effort in the acid rain, stepping over shell-shocked paving stones and slippery dog turds, into the teeth of a Siberian wind, in her Burberry raincoat and matching rain hat, whirling on her silver-topped cane like Punch on his stick, or a Burberry-coloured plastic wind-mill, or Captain Hook on deck in a storm — as tough as an old one-legged turkey and just as hungry. They decide to eat at a *tapas* bar, but Rose refuses the squid, the peppers, the spinach, the fish-cakes and the broad bean salad. Miriam finds herself apologising to the waitress and wildly eating olives, chilli peppers and several platefuls of bread. To Miriam's relief, Rose finally settles for a bowl of onion soup. Afterwards they take a taxi to Miriam's dingy base-ment flat, descend the stairs to enter the front room which is taken up almost entirely by the badly tuned recondi-tioned piano that Miriam is storing for her daughter. Rose is very tactful about the state that the piano is in though she implies she expects this from Miriam. Rose mentions her own acute ear and perfect pitch — she can tell in exactly which key the distant church bell is ringing.

An unseen warbler trills in the garden.

Rose sits down at the piano to play Beethoven. Her solid gold Katz and Lurie earrings circa 1930, tremble in her ears as she quietly moves her stiff body, her fingers sketchily running over the keys. Suddenly Rose bangs both hands down on the keys in frustration. "I can't play anymore," she says. "I'm too old."

She begins to tinker on the piano with the old songs she used to sing when Miriam was a child — her own mother's

102

songs. First she plays *Oh You Beautiful Doll,* then *Old Man River.* Miriam finds herself singing along.

Suddenly her mother does something she has never done before.

Rose Meyers rises and goes to the kitchen. She makes her daughter a cup of tea and brings it to Miriam, who sits utterly still, then receives it like a chalice.

A weird feeling suddenly rises in Miriam as she takes the cup from her mother's hands. Something moves in her bowels. It pushes up into her throat, into her eyes. Fluids pour from her, tears and snot and sweat and blood, bathing her in salt and slime. Gales course through her and break from her arse, her throat, her nose. She collapses inwards like a black hole. Her body changes into the body of a starving child. She metamorphoses into the maid Stephena. Somewhere inside the black churning fluids in her head, words try to form themselves. She bites her tongue so that they don't slip from her wide slavering mouth.

Ruth Behar

Fortuna Egozi Pierces Her Ears

When Fortuna Egozi was a baby in Cuba her mother was going to pierce her ears, but her father wouldn't allow such a thing to be done to his little daughter. He was amazed that she was a complete human being, with ten little toes and ten little fingers, a little mouth, everything. *"Mira, está completica,"* he kept saying. *"No le falta nada. Mira sus piesitos, mira sus deditos, mira su boquita."* He didn't want to see his perfect baby girl cry and so she left Cuba with her ears intact, as unscarred as the day she was born. The years passed, and growing up in America, Fortuna was often tempted to get her ears pierced. But she always resisted, staying true to the story she'd heard about her father's wish to protect her.

Upon learning that Fortuna didn't have pierced ears, her friend Leonor Rodríguez, who was also Cuban and her colleague in the Spanish department, shook her head in dismay. The two women, who grew up in New York and felt like foreigners in their Midwestern college town, met for lunch every other Wednesday at Eastern Accents, a pan-Asian restaurant across the street from Aunt Agatha's, a mystery bookstore. As she poured globs of hot sauce onto her bi bim bop, Leonor exclaimed, "I can't believe you don't have pierced ears. How did you manage to get out of Cuba without having your ears pierced?"

Fortuna told the story of how her father had forbidden it. Leonor remained unconvinced. "A Latina has to have pierced ears," she announced. "It's tradition. And those gold bolitas look so pretty on a baby girl, don't you think?"

Half in jest, Fortuna told Leonor that she would pierce her ears when Leonor pierced her baby girl's ears. Hearing this, Leonor brightened. "I'm going to pierce Ariannita's ears on Friday. Want me to find out if you can get yours done at the same time?" Fortuna nodded hesitantly. She wasn't ready to go through with the ear piercing at such short notice. Leonor was often absent-minded and Fortuna counted on her forgetting to make the appointment.

The next day Leonor called and left an excited message on Fortuna's answering machine: "Just reminding you that Ariannita's getting her ears pierced tomorrow. I'm taking her to a salon that my pediatrician says is the best in town. Why don't you come get your ears pierced? The lady said she'll do you after she does the baby." Even though Fortuna didn't call back, the next morning Leonor showed up at her doorstep with Ariannita. "Come on, Fortuna, don't keep putting it off. Think of all the beautiful earrings you'll be able to wear."

The baby's ears were pierced first. Her head had to be held still by Leonor and the baby wailed miserably as one ear and then the other were attacked by the cold steel hole puncher. Leonor prodded her breast into her daughter's mouth and tried to console her. "It's okay, *mamita*, it's okay. The booboo will go away soon and you'll be able to wear the pretty gold bolitas that your *abuelita* gave you." The baby sucked greedily. Coming up for air, her wretched cries grew louder and she cuffed her hands over her ears, as if to keep them safe from any further mutilations. The salon lady said, "Look at her, isn't she a dramatic little one? You'd think we had cut off her ears!"

Fortuna considered changing her mind, but there was no going back on her decision. She'd chosen her studs and the salon lady was dabbing alcohol on her ears and saying, "Okay, ready?" When Fortuna didn't reply right away, the lady grew impatient. Two rows of hoop earrings hung from the rims of each of her sagging ears. "Look, honey, I'm running late. The baby took a long time, so if you have any doubts we can leave it for another day." Fortuna told her to go ahead. Earlobes, she'd always heard, were fleshy skin without nerves. As the gun punctured each ear, she was surprised how much the piercing hurt. With the pain came anger, an indignant rage, to be more exact, about the falsehood of claiming this barbaric little operation was painless. Her lobes felt as if they'd been run over by a two-ton truck, stabbed by a thousand knives, scalded on a hot stove. She wanted nothing more than to shriek like the baby, collapse into a warm milky embrace, and be comforted with sweet words. When the ordeal was over, she touched her wounded ears gingerly and feared they'd be dripping blood. The salon lady said, "Done. That wasn't so bad, was it?" Fortuna felt like slugging the woman, but she glanced in the mirror and saw the studs sparkling in her ears like shooting stars and decided it had all been worth it.

On her return home, Fortuna expected her husband to notice her newly pierced ears right away. But her husband Peter was a bookish man who wore thick glasses and was perpetually distracted. Finally she said, "Don't you see anything different about me?" He peered at her closely and said, "You got a facial?" She couldn't believe how unattuned he was lately to her physicality. "Can't you see I got my ears pierced?" she yelled. He looked again, his myopic eyes focusing on her earlobes. "Oh, yes, I see the earrings now. Very nice."

Fortuna stormed out of the room, leaving her perplexed husband to ponder why she was always so impatient with him. She went to her upstairs study and called her friend Amaryllis Goldstein in San Francisco. "Amaryllis, guess what? I finally got my ears pierced." Chuckling, Amaryllis replied, "Well, it's about time." Fortuna said, "You want to hear something sad? Peter didn't even notice." Amaryllis wasn't surprised. "Don't feel bad. The kind of men you and I married don't notice those sort of things." For years Amaryllis had been urging Fortuna to seek some pleasure outside of her marriage. Both Amaryllis and Fortuna married good American men who were faithful and caring, but a bit dull. Amaryllis had a theory about their marriages: "Look, Fortuna, we had to choose very safe men because we were uprooted from Cuba as children. We needed to marry men who'd never abandon us.

But there's a sexy world out there and it isn't sinful to have an affair." Amaryllis knew about affairs. She'd had several. "Look, as long as you're discreet and do it in a spirit of fun, it's okay. You keep on appreciating your husband. The process isn't one of subtraction, but of addition," Amaryllis explained. "Bringing a lover into your life is like having a yummy dessert without the fat calories." Hearing for years about Amaryllis's sexual adventures, Fortuna wondered if she was capable of such a thing. Long ago, she'd chosen shelter from the ravages of the world by becoming a professor and burying herself in teaching and academic work. She was much more shy than Amaryllis, and though she'd contemplated having an affair before, she was uncertain whether she could be so blasé and carefree about sleeping with other men.

But then Fortuna thought, "If I can pierce my ears at the age of 47, it's not too late to take on a lover." She began dancing tango. There was a club at her university that met on Thursday nights. At first, the men steered her around the floor and she felt pathetic, tripping over her own feet. She adored the passionate music, how the violins wept and the *bandoneón* sang, and worked at her dancing diligently. Submitting to the lead of the men was difficult at first, because she was used to thinking of herself as a feminist in control of her life and her movements, but slowly she came to enjoy relinquishing her need to be in charge. She wasn't the most popular *tanguera* in the club and knew she never would be. Fortuna lacked the flair of some of the other women, who showed off their flawless legs in skirts with slits up the side. Compared to these women, Fortuna felt frumpy, but she was glad there were a handful of men who seemed to enjoy dancing with her. She hadn't had an affair with any of them yet, but she was doing alright, she thought, just dancing the tango, playing at the fantasy of seduction with men she knew by the scent of their after-shave.

The months passed and on a humid Thursday night in July, Fortuna said goodbye to her husband at the door and drove off in the Subaru to her tango club, arriving after the lights were down and the dancing underway. Driving to the club, her husband's words echoed in her ears. "You're going tango dancing? It's Tisha B'Av, you know." On Tisha B'Av, the day marking the destruction of the First and Second Temples of Jerusalem, Jews sat on the floor in mourning, the ark covered by a black cloth, and chanted from the Book of Lamentations. It was a haunting, primitive ritual that Fortuna had found very moving on the one occasion she had witnessed it. She knew that on Tisha B'Av in 1492 the Sephardic Jews had been expelled from Spain. No question about it, Tisha B'Av was a day of Jewish misfortune, a day to fear and respect, but Fortuna didn't want to be with other Jews sitting on the floor amid inconsolable memories. Her husband's righteousness annoyed her. "Pray for both of us," she had said. "I need to dance tonight."

As her husband prepared to go to synagogue, she squeezed her voluptuous body into tight black pants and a tight black top, and gathered her hair into a chignon to show off her first pair of dangling earrings, orange and black coral set in gold. The earrings were a gift from her mother, who smuggled them out of Cuba, along with other jewellery, by hiding them inside the belly of Fortuna's rag doll. She was happy to be able to stop at a red light and admire the earrings in the rearview mirror, moving her head from side to side to hear them jingle. But what torture it had been to get them into her ears. Even though the salon lady had promised that in six months she'd be completely healed, her ears were still sensitive and the piercings continued to feel unnatural to her. To insert the earrings, Fortuna needed a mirror to see exactly where the little holes were, and it took her a good deal of time before she successfully manoeuvered them into place. Removing them, she knew, would be much more difficult. She'd learned that if she rushed and pulled too hard on the posts, she felt she was ripping flesh. Fortuna had faith that getting earrings in and out of her ears would become easier with time. Eventually she wouldn't have to look in a mirror, it would all be second nature.

No sooner had she slipped on her red suede dancing shoes when she saw the stranger across the room. He was tall and lean, yet his arms were muscular and his legs powerful beams holding him up. Was he middle-aged or older? In his fifties? Or sixties? Fortuna no longer felt she was a good judge of age and lately tried to see everyone as younger, so she could see herself as younger too. The man was old enough to be bald, but he was blessed with a mane of thick, dusty blond hair pulled back into a ponytail. His blue eyes shone like a cat's in the half-light of the tango club. Fortuna thought he looked outdoorsy and sunburnt, like a lumberjack, a man who should be wearing flannel shirts and thick boots and be out in the forest chopping trees. In his two-tone dancing shoes, he moved with more grace than the young men in the club, flirting with the music like a torero flirts with the bull. He'd wasted no time and was dancing with the best dancer in the club— red-haired Amanda, a house-cleaner by day with a model's figure. He led her effortlessly around the floor, and Amanda, who always kept her eyes open when she danced, refusing to surrender to any of the men, was on the verge of drifting off.

Fortuna pretended to watch their footwork. She didn't expect this gorgeous man to ask her to dance. When he came and offered his hand, she said, "Me? You want to dance with me?" And he replied, "Yes, with you." She was sure he was just being charitable, but she gratefully took his hand.

In his arms she felt sensations she'd never felt before. She trembled from the excitement of pressing her body against his. His strong hands on her back, the smell of the green woods that seemed to emanate from him, aroused her and made her sink into his embrace like a floppy puppy. She was certain she was dancing terribly, that after one dance he would say "thank you" and return to Amanda. When she danced with men who knew how to dance the tango, she closed her eyes and fell into a deep trance and forgot who she was with. The men were simply vehicles to guide her and hold her steady as they navigated together through space to the rhythm of songs about lost youth and lost loves.

Fortuna soon was dancing with eyes closed, song after song, in the deepest tango trance she'd ever known, a trance from which she didn't want to awaken. The stranger whispered in her ear, "I want to dance naked with you." His hands slid down low on her back. She knew it wasn't wise to let him be that forward under the watchful eyes of the members of the tango club, all of whom knew she was married and a respected professor at the university. But she yearned to surrender to him. Before the night was over they were going out in his Jaguar for "a cocktail," as he called it, and she was drinking the first "cosmo" of her life.

They sat with their thighs touching on adjoining bar stools. He stared at her breasts clinging to her black top, but she tried not to notice. She still didn't know his name. She drank her "cosmo" as he consumed her with his eyes. When she put down her glass he took her by the chin and gave her a kiss that left a taste of burnt sugar in her mouth. It was the first time she'd ever been kissed like that in a public place. She grinned and he kissed her again, just as fervently. The place was empty, but she saw the bartender watching with amusement as he mixed drinks at the bar. She could rise and say she'd had enough. Why didn't she? Maybe because—she was enjoying it. Her husband had never done anything like this, even when they were young.

"So you're married?" he asked, pointing to her ring finger. "Or do you wear the ring just to scare off potential suitors?" She looked at the gold wedding band; on the inside it was inscribed with her husband's initials, but she hadn't looked on the inside for a long time. "Yes, I'm married," she told him. "How long?" he asked. She had to take a moment to count the years since her wedding. "Twenty-two years," she said solemnly. He laughed. "So you want me to get you into trouble? Or out of trouble?" She didn't know how to answer. "What about you?" she asked. "Are you married?" Without a trace of regret, he replied, "Married three times. My first wife was my high school sweetheart. My second the mother of my two children. The third was a cute Spanish lady like you, except she was dumb and we had nothing to talk about."

Fortuna wanted to bolt into the night when she heard him describe the last wife. To steady herself, she searched inside her purse for her lipstick and he watched as she applied the raspberry gloss to her lips. "Why are you putting on lipstick? It's going to come right off, you know. I want to keep kissing you." He embraced her more tightly and kissed her hard on the mouth, then gently ran his tongue over the rims of her ears, which made her want to scream with insane joy. "Pretty earrings," he said. "They're from Cuba," she told him. "I had a feeling you were from somewhere Spanish. So what do you do when you're not dancing tango?" he whispered. "I'm a professor," she said. "I knew you were a smart girl," he replied. "And what about you?" she asked. "I'm a pilot. A retired pilot." Fortuna had to admit her surprise. "That's funny. I thought you were something else. Maybe a construction worker. Or a lumberjack. You're so strong. You make me think of the Wild West." He laughed. "From now on you can call me your Wild West lover. That is, if you'll let me be your lover." He undid his ponytail and Fortuna ran her fingers through his hair. She imagined herself as wife number four. She'd be the one to keep him by her side forever.

They finished their drinks and the bartender winked at her as they walked to the door. It was after midnight and still warm and muggy. She told herself to say goodnight and thank you, but she let him kiss her in the parking lot. Leaning against his Jaguar, he reached under her top and caressed her breasts. With his other hand he unzipped her pants. "No," she wanted to say. "Stop," she wanted to say.

She recalled the words of her friend Amaryllis Goldstein, "If it happens, enjoy it. *Gózalo*." But she didn't like the idea of doing it in the parking lot. "Let's go somewhere else," she said. "Wherever you want, honey," he whispered. "You lead." He revved up the engine and they drove through the desolate streets of her college town like prowlers looking to steal some happiness.

Fortuna directed him to the hotel downtown that she'd passed many times on the way to the People's Food Co-op. It was seedy (in more ways than one, she imagined) and just run-down enough to be tolerated in a town replete with expensive hair salons and used bookstores. There were rooms for rent by the hour. Not a place she'd ever entered or thought of entering, but it was perfect for a night with a macho deluxe. She strode into the room in her red suede dancing shoes and sat on the edge of the bed, waiting for him to start. He undressed her, touching her arms, her shoulders, stroking and kissing her breasts, working his way with his tongue to her tummy, her thighs, her ankles, her toes. She felt like a lightening bug glowing from end to end. He was a pro, she realised, definitely a pro. He entered her from different positions, teasingly, not staying inside for long. Dormant pleasure burst from every part of her body. She screamed. Wept. Laughed hysterically. Begged him to stop. Begged him to keep on going. "You're driving me crazy," she murmured. "Crazy."

Suddenly the venom in his voice scared her. "Can you shut up now? When are you going to give me a chance?" She'd had her eyes closed, as though they were still dancing tango. Her mouth trembled before she could speak. "I'm sorry. Has it not been good for you?" He gave her a look of contempt. "Turn on your stomach," he said. "I don't want to see your face."

He'd gone soft and angrily pumped up and down trying to grow hard inside her. His head pressed against her head like a brick crushing her jaw. She felt as if the ceiling had fallen on her. Everything ached — kidneys, liver, ribs, womb. He pulled on her nipples with his calloused fingers.

112

"Slut, you better relax and let me enjoy this," he yelled in her ear. "You're going to get it if I don't come."

It wouldn't end and it wouldn't end, but finally it did, when he gave up. He peeled himself off her body and she turned and saw the injured look in his eyes. "I hope I didn't hurt you," he said. "I didn't hurt you, did I? You're a nice person. I didn't want to hurt you." He slipped his long legs into his pants and retrieved her panties and bra from the floor and passed them to her. She felt herself go mute, as if she'd swallowed all the words she'd ever known. "Cat caught your tongue?" he said. She couldn't look at him. She tied the ankle straps on her red suede dancing shoes and smoothed her hair with her hands. When she touched her ears, she noticed she'd never taken off her earrings.

In silence he drove her back in his Jaguar to the lot next to the tango club where she'd left her Subaru. Hers was the only car there. It had begun to rain and Fortuna rushed to get inside and turn on the engine. When she looked back, he was gone. She swung her car onto the road and drove for a bit before realising something wasn't right. The darkness was thick and overwhelming and it wanted to gather her up like the ocean.

Then she saw that she'd forgotten to turn on her headlights. She flipped them on and the world was illuminated — wet, glistening trees, closed stores with their alarms set to go off at the slightest disturbance, sleeping babies in their cribs who would grow up to learn their parents no longer loved each other, the useless cries of the dead to the living. In the rearview mirror she caught a glimpse of herself, mascara smeared, lips dry and cracked, eyes hollow. "This is what a Tisha B'Av adulteress looks like," she thought.

Fortuna approached the entrance to the freeway and had an urge to jump on and drive until morning to wherever destiny took her. Open to life's infinite possibilities was how she felt. A little broken too. But it hadn't all been bad. Not in the least. They'd had fun dancing. There'd been some pretty amazing sex, real hot lust, before he

113

turned mean. And she liked the taste of a "cosmo." She was still in one piece. Nothing to worry about. But she kept driving home. Soon she'd be in bed beside her snoring husband and tomorrow would be another day. No need to say anything. Her husband wouldn't notice, just like he hadn't noticed her pierced ears. Nothing to feel guilty about. As her friend Amaryllis Goldstein had said, it wasn't a process of subtraction but of addition.

It took no effort to drive, the car knew the route home and seemed to be driving itself. That gave her confidence. Now and then, for a split second, she dared to close her eyes, driving the way she liked to dance tango, in a trance, not seeing, but trusting.

Trusting.

Trusting the universe still loved her as tenderly as her father did when she was a baby girl in Cuba.

The porch light, turned on for her by her husband, would be shining brightly in the last hour of darkness. She'd slip into the house as quietly as a shadow and remove the earrings that had come with her from Cuba, hidden in the belly of her rag doll. Moving her head from side to side as she drove, she heard the earrings jingle again. Earlier that evening, she retrieved them from the black satin case in her bedroom, precious jewels from a country she had lost. Fortuna knew it would be more of a struggle to take them off than it had been to get them on. Even though she was tired, she'd have to be patient. She was a few blocks from her house when she imagined herself already holding the earrings securely in the palm of her hand, touching the coral that long ago had been snatched from the sea, and tiptoeing up the stairs to her bedroom to return the earrings to the safety of their black satin case.

Mois Benarroch

Again in Front of the Sea

And if water
has memory it should remember
me swimming on the other side
if water remembers all
those who swam away their blood
in history I am watered
if salt has memory
it should dry the blood
anchovy, sole, hake
I remember your taste
like a fruit tree of ancient flavours
like olive oil
from the beginning of a century.

My Hometown

There are days I only think of it,
As if there were nothing in the world
but longing.
Other days, life and its banalities cover
everything
and I walk feeling that no-one
will ever understand
my language.
As if I was walking without legs
and the distance between me and the earth
just grows and grows
still I don't fly
it is an imagined
walking
an imagined world
instead of
a solid land.

The Hamas Terrorist

After Wysalva Czymborska "The Terrorist, He Watches"
and dedicated to Asaf and Meital and to all the victims
who lost legs, lives and futures.

1.

In a few moments he will blow himself up
he is young, has no children
has no wife, in a moment
nothing will be left of him.
No one will know who he was
he left home years ago
and disappeared
forever.
I am sitting very close
drinking an espresso
and smoking a cigarillo
my friend asks me to come with him
to the place of the bomb
I tell him I am tired
which is not true
and that I will wait for him.
He doesn't know and I don't know
that in a few minutes
the terrorist will explode
the hope for peace will explode
and that Meital's leg will explode
and her brother Asaf will go to heaven.
Meital's husband, a doctor
will hear the bomb and run to help the wounded
not knowing that his wife and her brother are there.
I am savouring the espresso.
It is a sunny day in Tel Aviv
and after this bomb
nothing will be the same again for months
people will be afraid to come back here

Dizengoff Street will be deserted.
No one can stop him now
it is too late
he will die for Allah
and for being young, virgin
and indoctrinated.
Even if I go there I can't stop him.
My friend disappears.

2.

Suddenly there is a boom
and then there is silence.
Fifteen seconds of silence
like the moment before God created the world
or it is like the silence before
being born.
It is a screaming silence
that can cut the air,
then there are police cars
shredding the silence
first comes a Peugeot 205
one, two, three,
fifteen of them,
then the ambulance comes
then people come from the place
they have to tell the story
they talk to everybody and to themselves
a mother doesn't know what happened to her daughter
people are making calls
on telephones and mobiles
very soon the whole system collapses
this is the centre of Israel
Dizengoff centre in Purim
everybody is here or could be here.
I sit,
hear what happened
don't know what happened to my friend
(he reappeared five hours later)

I am left speechless
for half an hour
I stand
try to talk to the waitress
I can't manage a sound
I go back to my seat
drink the water left.

3.

I think of the whole day
then I am really afraid.
How I bypassed the place of the bomb
a place where I always go or pass through
I took many side streets
and my friend didn't understand why
he just followed me
I wanted all the time to go back to Jerusalem
"Half hour by the sea
That's enough for me"
I said
but he wanted a coffee
"let's drink it here
in Sheinkin
and then go back"
but he insisted
he wanted to drink it in Frishman,
and so on for the whole day.
He has promised not to insist again
and just follow me.

4.

My religious friend said it is a sign
but a sign of what,
of being right or being wrong.
What kind of smoky shadowy cloudy
world
is this
that when there is a sign
we can't decipher it.

118

Erez Bitton

Summary of a Conversation

What does it mean to be authentic,
to run through the middle of Dizengoff and shout in
Moroccan Jewish dialect:
"Ana min el-Maghreb, Ana min el-Maghreb"
(I'm from the Atlas Mountains, I'm from the Atlas
Mountains).
What does it mean to be authentic,
to sit in the Café Royal in brightly flowing robes,
or to proclaim out loud: My name isn't Zohar, I'm Zayish,
I'm Zayish.
Neither this nor that,
but despite everything another language moistens the
tongue to the point of renting the gums asunder,
and despite everything the repressed and beloved aromas
are overpowering
and I fall between the circles
lost in the medley of voices

Moroccan Wedding

1.

Who never saw a Moroccan wedding in their day –
We heard we heard
your blessed hands arched over the *tam-tam* drums,
Sarah, Dodo's daughter.
From one end of the village to the other end of the village
Arabs and Jews arrive.
We saw we saw
the kegs of *arak*, the spits of roasted pigeon,
the layers of dates amongst the seven kinds

at the entrance to the house,
the proud jugs of olives.
Your blessed hands arched over the *tam-tam* drums,
Sarah, Dodo's daughter.
Arabs and Jews, Come in!
Slowly our hearts expand and our souls rejoice.

2.

Ayima
ten birds want to sever themselves from my torso.
Dear, as dear to my soul
as a Buskri date
which is the sweetest date of all
your lips are two dates
Buskri dates which are the sweetest dates of all
Ayima
I bear the light of that evening like the unsung burden of
    happiness.
Ayima
I feel like the land is two cubits lower than I am
my dear, dearest to my soul
your neck is like a fine handprint,
like the finger of fingers
adorning the fetters of my heart.
And they will still claim: Since your wedding there has
    been no wedding like
your wedding

3.

I also want salad of baked peppers, skinned at the start,
and seasoned with ten spices,
mother,
I also want bread and a hard boiled egg with *lebzar* and
    cumin beaten into it.
TE TE TE TE TE TE
TE TE TE TE TE TE TE TE TE
on the *tanbul*
Naq-te'ish, that you may live, Sheikh Hassan.

120

Drink a glass of *arak* with me. Sheikh Hassan.
You didn't have to bring all those gifts, my dear Abu
    Muhammad.
And you, playing the *tanbul*,
why are you off all alone in the corner while we rejoice in
    your music.

4.

Whoever hasn't been to a Moroccan wedding,
whoever hasn't seen Grandmother Freha
climb the scales of desire in the ears of the bride and
    groom,
whoever hasn't sat on the ground on bright featherbed
    cushions and Atlas Pillows,
whoever hasn't ripped the bread with their own two
    hands,
whoever hasn't dipped into a flowing salad and washed it
    down with wine
from Marrakesh,
whoever hasn't breathed in the fresh yearning of our
    fledglings,
whoever hasn't been to a Moroccan wedding,
here is a ticket.
Come on in
to the disturbances
of the heart
that you couldn't ever kill.

Benjamin Black

Breaking Ranks

As soon as I step across the threshold, I will be transformed from an Israeli citizen into an illegal draft dodger.
I check my bags in and head to passport control.
Surprisingly, there's no queue. I hand over my British passport and my exit permit. The woman keys in my details and
sits staring at her computer screen for what feels like several
minutes. Normal procedure, I try to convince myself.

My palms are sweating. I pray that beads of sweat are
not gathering on my forehead. Why didn't I shave? Jesus.
How could I be so damned stupid? So I don't make a habit
of shaving. But if there was ever a time to look smart, like
I was actually going on a business trip, now was that time.
I'd blown it.

"Where is your Israeli passport?"

"I don't have one."

"But you are a citizen, no? You have an ID card, right?"

"Yes."

"Can I see it please?"

"No problem. I just haven't had time to get to the
Ministry of Interior to pick my passport up yet. I'll get it
next week."

I hand over my ID card.

"Where are you going?"

"London. Business trip."

"Show me your ticket please."

I oblige. I had to buy a return in order to get my exit permit, even though I knew I'd never be on that return flight.

"You have a three-day permit."

"I know. I'm returning Thursday."

She pauses, punches some keys and then stares at the
screen for what seems like another excruciatingly long
time. Then she stops.

I watch her closely as she lifts her hand, and then lowers it, stamp grasped firmly in her palm. She saturates the exit stamp in black ink and then bangs it firmly onto a page in my passport, permanently staining it. And with that she seals my destiny.

The round stamp simply states the date and the following: "Ben-Gurion Border Patrol. *Yetzia* — exit."

She was just a passport control officer, but as she handed me back my passport, I looked her in the eye as though she were the chief of staff of the IDF. I swallowed hard, bit my bottom lip, skipped a heartbeat and reached out to clutch my passport to freedom. I lowered my head before walking on.

In the departure lounge, my flight had already been called. I rushed to the gate and, as I boarded the plane, I took one last look behind me.

A security guard was mumbling something into a walkie-talkie.

I left home and entered exile.

***

Over three years have passed since May 1998 when I left Israel for the last time, and became a draft dodger living in exile for the first time. Since then, barely a day has passed when I have not, consciously or subconsciously, thought of home.

Looking back, I take no pride in being a draft dodger from the IDF. It may sound like a hip honour to hold, but under the surface it's a bitter reality. I did not depart Ben-Gurion international airport, just before my call-up, with a smile on my face. I left my soul behind.

But I have no shame either. I returned to Israel in 1994 to live in a country that had just embarked upon the road to peace, after Rabin and Arafat had signed the historic Oslo Accords and Israel and Jordan had just declared an end to war. I arrive home to become a living part of that peace crusade.

Some say I am a coward. Others say that I missed out on a great life experience. And there are those who admit that, while it wasn't great, it wasn't that bad after all. Very few people think I made the right choice. So be it. I don't know. And I may never know.

What I do know is that I can sleep at night in the knowledge that I stood up for what I believe in and didn't conform just because the vast majority were, and still are, conscripting. I only wish that national service was an option. Then my address would still be home, not exile.

There is a list. I guess it's a "black" list. A list of people barred from entering Israel. Immigration officials at Ben-Gurion international airport have a copy of the list. Staff at the seaports and land crossings have one. So does every Israeli embassy the world over.

There are some obvious names on the list. They won't roll out the red carpet for Saddam Hussein. And there's no love lost for Libyan leader Mummar Gaddafi. But these guys are unlikely to make a personal appearance at Israeli immigration. They usually send someone — or something — in their stead. Like scud missiles or aeroplane hijackers.

The list isn't geared for the likes of Palestinian Authority Chairman Yasser Arafat. He has seriously sneaked into Israel several times to hold "back-channel" meetings with prime ministers to try to complete the peace process.

No, this list largely comprises thousands of Islamic fundamentalists belonging to the military wing of Hamas, Islamic Jihad and Hezbollah, among other terrorist organisations. Like PFLP-GC leader Ahmad Jibril or his comrade in arms George Habash. Not to mention Fatah Revolutionary Council Leader Abu Nidal or Hezbollah militiamen like Sheikh Muhammas Hussein Fadlallah.

And me.

I'm up there alongside these thugs — and countless other draft dodgers who have fled the country, trading flak jackets for freedom.

124

I didn't know about the existence of the list, in its formal sense, until I decided to check with the Israeli Consul-General about the law regarding Israelis who had dodged the draft, who were AWOL, or, as it is know in Hebrew, ARIK.

I had been led to believe that there was a general amnesty after seven years in exile. And, having endured three years, I wanted to be sure that if I sat tight and suffered another four years I could return home. On a whim, I called one day to check the score.

"Do you want me to see if you're on the list?" the woman on the end of the telephone line asked in Hebrew.

"Y-y-y-yes," I stuttered unconvincingly, trying to buy time.

What list? I knew I had broken the law, consigned myself to exile, would be imprisoned if I tried to re-enter the country, but I was amazed that there was someone around the corner who might know, by consulting a list, that I'd committed this crime.

"What's your name and date of birth?" she asked matter-of-factly.

Midway through my vital statistics, a shiver ran down my spine and grabbed me by the genitals.

"Wait! Wait a minute," I said in short, sharp Hebrew.

"If I give you my vitals, then I guess, you guys could come and take away my … vitals. Right?" I suddenly began panicking that, by now, she knew my name and where I lived.

"No," she replied, somewhat unconvincingly. "We have no need." At this point my left brain reminded my right brain that I had once suffered from a viral strain of pneumonia and a lung abscess, am chronically B-12 deficient, scream at the mere suggestion of an intravenous injection, faint at the sight of blood and that if the IDF wanted to flex its military muscle I'd be at the very end of the queue. So why the hell would they trek all this way just to bring me home and then lock me up?

"OK," I sighed, and parted with my vitals. In an instant, I felt denuded.

There was silence. An eerie silence that seemed to last a life-time. I could visualise the computer's database processing a check through the list, trying to find my name amid all those terrorists. The longer time went by, the safer I began to feel. My mind shifted effortlessly into overdrive. Maybe, after all, I had become one of the lost statistics, a mistake, a deletion, an accident. Human error. Any number of possibilities. All that worry, concern, fear, neurosis over nothing.

Ice-cold, with next to no hint of emotion that my future was in the balance, she finally cleared her throat.

"Ben — yes. You are on the list."

It was official. Here, talking on the telephone to the Israeli embassy in Australia, having escaped military duty three years before, was the first official confirmation of my status.

I knew I was a draft dodger. I also knew that the military police had been looking for me after my conscription date. Anat had e-mailed me to say that days after I left, a draft order arrived in the mail and, later, a few messages were left on the answer phone and more orders arrived. Then an order was sent by registered post. The little old lady downstairs, who permanently smoked a plastic cigarette and limped around with a four-pronged walking stick, took the liberty of signing on my behalf. Anat got back from the beach to find her waiting, mail delivery in hand. Furious, Anat kindly asked her never to act on her behalf again (although it was very thoughtful, typically Israeli and came straight from the heart). The mail delivery led to another barrage of phone calls and messages.

While I knew that they may have given up looking for me in Israel, I didn't realise that I would be blacklisted on every single Israeli government computer terminal around the world. I didn't know whether to smile or sulk: on the one hand, it confirmed what I already knew deep inside. No big deal. No drama.

She asked me if that was all. "Hell no!" I felt like yelling. Now that I knew I couldn't sneak into Israel with my

British passport, I wanted to know how I could get back in without being banged up in a cell with a bunch of criminals who could smell the scent of fresh blood arriving.

Instead I tried to remain calm and said, "Err … let's say, hypothetically of course, that I had to return urgently. What would I do?"

"You have to make a request in writing through the embassy. We send it on to the army and they will respond within two or three weeks. In all likelihood, they will let you enter."

My eyebrows leaped towards my hairline, lines on my forehead immediately subsided, my ears pricked up.

"But," she cautioned after a long pause, "you will have to report to the army headquarters and resolve the issue with them when you are there."

Having offered the prize, she immediately snatched it away again. My face sank.

"OK," I said pretending to be composed. "So, let's say I did that. What would they do?"

"They may decide to close the case," she said blankly, swinging the pendulum back in my favour again. "Or they may take the matter to the military court."

I suddenly felt like a kid who'd just been told that, in fact, after all these years of blind belief, Moses did not part the Red Sea. "You m-m-m-ean," I stuttered in Hebrew, "that I could actually be let into the country, but then wind up in prison?"

"Potentially," she replied.

I required clarification. "Let me understand. You're telling me that you can probably get me back into the country, but can't guarantee that I'll get out? Why on earth would I contemplate risking my free life for a life, or even a few months, no, one single day, behind bars?"

She responded on the defensive. "Look, I'm just telling you the facts. If you want to apply to enter the country, write to us."

"OK," I said, trying to extract the heat out of the moment, but really wanting to re-confirm that I wouldn't get home to find a dodgy-looking car parked on the street outside my flat with two Mossad agents inside wearing sunglasses in mid-winter and pretending to read *Beano* magazine upside down.

"Is that all?" she queried, clearly fed up with my persistence.

"Yes. Well, actually, no. Would you happen to have my Israeli ID number on file?"

"2034 …", she began.

"23968." I finished, my memory bank suddenly jolted into remembering my identification number which, for the duration of my time living in Israel, was my password — and passport — into civil life. Truth is, you can barely fart in the country without someone asking to see your ID card or, at least, what your number is. Without an ID card, the taps are turned off, all roads are closed, all avenues sealed. Life in Israel without an ID card is simply not worth the hassle.

"Thanks," I said, trying to sound remotely thankful.

"Good luck," she threw back at me, more as a convention than a courtesy.

Delirium

Roohieh Darakhshani

In the morning Arash awoke with a headache and feeling terrible. He took some painkillers, dressed and went to the door. When his mother asked him not to go to work he said "Don't worry, I'll be alright soon."

At the office his headache grew worse but he carried on until mid morning; then he could not stand it anymore. He left the office and called a taxi, but headed back home instead of going to see the doctor.

The apartment door was open and he slowly climbed the stairs, holding his hand to his painful head. He called to his mother but there was no answer, so he went to his bedroom. He glanced at his newly-made bed but unaccountably took his pillow and a blanket and staggered into the living room. He made himself a bed on the sofa and gratefully lay down. He felt very thirsty but could not make the effort to go to the kitchen for a drink. As he lay on the sofa his tired eyes were caught by the rhythmic moving of the pendulum of the clock on the wall. He felt unsettled as he lay there – sometimes covering his head with a blanket and sometimes staring at the moving pendulum on the wall.

TICK TOCK TICK TOCK TICK TOCK
TICK TOCK TICK TOCK TICK TOCK

This normally friendly sound became more menacing with every movement. Arash peered anxiously at the source of the sound and then hurriedly covered his face but could not resist looking back at the clock that had been in this house since his uncle had bought it as a present for his birthday.

Arash had now grown into a young man, but the clock was still the same. It seemed that during those years the clock had developed a kind of hate and hostility towards Arash and now that he was alone and vulnerable it was going to take its revenge.

It opened its mouth and laughing wildly said "Ha! Ha! Ha! It was you always laughing; now I am laughing at you. You and I came to this house at the same time. I was hung on a nail on this wall and forced to work and the only attention I was given was by a big man with rough hands who cleaned me with a stiff brush. From the same time you have been loved and cosseted. Your mother and father embraced and kissed you and the nursemaid took you for walks in the fresh air. When you were ill you were lovingly cared for and all the time you were free to play with your friends whenever you wanted. But for all of that time I was hanging on this hard, uncomfortable wall. On hot days I hung in the dust so that I could not breathe properly. On cold days I shivered in the cold draught. Even the little alarm clock at the side of your bed was touched and moved — but no one touched me. It is only today that I can take revenge on you for all this injustice and favouritism."

With the last sentence, while the clock was laughing fiendishly, it showed its vicious teeth – which Arash had not known about until that moment – the ticking became louder and seemed nearer to him which made Arash's heart beat wildly.

He put his head under the pillow so that he could not see the clock coming towards him but the sound of the laughing came through the pillow and he could feel the swish of the pendulum beating round his head. With a feeling of panic he tried to get up and escape from the scene but he did not have the strength. Arash wanted to ask the clock for mercy; he wanted to say the injustice was not his doing — it wasn't his fault that the clock was hung there. He wanted to tell the clock that he had always liked it and thought of it as a friend. He had always relied on its good timekeeping for school and now for work.

Before he could say any of this, he noticed that the clock had grown huge and covered the wall! The clock's

130

pendulum became like a huge hand with horrible claws reaching out to him and clutching at his throat. Arash felt suffocated and his heart nearly stopped; his head felt heavy and his tongue was swollen. Under the striking pendulum his body was painful but he somehow found the will to live and defend himself. He would not be overpowered and killed by an inanimate object that was normally under his control. He twisted and struggled to reach and drag the pendulum from his throat but his hand touched nothing. Feebly and helplessly his hand fell beside him and he opened his eyes to see the clock laughing defiantly at him from the wall but it had withdrawn the horrible hand. As his eyelids drooped wearily, the clock sneered "Do you see that you have everything. You who have human power and thought. You who have inherited pride and selfishness from your forefathers. You were begging me — an inanimate — for forgiveness. Your pride was broken and you, a human being, were lower than everything else."

Arash again opened his eyes and looked wildly around, finally staring at the clock and muttering deliriously, so that his mother on entering the room was alarmed by his manner. The clock, to his mother, was just a normal clock hanging on the wall ticking the minutes away but Arash was watching it fearfully, and suddenly cried out "That …e..e…evil c…clock, th..that u..u..unfaithful clock… I..I am frightened of it. Take it away; it was choking me with a horrible claw. It was laughing at me. It told me that I was free but that it is a prisoner on the wall… Ah! My head, my head… mother take it away please, it is beating me again." Arash with a moan fell back on his pillow, unconscious.

His mother left him for a moment while she phoned for an ambulance and then returned with a cool cloth to bathe his fevered head, while she waited for the ring on the doorbell.

Ariel Dorfman

Prologue: That Deafening Noise is the Garbage Truck

Today the cup broke;
How could I be so clumsy.

It made me very sad when it broke,
It was the one we had bought right after
    We left the country,

One that we were fond of,
You could say it was almost
    Our friend,

Bright red with white spots
For drinking *café con leche*
    In the mornings,
Those first mornings at the beginning.

So that there wouldn't be any slivers left,
Any sharp bits to surprise us afterwards
In our soup, our feet, our eyelids,
I picked up all the tiny fragments
    Squatting
At first and then on all fours,
With the infinite care of a punished child
Doing a chore over again
    Quietly, quietly,
And slowly.
    We had it for
    More than four years.
Today I broke a cup
And my exile began.

The Telephone. Long Distance.
Bad News, says a familiar voice.
We have to organise a campaign.

And if it were you?
and if this time
   it were you?

before they say anything
before they add a single word

   like a cat that walks through darkness
   your memory cuts through me
   like a kick
   it cuts through me
      Your body
   like a white cat that walks and shatters
   the darkness

but it's another name, it's another
name.
   Suddenly
everything lasts suddenly
   stiff and twisted
like nails in the suddenly so close
hand
   I am flooded with
      the lonely horror of relief
because it isn't
   you.

How can I feel
   this unspeakable relief
      like cats
dirty cats
   that I smother so I don't have to look at them,

how can I feel this relief
because this time
    it isn't
        you?

I write down the facts carefully. I hang up the phone and begin to call the newspapers one by one to give them the name of the companero *who has been arrested, the name of the* companero *I don't know.*

The Telephone. Long Distance. Bad News.

And this time?
   who is it
       this time?
start to make plans
   this time and the next
       time
learn to develop
       contacts
   differentiate
   use
       contacts

measure how much space
       less and less space
   is left in the newspaper
contacts
keep up contacts
       like other people put away preserves
       or their favourite clothes
       or wine in a good cellar

for another day
   and other phone calls
       for friends
           who haven't been caught yet
      relatives *companeros companeras* fighters
           who haven't been caught yet
contacts
learn not to abuse
   my
   goddam contacts

   Do you know something?
   We rank the life

                    and death
          of others
          as easily as we used to
          make shopping lists
          for the week
may god have mercy on us.

I write down the facts carefully. I hang up the phone and
begin to call the newspapers one by one to give them the
name of the companero *who has been arrested, the name of*
the companero *I don't know.*

Moris Farhi

Bilal: The Sky-Blue Monkey

There are two versions of my family's origins. Each is attested to with oaths of honour that no self-respecting Middle Easterner would ever dare to take in vain.

The first, a grandiose notion, claims that our ancestral home was founded in Toledo, Spain, in the days when the Iberian peninsula was a haven of co-existence between Jews, Moors and Christians; that the family climbed the rungs of nobility carrying the elegant name, De Flores — *perah*, the Hebrew source of our present surname, Perahya, means "flower" — and that our direct forbears had been gallantly rescued off the Andalusian beaches on one of the few good days in the years of the Inquisition, by the Ottoman Turks, probably by the great Admiral Barbaros Hayrettin himself.

The second, an even more grandiose version, traces our lineage all the way to the first century of the Christian Era when the Romans, after decades of war, had finally conquered Judea. An extraordinary episode of those times, it will be remembered, occurred in 66 CE, during the siege of Jerusalem, when the celebrated Rabbi Yohanan ben Zakkai persuaded General Vespasian — later to be crowned emperor — to allow him to leave the doomed City of David for Yavneh on the Mediterranean coast, with a retinue of scholars, so that while the Romans did as they pleased with the Kingdom of the Lord, he, ben Zakkai, and his theologians could save Judaism by redeeming its essence for posterity — a task they accomplished, in a century or two, by compiling the Talmud. One of those exegetes, the Pharisee, Eliezer, invariably praised as "ben Zakkai's brave and devoted companion", was, so this second version proclaims, our first known ancestor.

***

A good start, don't you think, Mami and Papi?

You may well ask: why I am writing this? And why secretly in the middle of the night, when you're both fast asleep?

I really don't know.

I imagine I'm writing it for you — even though it's really for me and, in any case, much of what I might write won't be unknown to you.

Then again maybe I'm writing it for my friends. Waving them goodbye, as it were …

I have a fear that keeps tearing at my innards. I'm trying not to look at it. I don't want to recognise it. Or give it a name. The mother of my English — sorry, Scottish — friend, Robbie, a very sad woman since the death of her younger brother in the war, once told me that the moment you put a name to a fear it takes on substance.

And yet, I want to leave something like a testimonial behind me — just in case. I want to leave an impression of who we are, what we do, how our life is and has been, how blessed I am to be your son, how your love for me means everything to me, how it gives me strength, how I keep wanting to love you more, but don't know how. And yes, also how unhappy you make me — and, of course, your- selves — when you keep quarrelling.

Anyway, I'm writing down some of the things I want to say in case they prove to be my last words.

***

My father, Pepo, treats both accounts of our origins defer- entially. His eyes, which always reflect wonderment, shine all the more whenever elders embark on a retelling of one or the other version. But he refuses to subscribe to either — or so he admitted to me on a number of occasions when instructing me on the sensitivity one must acquire towards other people's beliefs and fantasies. Myths are fine, he says; in all likelihood, they reflect the divinity that all humankind possesses, but it is not right that existence should acquire meaning only when embedded in legends; reality, too, is meaningful; moreover, reality is immediate and demands prompt attention. (Actually, the first version, as I found out, if not a fantasy, certainly lacks historical accuracy: if Barbaros Hayrettin had indeed plucked our ancestors off a beach, it would have been some forty-odd years after the *Reconquista*; and the beach itself would have been in North Africa, not Andalusia.)

And so, whenever my father finds himself in less atavistic gatherings, he maintains that our family, like most families, is mongrel and that, if we think about it, this is a blessing because mongrels seldom suffer the hypersensitivity, not to mention the paranoia — indeed, the insanity — which are the bane of thoroughbreds. Moreover, since our pedigree derives from a variety of stock — Jewish, Spanish, Turkish, Greek, Bulgarian, Gypsy, Armenian, Arab, Persian, to name a few — we contain as much colour as the rainbow.

On the origins of the family's last two generations, however, some solid facts exist.

My great-grandfather on my father's side can be traced to Burgaz, Bulgaria. A barely legible document states that he had served there as an Ottoman functionary. Since he had also spent spells in Varna — like Burgaz, a Black Sea port — and in Ruscuk — also known as Ruse — Bulgaria's border town with Romania on the Danube, it is assumed that he had been employed by the Imperial Customs Department. Late in his life, probably around 1878, when Bulgaria became an autonomous province of the Ottoman empire, he emigrated to Izmir, the Ottoman port on the Aegean. There, he married my great-grandmother. Of her nothing is known save that, having given birth only to my father's father, she had not distinguished herself as a bounteous womb. (Nevertheless, one child was all a women needed to produce in order to triumph, as the saying goes, over Satan.)

Since, in Ottoman times, the registration of births and deaths was an arbitrary procedure, it is assumed that my grandfather was born in the early 1880s. This date was calculated on the basis that he had sustained a disability around the turn of the century, while serving in the army, and had died in 1915, still in his thirties, leaving behind a wife and three children of whom my father, aged thirteen, was the oldest. My grandfather's death, I have often heard said, exemplified the suffering endured by countless Turkish civilians at the time of the First World War: worn out by the effort to keep his family alive during the interminable food shortages, he had been swiftly struck down by an unspecified illness. The family survived only because my father had been lucky enough to find work as a child labourer. My grandmother, by all accounts fit as ten ewes, remarried and was widowed — at least twice — and lives to this day what my parents call "an interesting autumn in an existentialist milieu" in Alexandria, Egypt. Fatma, the Gypsy, who periodically visits our neighbourhood to read fortunes, attributes my grandmother's endless regeneration to her lustful disposition, specifically to her predilection for swarthy men. (I surmise — if I have rightly deciphered the whispers and winks — that her enviable life is that of a worldly-wise socialite popular with the non-commissioned officers of the British army.)

By contrast, my mother, Ester, a native of Salonica, the port city in Thrace, belongs to the so-called "Jewish aristocracy". This term, I have been told, can be traced to a tsarist monk, one of those White Russians who took refuge in Istanbul after the Bolshevik revolution. This mule, preaching in the Balkans in his acolyte years the demented message of *The Protocols of the Elders of Zion*, had observed in horror that, as a result of the education provided by the French-based Alliance Israélite Universelle, the Jews in the Ottoman lands, unlike their brethren in *shtetls* beyond the Pale of Settlement, were fast attaining emancipation; that this emancipation was at its most dangerous in Salonica, where autonomy in

140

community affairs and the pursuit of culture, wealth and cosmopolitanism had virtually transformed the city's Jews to an aristocracy; and that, therefore the long-feared Jewish domination of the world could be expected to start in that fiendish waterhole.

At the time of my mother's birth in 1909 — eight years before the Great Fire which. like a portent of the burnings to come, destroyed so much of the city's Jewish neighbourhoods — Salonica was still under Ottoman rule and had a population of about 180,000 souls, more than half of them Jews. In effect, as the tsarist monk had rightly stated, the Jewish majority, Europeanised in the main and economically vibrant, had earned the city the sobriquet of "the Sephardi capital". This situation prevailed, even after the Ottoman empire yielded Salonica to the Greeks in 1912. It is only now, in 1942, with Greece under Nazi occupation, that the Jews face annihilation. We know this from the desperate letters my mother receives from her sister, Fortuna, who still lives in Salonica.

My mother's father, a lawyer, could trace his line — crammed with physicians, artists and merchants — to Cuenca in Castile, which in its heyday, had competed with Toledo for the glories of the Spanish Golden Age. But during the Inquisition, between 1489 and 1492, Torquemada and his henchmen had set new standards of barbarism there. The few Jews to escape Cuenca's *autos-da-fé*, including my mother's ancestors, had adopted the name of the city, as their surname, in commemoration.

Given the differences in their backgrounds, not to mention a plethora of other considerations, I doubt whether even the Great Sybil could have foretold that my father and my mother were destined to marry each other. But then, if the books I've been reading are to be believed, marriages, in the main, are made in hell, not in heaven, and it is the demons who misdirect Cupid's arrows, not the poor little urchin himself.

Haci Hasan, the old cobbler — according to my father, the wisest man in our part of the city — dismisses that cynical remark as unworthy of my intelligence. He tells me it has become a habit with me to muse about events as if I were a European, seeking logic in everything, even in matters where there can be none, instead of accepting, as any sensible person in the Mediterranean basin would, the laws of fate that are the primary laws of existence.

Fate is unchangeable. Haci Hasan, who, it is said, became a dervish in the wake of his pilgrimage to Mecca soon after the Balkan Wars, is unequivocal about this. What is written on a person's forehead will unfold come what may. No writing, not even a cursory scribble on the sand, can disappear, since Allah has witnessed its composition. (I wonder if Rifat's storyteller hero, Mahmut the Simurg, knows Haci Hasan. They seem to speak the same language.)

My Scottish friend, Robbie, finds it difficult to understand the Turkish Jews' perfunctory acceptance of Allah. He says divisions between sects, let alone religions, are so entrenched in the West that they are unassailable. I put the question to Eli, who taught me Hebrew for my barmitzvah and who is working on his philosophy doctorate at Istanbul University under Professor Alexander Rustow, a Jewish refugee from the Third Reich. Needless to say, Eli who everybody says will become a professor in no time at all, rattles off the reasons without even pausing to think. In every culture where major religions rub shoulders — and, periodically, clash — the identities of the Ineffable One invariably commingle. Most Jews who have lived under Islam will admit, if they are honest, that, over the centuries, Elohim and Allah have become interchangeable — a solid journeyman who dresses now in a turban, now in a skullcap. Gods become uncompromising and merciless only when men in pursuit of some utopia or other — like Hitler and his Nazis — alienates himself from Creation and kills the love that exists between the Creator and the Created.

Anyway, back to Fate, the irrevocable, as defined by Haci Hasan. A strange and amazing force. It loves irony,

142

paradox and perversity and has a great sense of the absurd. But, since it is itself a tool of Creation, it also has integrity. Thus, while it indulges in all sorts of liberties and wanders off on curious detours as it ambles its ways towards its destination, it never loses sight of its position in the cosmic order. And though much of the time, its meandering appears to be a tactile relationship with the person under its charge. For most people, it has a real and continuous presence, like a once integral limb waiting in the limbo of amputations, to reattach itself to the body.

And it is immediately inventive, immensely innovative.

And so, true to form, in June 1927, within a few days of each other, it brought two men of totally contrasting natures — one personifying sweetness, the other rage — both now my great-uncles — knocking on the door of a famous Istanbul matchmaker.

I believe the conventional image of a matchmaker, in Turkey, as everywhere else, is that of a gnarled parasitic busybody. According to Uncle Jak — the good uncle — this particular woman, bearing the evocative name, Allegra, or "joyous", was not only an exceptional beauty, but also a student of Rousseau. She saw marriage as the only arena where women in general, and Middle Eastern women in particular, had the opportunity of defending themselves against the inequalities imposed on them by the patriarchal societies that ruled the world. Not for her the prevailing custom whereby men would discard, as and when it pleased them, their used, but perfectly adequate, not to mention well-lubricated, scabbards for new ones. Thus she always made sure that the couples, behind closed doors, at least, would have a parity.

The easiest equation, in her view, was to pitch a woman who rejoiced in the blessings of her loins with a pacific man who yearned for carnal delights: thus the woman would rule benevolently, the man would be invested with a permanent beatific smile and the two would live happily ever after. Other equations included matching strong men with timorous, dependent women — or vice versa — or

143

joining men and women who were so inanimate that they would drift through life often unaware of each other while producing children with acts akin to pollination. Most intriguingly, Allegra had scored her greatest successes when matching authoritarian men with headstrong women. Notwithstanding the sense of identity each equipoise gave the woman, the strategy also ensured that battles between husband and wife in such circumstances invariably ended in stalemate. And as stalemate after stalemate would push the contestants obsessively to further battles for at least one meaningful victory — which, of course, could never be attained — the continuation of the marriage was guaranteed. And if, as had happened on a few occasions, the battles ended in violence, the blame could always be ascribed to the stars or to the sun's spots.

Interestingly, because she had never married or been known to have liaisons with men, Allegra was often rumoured to have Sapphic tendencies. Her answer to such gossip was that in order to be clear-thinking and effective while doing God's work matchmakers had to be celibate, like the Pope.

Anyway, as Fate would have it, the two great-uncles wended their separate ways to Allegra within a few days of each other.

Jak, my maternal grandmother's brother, waxed lyrical about Ester, aged eighteen, his beautiful and remarkably modern niece in Salonica, who not only possessed all of the rubineous virtues of a Jewish woman but as singer, pianist and painter, was also an artist thrice over. Moreover — and how marvellous that one so young should be so wise — she still saw Turkey as the spiritual home of the Jews of Salonica, and would be prepared to come and live here.

The other great-uncle, my paternal grandmother's brother-in-law Saul, known as El Furioso, stated imperiously, as if rewarding an underling, that he had a nephew in Izmir, one Pepo, who worked in his drapery shop but who, no longer needing to look after his mother and siblings (his mother and sister had both married and settled, respectively, in Alexandria and Beirut; his brother had emigrated to Venezuela), had turned into one of those dashing, forceful young Jews, and was now having ideas *au-dessus de son rang*. Moreover, Pepo, who was also a veteran of the War of Independence — and that tells one a thing or two — wanted to spread his wings, travel a bit, chase some Jezebels, even study something that would put his considerable attributes to good use — study, *nom de Dieu*, at age twenty-five! The truth was, and Saul was loath to say it, Pepo had become indispensable to his business and had to be made to abandon all those grandiose ideas. What better than chaining him down to real life with an adamantine wife and — the things one had to do for the lesser members of one's family! — reward this loss of freedom with a minor partnership in the business?

The methodical Allegra duly visited first Salonica, then Izmir. And she contrived to meet, seemingly by chance, both Ester and Pepo. Thereafter she spent several weeks conjugating the two with various potential candidates in her books. In the end, guided by her special formula on equipollent couples, she decided that the spirited Ester and the enterprising Pepo were ideally suited to each other. For good measure — since Ester, as an aristocrat, would need something extra to consent to the proposal — Allegra concocted a variety of spells and potions. One charm, my father swears to this day, worked wonders with him: silk French knickers dusted with cinnamon powder to induce sweet turmoil in his genitals. Another, attar of roses on my mother's pillow to clear her mind of all thoughts except love for my father, was also apparently very effective.

Whether through professional acumen or through spells, Allegra's reputation for arranging an immaculate union was validated in no time at all. In a courtship that stunned even the matchmaker by its speed, my father and mother fell in love. Within weeks they were married — "in indecent haste", according to the gossip-monger.

145

On one of those luminous blue days when the gods frolic like dolphins in the sea and all barriers between parents and children crumble, I asked my father about his hasty marriage. With those eyes that look at the world in adoration, he admitted that, indeed, as the old vestals claim, he and my mother had been consumed by desire from the moment they met. But since like all good Jewish youngsters in those days, they had to observe tradition and would not have sex before matrimony, getting married as soon as possible had been their only course to satiate this hunger. So no truth in all that talk about me being conceived out of wedlock. I arrived in this world in seven months. I hope I will not leave it as prematurely.

No, I'm not afraid of the mission ahead. That will go smoothly, you'll see!

There was, however, another factor, which proved as strong as carnal hunger, that further contributed to the hasty marriage: my mother's love for my father's stories about his adventures.

Mother, as mentioned before, was an accomplished singer, pianist and painter. But, according to Uncle Jak, her gifts needed to be nurtured. They needed drama, strange characters and extraordinary episodes — in effect, compelling narratives. And my father, who, despite his young years, had lived an eventful life and who moreover was a virtuoso storyteller, provided these in abundance. (Sadly, Mother abandoned her artistic aspirations soon after my birth. In the impoverished early years of the republic only the very few could pursue a career in the arts.)

By all accounts, the story that clinched the marriage was the one about the battle of Sakarya, the turning-point in the War of Independence, during which my father served as a signalman in Atatürk's command post. In my younger days, this story remained my mother's favourite. She used to make my father tell it to everybody. She even made him write it down when his memory began to blur and he had to guess details that he could not remember

146

exactly. In later years, after the endless quarrelling had started, she stuck to her claim that he had seduced her with that story — poor, naïve damsel that she had been — the way Othello had seduced Desdemona. A brutal, worldly plebeian capturing the heart of an innocent maiden with a tale of war and bravery.

Actually, since the Sakarya story is one of my favourites, too (and since this, my composition, whether it turns out valedictory or not, has evolved into a hosanna, my sentimental celebration of my mother and father — alas, no brothers or sisters: Mother thinks one child, particularly if not a girl, is more then enough), I will attach that story, as written by my father, as an appendix to this piece.

A word here about the unhappiness that rules our house. I don't know when it began. Or how serious it is. My mother and father still appear to be very close and very interested in each other. For instance, they never go their separate ways. Not for my mother, bridge parties or after-noon coffees with other women. Not for my father, the secretive world of the Freemasons or nights out at new-fangled clubs with cronies.

But begin it did at some point.

Possibly, as Uncle Jak thinks, one sunless day, Mother took a look at Father and saw, in the brume, the shadow of a man who, though he had looked like a giant in yester-years, was now impaled on a crag, unable even to defend himself against a buzzard that was tearing out his eyes. Sickened by this sight — maybe even thinking that the buzzard might well be herself and not Uncle Saul's damned shop (which my father inherited after Uncle Saul's death), she ran hither and thither, shouting at God, "Did I abandon my music and paints for this? I threw away my life for this?!" That same sunless day, Father, who was indeed a giant, who could have been a savant, a statesman, certainly a great man, if only he could have studied, but who, in order to feed the wife and child he loved, burned his bridges and boats, wept tearlessly, as the

147

winds blew away his days, and asked in turn, "Is this all there is to life?"

The tragedy, according to Uncle Jak, was that Mother and Father had taken stock of their lives on the same sunless day. Had they done so on different days, one or the other would have noticed that their lives, though compromised and very much unfulfilled, were also rich beyond their imaginings: their son and their love for each other, for a start …

After that, the unhappiness advanced with sickening speed. Now, it is a constant. Mother accuses Father of some wrongdoing — always a silly thing like not folding the napkin properly or walking home in the rain at the risk of catching a cold, to save money, instead of taking the tram. Father tries to appease her by apologising. She responds by raising her eyes and demanding of heaven how many times a woman can forgive a man for the same stupidity. A long silence ensues. She starts again, reiterating her question. He censures her for escalating a minor disagreement into a major quarrel. That infuriates her; she starts accusing him of all sorts of misdemeanours, from being uncouth to mocking her Greek accent (which he actually finds very endearing), to not giving her enough housekeeping money, to surreptitiously looking, maybe talking, maybe even having fun with other women. Incensed by her imputations, he protests his innocence, then retorts that she would only have herself to blame if he did go and seek the harmony and happiness he craves with another woman. This enrages her all the more: a man who can distort truth so readily, without even a twinge of conscience, is not a man, but a brute, a Nazi, a Goebbels, no less. If he had his way, he would slaughter the world, starting with the wife he claims to love so much.

Last night, for instance.

It began, I'm ashamed to say, because of me.

Father was having second thoughts about my so-called boy scouts excursion to the Royal Hittite Archives of Bogazköy. The country was troubled, he said, orphaned by Atatürk's death. (Father worshipped Atatürk and has not

148

stopped mourning him), opportunist Nazi-lovers were crawling out of their holes. There was a growing economic crisis and these rats, together with right-wing elements in the government, were blaming the minorities, particularly the Jews, as its perpetrators. True patriots were either being marginalised or, as in the case of the poet, Nâzim Hikmet, were being thrown into goal. (Father loves Hikmet's work and maintains that had Atatürk been alive, he would have come to respect Hikmet's views. I suspect, deep in his heart, Father is a socialist — or, as they call them these days, a communist.)

Anyway, Father feared that if I went on the excursion to Bogazköy, I might be harassed by ignorant fellow-scouts or scout-masters, attached and ostracised as yet another Jew "who drinks the nation's blood'.

As if this was the opening she had been waiting for, Mother went on the offensive. (For once, I was glad she did, because there is really no excursion to Bogazköy; that's the excuse we — my friends and I — invented so that I can go to Salonica with Marko and smuggle out my mother's family.) She accused Father of being jealous of the education I was receiving while he had had to leave school at thirteen; in effect, he was oppressing me, trying to reduce me to a nonenity like himself; any day now, he would probably start burning my books; well, she was not going to let that happen, not as long as she was alive; she was not going to let him victimise her son as well.

Here is a snippet from that quarrel. I copied it down word for word:

He: "Victimise my son? My own flesh and blood. I'd tear myself to pieces for him!"
She: "There you go again with your violence!"
He: "I'd die for him as I would for you. You know that!"
She: "You'd kill us first — that's what you'd do!"
He: "Woman, you're mad!"
She: "Yes, I am mad — because I'm all heart! But you? A maniac — waiting to explode!"

149

He:	"I'm a loving man. You took me as a loving man!"
She:	"You've changed!"
He:	"No! All these years — have I ever hurt you? Lifted a hand to you?"
She:	"You've become like the rest. A man who runs around all day. Comes home angry. Ticks away like a bomb!"
He:	"A man who is trying to put bread on the table."
She:	"Oh, yes, never hit a hungry person. Wait for her to finish her bread, then — wham!"

And so it went on. And so it always goes on. And the horror is, she knows — as I do, as everybody we know does — that Father, despite his shortcomings, despite his frustrations, has no violence in him and is truly a loving man.

A few months ago, after an exceptionally bitter quarrel, I heard my father leave the house in a fury. There was a blizzard raging outside. Thinking that he was either going to desert us or kill himself, I went after him. I followed him down to the sea. I watched him as he sat on a capstan and started smoking. He had not taken a coat or a jacket — just a thin sweater on which the snow was settling. I remembered how Naim's sister, Gül, whom I adored and still miss very much, froze to death on a park bench like a homeless person. Afraid that my father, too, would freeze to death, I went and sat next to him and put my arms around him. He stared at me, seemingly surprised that someone still cared for him. Then he hugged me fiercely as if wanting me to become part of his body. Eventually, joking that we would soon turn into snowmen, he took me to the local *mahallebici* for some hot soup. As the warmth seeped back into us, I asked him why Mother had changed so much, why did she keep accusing him of having a brutal nature. At first, he hesitated to talk about her; then deciding that I was old enough to know, he told me a bit about her past. He said that Mother's father had been a violent man who had, on one occasion, crippled his wife by pushing her off a balcony. He told me that, on another occasion, when my grandfather was beating up my grandmother, Mother had threatened to shoot him with a hunting rifle. According to doctors, Father explained, exposure to such violence leaves terrible scars on sensitive minds. Perhaps under different circumstances, she could have lived with those scars without much trauma, but now, with war raging all over Europe, with the Nazis in Salonica persecuting the Jews, persecuting her family, Mother could see nothing but violence and brutal death all around her. But she could be helped through this awful period. With love and patience. Then again, a single piece of good news like her family being safe would probably bring her, in no time at all, back to her old self.

It was after that conversation that I decided to find a way of saving my mother's family in Salonica.

***

So, this is what lies ahead.

My friends, Naim, Can, Robbie and I have devised a perfect plan.

We will save all five members of my mother's family: my aunt, Fortuna; her three children, David, Süzan and Viktorya; and my grandfather, Salvador. Initially, I had been against including my grandfather in the rescue because of his violent nature, but then decided that it would be ungallant to exclude him. Sadly, Fortuna's husband, Zaharya, died a few months ago, after being sent to hard labour by the Nazis.

We have passports for them all: Turkish ones, which, we have been told, will be honoured by the German authorities because Turkey is still neutral in this war and, following the occupation of Greece, a neighbour to be wooed. We procured the passports by exchanging them with British ones. We got hold of the latter thanks to Robbie, who can go in and out of the British consulate because his father is a grandee there. The exchanges were made through the intermediacy of Naim's classmate,

Tomaso, a Levantine boy whose family controls all the smuggling in this region. Tomaso also introduced us to Marko, his mother's young brother, who although only twenty-five, has the reputation of being the best and the most daring operator in the Aegean; moreover, it is said that his boat, the *Yasemin*, can run circles round any patrol boat. So Marko will be our saviour. Originally, Naim, Can and Robbie were to have joined us. We had invented a good excuse to be away from home — the boy scouts excursion to the Hittite Archives in Bogazköy that I mentioned earlier. But, alas, Naim and Can are needed to help out in their fathers' shops and Robbie has to stay at his mother's side because she is not at all well.

So it will be just Marko and me. We will slip into Greece, make our way to Salonica, find Mother's family, hand them the passports and slip out again.

We'll be back in a week.

We sail the day after tomorrow.

***

God, I was hoping to say much more.

Well, another time …

Oh, I nearly forgot. I had a strange dream last night. I don't normally remember dreams. Only the sexy ones that wake me up all messy.

Anyway, this dream. I was in ancient times. Watching a religious rite. People were piling their troubles and wrong-doings on to the back of a *kapora*, the traditional animal of purity, the scapegoat, in effect. But in this case the animal was a monkey, like Cheetah in the Tarzan films, only sky-blue in colour. When this monkey was so loaded that it was staggering about, they dragged it to an altar where a priest stood ready to slaughter it so that in death it would take away with it all the people's misery. As the priest prepared to cut its carotid artery, the monkey turned and looks at me.

It had my face.

Bizarre.

When I get back, I must ask Ruhiye, Uncle Jak's maid, what it means. Like most descendants of the Yürük, the original Turkish tribes from Central Asia, she is good at explaining dreams.

So …

TO BE CONTINUED...
WHEN I GET BACK …
WITH GOOD NEWS, GOD WILLING …

Predrag Finci

The Traveller

Ubi sunt

The lake was down there. And even if it was not, it was quiet, deep, bottomless. On winter mornings, I emerge from the house and wend my way down to the river, to the dam. With the tip of my pen push through the icy surface, through to what is no longer. *Mais où sont les neiges d'antan?* What proves that what was really happened? What proves that what we felt really existed? Wherefore the time that abandoned us? Much of what I loved is no longer, and it cannot be affirmed at all, except by my impressions and deceitful memories, the mist of the elusive. I can still see the overcast morning sky, I still try to describe it, to capture the sensual, the elusive beauty, that reaffirms itself in its elusiveness, to reach out for something that is breaking away further and further, and yet it feels ever closer. I like the clouds, far and away... "I love the clouds... the passing clouds..." He used to watch them in the mornings. I still sometimes believe that imagination is more real than reality, although it is clear to me that such reality, no matter how close, is far, too far, like the dark cloud which sucked in what I left behind, darkness where dwells what I never reached, like mist in which I seek something that is neither here nor there, and yet I know that it exists...

The cycle

Short agency note: "A group of some hundred refugees from Sarajevo, mainly Sepharadic Jews, arrived in Madrid". The note said nothing else. Different thoughts spring to mind. Suddenly, in the midst of all this confusion, I remembered an old-time TV drama by Filip David[1]. As I recollect, its title was either *The Golden Gate* or *One*

154

Day My Yamel. Misa Janketic [2] starred in it, and Arsen Dedic [3] sang "One day, my Yamel..." The story was resonant of the old British classic *The Dead of Night*. In both cases I was overwhelmed by the intertwining of reality and dream, imaginary and real, and above all by the mysterious repetition of the wondrous law of the cyclic path of human destiny.

The agency note said little. I do not know if Madrid was the final destination of Sarajevo's Jews or just a stop in a new vagrancy. But there is a definite symbolism in their arrival in Madrid. Exactly five centuries ago a great exodus of Jews from Spain began. They were expelled by Ferdinand II and Isabella of Spain. The Jews loved Spain. In their new homes for centuries they preserved Spanish costumes, habits and culture. Legend has it that, when leaving Spain, they were unable to take much with them, but each hung around his neck the key to his house. They vowed "one day we shall return". They did not. Many of those settled in Bosnia. Now, once more, they are travelling the route to uncertainty and hopelessness, running away from the menacing horror of destruction.

Their houses in Spain are no longer there. They are gone, just as their homes in Sarajevo may go. They are gone like the houses of their friends and neighbours. Long ago Jews ran away from a cruel government. Those who agreed to obey could stay but had to be prepared to make many concessions, one of which was conversion to Christianity. But the cycle of hell is never one. Nightmare again overcame dream (A dream: I have a feeling for a moment that this horrible war cannot be real, that it is only a nightmare, because I cannot comprehend so much madness. I cannot accept the fact that this horror was inevitable, that darkness had to cover the earth. I shall wake up, I keep thinking, and all this will vanish...)

Those who recently came to Madrid are well aware that the power of the fire and sword hangs over all of Bosnia[4];

a power no one can expect to survive. It is manifested in a bestiality that finds its fulfilment in destroying everything that opposes it. It is a cruelty that makes "Jews" of all of us. I am not in favour of historical parallels and comparisons, because I find them inaccurate and banal, but I think that the suffering of any one person has something in common with the destiny of other human beings. Sometimes it occurs to me that everyone has experienced everything, and has existed in every period of time, enduring contradictory fates. I believe we have existed since the beginning of time, that the whole of mankind is one and the same generation "kindling in measures and being quenched in measures", just one general destiny in which everybody is given to experience everything. We repeat that which has already happened and will happen again, even though, as philosophers well know, the "same" is not "equal".

This is one of the reasons I could never understand a lack of compassion for another being's misfortune. In the situation of common misfortune, the moral imperative requires us to resist the temptation to be criminals. When after hundreds of years a Sepharadic rabbi found himself in Madrid, he could not help but cry. How long will my Bosnians have to roam in the hell that has befallen us? How long will it take before my fellow townsmen return? How many of them will cry over the life that has vanished and remains only in their memories? And how much menace will remain, only emphasising that the sinister path will be taken again? But, has it not been written a long time ago: "One day, my Yamel, thou shalt come before the golden gate..."

The Bus
Does it have to be every generation? Does everyone have to hang a key around his neck? Does every family have to be broken by a journey? The engine rumbled and then silence. I recollected the stories on the influence of the negative vibrations that can stop a bus and I try to think

156

positively, aware that every one of the travellers is petri-
fied.

We had been going to the Jewish Community premises
for days on end and kept asking:

"When will the convoy set off? Will there be one at all?"
To many the "Jewish Convoy" was the last resort, because
life became impossible in the besieged, destroyed and dev-
astated city of lawlessness and anarchy. It is the reason
why many people left everything behind them again, and I
understood those poor people completely. I myself felt that
life alone was more important than all the possessions,
painting and books I had left behind me for good. Each and
every one of us, some 150 people, carried their possessions
in a couple of suitcases or two. We would leave them
behind only in order to escape destruction.

The three buses set off at last. I see my neighbour waving to me through the window, I see my policeman friend
smiling sadly, I see the swollen red face of the President of
the Jewish Community; an entire nation departing. We
are crossing the bridge when a penetrating, shrieking
female voice cries out: "My Sarrrrrrrrajevo". The silence is
broken only by the lighting of cigarettes and muffled
breathing. My Sarajevo? I am 46 years old. I was born in
'46. 46 and 46 makes 92. Five hundreds years ago, in '92,
the expulsion from Spain began. Nine and two makes
eleven. One is the number of the beginning, one is the
number of the end. If I stay — I was saying to myself —
troubles await me, if I leave, suffering awaits me. And
now, while I watch apparitions behind me and fog before
me, I know that I am parting with a landscape of memories, that I am leaving what used to be my life in order to
preserve what could be my life.

And this is why I am among these people, who have but
one concern: how to get out of Sarajevo. Why did they go,
where are they heading? It does not matter any more.
Eventually they will ponder on it. Later they will cry. Now,
they are all still and stiff. They are all sitting motionless,
no one complains. No one asks when we are due to arrive;

no one asks why we stop so often. In the long journey through the night, no one will ask for anything. An exhausted body, deprived of bread and water, which has survived thanks to the determination to survive; not by a conscious will but by an elementary instinct. Not even the children cry. (I found out later that in one of the bags a fat cat named Count was asleep.)

We pass through "Serb territory". They wave to us, maybe the same hands that shell us are now waving. An older man in dark uniform enters the bus: "Fuck your Alija", says he instead of hello, asks us to hand him over all the letters, pushes them into a bag, looks at the passenger list: "Which of you are Muslims?" Silence. "Who is a Muslim in this bus, there are two Muslim surnames, I am warning you…" Frozen looks, breathing stops. And then, the man in charge of the convoy enters the bus and whispers to him. The bus continues its journey. Another familiar face at the new check-point, and, sure enough, I would meet a dear friend at the next check-point, which is Croatian. Close friends before the war are now a world apart. I cannot quite say I did not anticipate it, for I learned during the war that even the darkest premonitions come true.

This is why all of us obediently and humbly show our documents at a Serb check-point, hand over the hidden letters, silently put up with undeserved insults, only in order to continue the journey — a flight from hopelessness and despair, a journey of hope. It is the physical fulfilment of the desire to leave a city where rain keeps falling and people are dying of thirst, where cold air comes in through broken windows, while one cannot get out to breathe fresh air, where fires burn everywhere, and yet it is so cold, where the earth turns into a cemetery.

Although one grows tired remaining awake the whole night the phantom of liberty does not let me sleep. I cannot help overhearing the nebulous chatter of a man who inaccurately but vividly declares that we are all "people of the deluge", then I look out the window again, surprised that I can look without fear, that I'll be able to stroll

158

around without fear of snipers, that I'll be able to breathe. I see a food store, and a food advertisement, I see open news-stands, unbroken windows, in a village that looks like a metropolis to my numbed senses. I gaze at the world as if I see it for the first time. I look and try to retain everything, but in my bewilderment I forgot it all.

We are coming nearer and nearer to our destination. I already hear impossible questions about the time of arrival, a remark here and there, and hushed mumbling. How quickly one forgets one's misfortunes! It occurred to me that awareness is a trait possessed by only a few. If it were different, would this war have broken out, would there be any of this horror that so graphically reflects the worse in human nature?

Somewhere in Croatia, on the Adriatic coast, we encounter a road accident. Two fellows come out of our bus and give assistance to the wounded passengers. They do it skilfully, calmly, without a trace of nervousness at seeing blood and hearing cries. But I know what they feel and how they will continue to react when they hear the whistle of the wind, the roar of the waves, the call of the child, the sound of a word.

It was broad daylight when we finally arrived. My wife told me she had never had a more comfortable journey. Sure enough, for we had never craved reaching our destination more than now. I tried to restrain myself during breakfast, not to eat with gluttony, to use a knife and fork, not to hide cigarettes, as I did in the war, when they were scarce. Before I fall asleep, I think about how I was and that again I must be. Then, I fall asleep. I did not dream. I come from a dreamless night. And tomorrow, on the road again... And then on to a voyage, across the sea.

[1] Filip David (1940), a prominent Serbian writer of Jewish origin. His TV-drama 'One day my Yamel' was transmitted on TV Beograd in 1967.

[2] Misa Janketic (1945), a popular Serbian actor.

[3] Arsen Dedic (1938), Croatian poet, composer and singer.

[4] The war in Bosnia started in 1992 and finished in 1995.

Juan Gelman

My beloved Buenos Aires
Translated from Spanish by Miriam Frank

Seated on the edge of a broken chair
giddy, sick, barely alive
I write verses that once wept
for the city of my birth.
They must be trapped, for here
were born also my sweet sons
who amid so much affliction bring such tender delight.
One must learn to resist.
Not to go not to stay,
to resist
though there surely will follow
more sorrow and forgetfulness

Poem written to his granddaughter
or grandson
Translated by Miriam Frank

I write to you on a bit of paper
fallen from my son's notebook
with a cow a donkey
all that remains
this letter which I'll never send you
holds delights and sorrows
and if you read it
you would be filled with tenderness
for I was writing nothing
but the birds were singing
blue on the left
flying to your shadow and hushing
with eyes open
like memories in the night

Prayer of an Unemployed Person

Translated by Miriam Frank

Father,
come down from heaven, for I've forgotten
the prayers grandmother taught me.
Poor woman, she's at rest now.
She needs no longer do the washing, cleaning, no longer
worry all day long about the laundry,
no longer keep watch all night, woe after woe, praying,
begging for things, gently chiding you.

Come down from heaven, if you're there, so come down
for in this corner I die of hunger;
for I know not what use it was to have been born,
for I look at my rejected hands;
for there's no work, none.
Come down a while, gaze at
this thing that I am, this broken shoe
this anguish, this empty stomach,
this city with no bread for my teeth, the fever
gouging my flesh,
this sleeping thus
under the rain, punished with cold, harassed.
I tell you I don't understand, Father, come down,
touch my soul, look into
my heart,
I have not stolen, not killed, I was a child
yet they punch me and punch me,
I tell you I don't understand, Father, come down,
if you are there, for I search
resignation in me and I have it not and I'll
grab my fury and whet it
to hit out and burst
into a blood-full scream

From **Dibaxu**

Translated from Spanish by Miriam Frank

the bird abandons itself in its
flight/yearns to forget its wings/
to rise from nothingness to the void where it becomes
    matter and lays down

like light in the sun/it is
what it isn't yet/like the dream
whence it comes and doesn't sally forth/it traces
the curve of love with death/it moves

from coincidence to the world/it chains itself
to its moment's labours/removes
the pain from pain/draws

its clear delirium
with open eyes/singing
incompletely

Farideh Goldin

Memoirs of an Iranian Jewish Woman

Pilgrimage to the Tombs of Esther and Mordekhai

"This is it?" I was shocked at the sight of the building. We had come such a long way to see the drab square brick monument. Maybe if my uncle had not built up the trip to be such a fantastic adventure I would have not been so disappointed. I hadn't expected a palace for a burial ground, but a Persian monument decorated with blue tiles, like the mosques colourfully scattered throughout Iran — in Esfahan, Shiraz, Tehran. The Moslems had conquered Persia much later; nevertheless, the Achaemenids had Romanesque columns, carved images of beasts, flowers and soldiers in stones decorating their palaces and their tombs. I expected to see a glittering gold or silver dome marking the burial place of our courageous queen. Instead, there was only a plain square brick building. Rather than the hands of Persian artisans and stone masons, strong winds, rainfall, and ice had shaped the sand coloured bricks through the last two millennia.

"Is this truly the burial site of Esther and Mordekhai?" I asked Eliahou in disbelief. The poor sat cross-legged on the grounds, their lunches of yogurt and flat bread spread over kerchiefs. A few vagrants squatted on the worn out steps, their greasy fingers extended through the sleeves of their patchy overcoats, gesturing for alms.

The *ziarat* was meant to be the highlight of our trip. Every year Esther's story was retold in all its awesome details: love, treachery and heroism. The most beautiful women of each region had been brought to the king's palace so he could choose a new queen. The beautiful Esther had groomed herself for King Akhashverosh, her black eyes red from crying, her spirit gloomy for having to

163

leave home. But her uncle Mordekhai, her only family alive, had encouraged her to be brave. Maybe God was placing her in this fate for a greater purpose. Among all the virgins, the most beautiful woman of each province was ordered to the court by the royal decree; but a Jewish woman was chosen to be the queen of the most powerful man, the King of the Persian Empire.

Then, after she held a position of respect and power, Esther had endangered her life to stop the murder of the entire Jewish community by the evil vizier Haman. How could she then be buried in this simple place? If not as a Jewish heroine, then as a Queen she deserved better. I thought of the room in the ruins of the palace, Takhte Jamshid, outside Shiraz that I was told was hers. The large room was made of the finest stones, polished to such a degree that they reflected the queen's image as mirrors do. The king wanted his queen to be surrounded by her own beauty. Where were such fineries then for her tomb?

A strong sense of longing overtook me. "I want to go home," I whimpered. "I want Baba."

"He is in Israel with Nahid. You know that," my uncle said.

I was at an awkward age, with a scrawny body and chicken legs. I had never been away from my father for such a long time, never spent so much time with my mother. Baba had been away for only a few days, but I already felt that I had forgotten his features. Now that the excitement of the trip had died off in disappointment, I especially needed the comfort of a familiar place, where my father's clothing hung in the closets, where the scent of his cigarettes was a part of the house.

I refused to enter the mausoleum, crossed my arms and puckered my lips, expecting the filth to be also in the inside. Holiness couldn't exist in squalor, I thought. My mother covered my hair with a kerchief and pushed me up the broken steps. We entered through the threshold of the heavy wooden doors. The room was dimly lit from the natural light of a skylight. The sweet fragrance of rose water

164

surrounded us, mixed with the smoky smell of candles burning in remembrance. A large dome in the middle of the room was covered with silk fabrics in bright colours, some with gold threads. Women crowded around the sepulchre crying, some beating their chests, a few spread even more cloths on top; all lips moved in silent requests, quiet prayers. A younger worn-out woman held tightly to the bars crying and had to be forcefully peeled off to make room for the crowd behind her.

In a carved opening in the wall in front of us a Torah scroll stood upright in its silver round casing, decorated with velvet fabric and gems, crowned with silver. My mother and I bent to kiss it. I prayed for my sister's healing and her and my father's safe return. I don't know what my mother prayed for but our faces were covered with tears as we stood up.

I had not seen the tombs yet. They were hidden underneath the offerings. I knelt by the bars, removed the layers of fabric and stared down the deep room underneath. Two simple gravesides were lit artificially. The rest was darkness. My uncle bent over and told me that those who wished very hard could be transported to Jerusalem through a secret passage underneath.

I closed my eyes and willed to be in Jerusalem with my father and Nahid. I imagined being transferred down to the gravesides, musty and dark. I reached to find the walls to the tunnel, slowly making my way through its dark narrow muddy sides. I could not see anything. I cried for my father, "Baba, Baba." I called for my sister, "Nahid, where are you? Do you see me?" An echo came back, and I was trying hard to hear the words, but a hand grabbed me by the shoulders and removed me. My time was up.

Fear permeated our lives

Fear permeated our lives. I didn't know then that the frequent attacks on the *mahaleh* had not only instilled terror in my grandmother's generation and those before them who had witnessed such rampages, but also on those of us who heard the horror stories connected with the raids.

During the Moslem holy month of Moharam, my family was especially careful. "Don't wear colourful clothes," my grandmother reminded us. It was a month of mourning, of wearing black. None of us wanted to provoke hostility by any implications of happiness. The men came home early every night, bringing their work home if they could, although there was not much business at such times, since most of their customers were Moslems preoccupied with their rituals of grief. Although fearful, we were also curious, and even entertained by the parade of mourners. "They are coming! They are coming," some neighbourhood child would call out, running ahead to inform us of the procession. All activities stopped. The herbs were put under a colander, the meat was thrown on a slab of ice, and the rice was put away hastily. I slipped on my rubber tyre flip-flops like everyone else; my mother, grandmother and aunts grabbed their chadors. I was only six and did not need a full body covering; instead, I wore a kerchief for modesty. We rushed out through the heavy doors to the dirt-covered alley-way, ran under the arched entrance of the *mahaleh*, and out to the large paved sidewalk of Moshir Fatemi Street. Women in black chadors and shopkeepers in dark attire lined up solemnly on the pavement by the narrow watercourse that separated us from the marchers.

The muezzin could be seen in the distance, standing on top of the minaret covered with decorative blue tiles, a mix of delicate floral motifs and bold Koranic verses. Its tall cylindrical shape reached out to the sky, an arm straining to bring the holiness of Allah's spirit to Earth. Cupping his hands around both ears in concentration, the muezzin finished the noon prayers. *Allah o akbar*, God is great; *Ashhado Allah va la Allah*, I testify that there is no god but Allah. His haunting voice travelled through the empty street, filling hearts with the deep sadness of the day. As

166

his prayers came to an end, men poured out of the Great Mosque chanting from the Koran.

Banners were carried in front of the procession by two young men with stubby beards, dressed in mourning clothes. First came the black banners, setting the mood of the day, with the familiar Arabic words written in contrasting white: *QULOU: laillaha illa Allah ve Mohammed rasoul Allah*, people proclaim that there is no God but Allah and that Mohammed is his messenger. A loud cry escaped from the spectators: *Allah o akbar*!

Red banners, for the blood of martyrs, were displayed next to the marchers. The green ones, symbolising life, bore their names: Hossein, his family, his followers, all seventy men, women and children, who were slain so brutally in the desert of Karbalah while thirsting for water. A banner of plain white fabric, devoid of any lettering, was marched by us. It was also the colour of death, the colour of a shroud.

The emblems came next, decorated with tassels in deep greens of the fields and blues of the oceans, which are the sources of life. Some were embossed with the word ALLAH, some with names of the Imams. Large poles draped with green silk fabric and decorated with jewels bore the metal imprint of Fatimeh's hand (the Prophet's daughter). Two solemn-looking men, unshaven like the rest in a sign of mourning, held tight to the corners of a large painting and took small deliberate steps.

From the heavily decorated and draped picture frame, the serious eyes of Imam Ali, the most revered Shi'ite leader, looked out over the crowd of mourners in every corner. He was wearing an impressive Arab garment, a black caftan, on top of a white shirt and a long black piece that covered his hair and draped over his shoulders. The painted image showed the Imam's body reposed on a heavy wooden chair, strong and determined. A wide curved sword rested on his lap, dripping blood. I shivered in fear that it was the blood of the Jews, that it could have been my blood.

167

A sacred palanquin decorated with flowers and colourful fabric was carried on the shoulders of four men. On each side of the symbolic coffin, unshaven men carried framed pictures of the martyrs. A lone mourner struck brass cymbals one against another, creating a rhythm for the steady footsteps.

The bravest were in front. Shirtless, they displayed bold chests. Each wore a wrap-around sash, or a loose pair of black cotton trousers. The scant clothing gave them little protection from the brutal midday sun. Right feet came down in unison on the first beat of the cymbals. The marchers flung both hands automatically over their left shoulders, clutching in both hands wooden rods attached to a bundle of heavy chains. Bloodied metal rested on tender skin for a moment: left foot in front, the chains going over the right shoulders to land on bare backs. Their bare feet contracted in agony as they touched the hot, paved road. They were the strongest believers. The blood dripping from self-inflicted dagger wounds on their foreheads told of their unrelenting commitment.

Beautiful horses were displayed as though ready for war; sharp swords and daggers hung from their sides. White doves dipped in blood rode on the back of the war horses in place of the soldiers who never had a chance to fight.

The *sineh-zans* came next. With each beat of the cymbal, they raised both hands to chest level, then above their heads, building a momentum that ended with their open palms slamming on their chests with their fists or their heads with the palm of both hands while moaning.

Younger men dressed fully in black entered the arena with lighter instruments, followed by teenaged boys who beat themselves with only two or three chains. "Hossein is dead! Hassan is dead!" The flagellants chanted in unison as they carried their beaten bodies from the great mosque to the Shah Cheragh shrine.

Young girls wrapped tightly in black chadors were the only females allowed to mingle with the marchers. They

168

represented innocence, purity, and compassion. The girls carried heavy containers of water and metal cups on their backs. They offered it to the soldiers of God, suffering in the unbearable heat, in contrast to the evil army that had allowed the holy men of Karbalah to die of thirst.

This religious enactment always fascinated me and everyone else in the ghetto. We were allowed to stand next to the Moslem spectators to watch the ceremony respectfully. Day after day, for the first ten days of Moharam, mourners cleansed their souls of evil by self-flagellation, acts of charity, and a state of constant mourning. Every day, I watched the parade in absolute awe, trying to understand the implications of the rituals, enacted so fervently.

The history of Shirazi Jews had not been documented then. When I was a child, many of us were still lost in ignorance and illiteracy. Elders of the community, their stories frightening, were our only source of information and historical continuity. Again and again, the Moslem clerics had initiated attacks on the Jews as holy wars. The ghetto had been decimated time after time.

Our elders retold the stories of horror, remembering times when pogroms had been carried on through the ghetto. Lost in their deep sorrows, highly emotional Moslem men recreated in the Jewish ghettos the story of a war lost long ago. Wanting to avenge the dead, the mourners carried on a jihad, a holy war, against the Jews, to imitate Imam Ali who had shed blood for the advancement of Islam. The killing, they believed, would bring personal salvation and global peace. It would expedite the resurrection of the messiah, the twelfth Imam, who would reappear when all nations accepted Allah as the only God and Mohammed as the final prophet to replace all before him.

Although the horrific tales were etched on my memory, I still needed to believe in the goodness of the people living side by side with us. Somehow I wanted to believe that if I knew them better the rumours would prove false. I begged my parents to allow me to watch the parade on the night

169

of Ashura, the last night of the mourning period. I had heard much about this night through rumours from those who had dared to be present at the ceremony. Mostly, we cowered in our homes, doors locked, never answering a knock, jumping anxiously at the slightest noise.

Only once, when I was six years old, did I have a chance to venture out on this most solemn night. The men were away working. We, women and children, were too afraid to stay at home by ourselves. Before dark that day, my grandmother, my mother, my unmarried aunt, and I left our house, which was too close to the parade route, for Aunt Shams's house. She lived deeper in the maze of alleyways in the *mahaleh* with her husband's extended family.

That night we were all bolder. Maybe the sheer number of women together gave us courage. My aunt and her sisters-in-law gave everyone black chadors to wear. There was one folded in half for me. We walked through the dark alleyways to another main gate, trying to look inconspicuous, walking solemnly like Moslem women.

The orders were not to talk at all. The hint of a Jewish accent could bring trouble. Trying to act invisible, the older women directed us to a large tree close to a gate so small that even I had to bend down to exit the ghetto. The tree provided a sense of security, allowing us to huddle against it and feel less noticeable. All this preparation and the anticipation of a potentially dangerous event caused my heart to pump blood faster than even before the march started.

The total darkness of the street was eerie. A few street lamps usually broke the blackness with their yellowish glow, but on that night these were turned off. Women's black chadors, and the men's dark clothing made the darkness even deeper. The silence of hundreds gathered on the parade route added to the blackness of the night.

The flickering of dim lights in the distance announced the approach of the parade. Soon hundreds of men, their faces invisible in the darkness and their battered bodies wrapped in white burial shrouds, moved down the street.

It was a march of the living dead. They shuffled their way to the tomb of the prophet looking for victims' body parts to take for Imam Zaman, the Imam of the "time to come". On the Day of Judgment, as it was told, limbs would come together to return the righteous men to the Garden of Eden. The symbolic act of gathering the blood-ied body parts was to remind God of the sacrifice of the best, of the holiest. In return, God would resurrect the invisible Imam through whom man himself would be returned to life.

The human shroud stretched in groups of twenty or more across the wide street, walking slowly, chanting Arabic verses from the Koran, reciting melancholy Persian poetry, announcing the night of Ashura in a haunting murmur. They carried long candles that slowly melted, giving little light. In the total darkness, the two sources of light became one, the Earth joined the heavens. The twin-kle of the small flames connected the street with the black sky of Shiraz, covered with stars.

As the last of the dead passed, our small group came to life. Moving away from the tree, we found our way to the small gate, bent down one by one, and merged with the greater darkness of the *mahaleh*.

The Question of Virginity

Winter was finally over. No more snow would fall to bring down the thatched roof on our heads as we slept. My father hired labourers to patch the roof before spring showers poured through the makeshift strips of metal cov-ering the holes. The green leaves waited to push their way through raised spots on the rose tree. White petals burst out, perfuming the air, flavouring our teas. Sparrows sang again among the orange grove.

My mother and I sat across from each other, rubbing the soap into dirty clothes. I took my eyes off Maman's nails, thick and cracked like those on the hoofs of a mule.

171

Instead, I stared at the clear blue sky stretched over the orange trees. I wondered how the birds had sneaked back without me noticing them. The sun made rainbows in the bubbles. I made them bigger and bigger, prettier and prettier, while trapping them between my two thumbs and index fingers like a heart. I blew the rainbow in the air. My mother smacked me with her soapy hand; she had winter in her heart, washing and hanging the clothes in silence.

I didn't want to help her anymore, so I went looking for my grandmother for something more exciting. Like the facets of polished ruby in my father's workshop, the geometric designs of a Bukhari carpet surrounded Khanom-bozorg. Facing the open French doors, my grandmother ran a wooden comb through her henna-coloured hair. The morning sun filtered through the large rose tree and brought in warmth mixed with strange shadows. The house was quiet.

My grandmother felt my gaze and turned to find me perched at the door, an invisible shadow with the darkness of the hallway behind. She fanned her right hand fingers towards herself, motioned me to come closer, and gently sat me on her lap. Khanom-bozorg combed my hair, splashing a few drops of water on it to harness the unruly mess. When the black hair hung softly, she cleaned and pulled hair from the comb's teeth, and braided my hair into one single strand. My head hurt but the price of pain was worth the moments of love and intimacy. I took the comb with its missing teeth, two in the middle just like mine, and wove hers into two braids the way I knew my grandmother liked, very close to each other, hanging side by side on her back. When I was finished, Khanom-bozorg covered her hair with a large flowery kerchief and tied it loosely under her chin. She opened her mouth in a toothless smile and made a scary face. I covered my mouth with both hands and giggled. Then I ran to get her false teeth from a chipped water glass on the mantelpiece. She thrust them into her mouth and over her jaws to adjust the fit, drawing out more giggles.

She examined me critically. The colourless dress hung on me like a wet sheet hung on a tree to dry. The leftover fabric thrown together carelessly, wrinkled after being slept in the night before. I was suddenly ashamed. The dress was big to accommodate a year of growth. My mother had dressed me in mismatched trousers and a long-sleeved shirt underneath the dress. As fall led to the colder days of winter, more layers of shabby odds and ends would be added in an effort to keep warm.

"Feri," she addressed me with my nickname, "don't you have anything better to wear?" She made a face. She knew our financial situation; after all, we lived in the same house as one family. As the eldest she was in charge of the household allowance. I knew that. I recognised this as an indirect way of criticising my mother and felt my usual pang of insecurity that came when the two women I loved used me as a tool against one another. I tried to evaluate the situation, averting my eyes. In an Iranian gesture I threw my head back for a "no." "Anything cleaner?" She squinted her eyes. When no answer came, she sighed, "Run and ask your mother." I hesitated, fearing my mother's anger that would undoubtedly come. "Well do you want to go out or not? I can stop by your aunt's house and take one of your cousins, if you don't."

She knew I was dying to get out of the lonely house. I tiptoed to my mother, who was still in the same position I had left her, in the backyard washing the dirty clothes in a large, soapy, aluminum wash tub. I could see her back, bent and rounded. Her short curly hair was a mess in need of a haircut. Her hands were rough and raw from the rubbing and contact with cheap soap. Her dirty, deeply cracked heels hung out of a pair of rubber flip-flops. I couldn't bear to watch them. She was sitting there alone, in silence, mumbling stuff to herself, just stuff. I felt sorry for her, for her hard work, for her loneliness. My job was to hang the wash on the clothes-line, and part of me felt ashamed for leaving her by herself. At the same time I hated her for creating such emotions in me.

173

I swallowed hard and asked, "Maman, is there anything clean for me to wear?" She turned, obviously embarrassed to have been caught complaining to herself, and looked at me with a child's eyes, vulnerable, hurt. "Going out with your grandmother, haa?" she mumbled. I stood there, not knowing what to say, hating her and pitying her. She pointed to another dress hanging on a tree without looking at me and disappeared again into her own world. I grabbed the dress, changed quickly. Threw the dirty one on the pile next to her, and happily ran back to my grandmother.

Khanom-bozorg pointed to a large sugar cone sitting on the mantel to be brought to her. I pressed the heavy piece against my stomach as I carried it and laid it down on a large flowery napkin. She tied two opposite corners on top of the cone and then the other two. It was a pretty package. I was curious to know what it was for, but knew not to ask any questions. I didn't want to be called a *verag*. The despicable adjective was attached to me, and I couldn't cleanse myself of its negative connotations. Adults didn't appreciate too many questions from children: I had learned to draw information by deciphering the circumstances and by listening and watching. I knew we had to be heading to a *simkha,* a happy event, since the sugar cone was used as a gift for such occasions. Khanom-bozorg adjusted a white calico chador with tiny black polka dots on her head, making sure the sides were of equal length. I picked up the gift and followed her. We walked down the old stone stairs to the yard and stopped by my mother's station. While my grandmother gave her instructions for the day's chores, I refused to make eye contact with Maman, refused to feel like a traitor. I was heading out for adventure and would not allow anyone to ruin it for me.

My grandmother and I walked down the narrow alley-ways of the *mahaleh*. Khanom-bozorg gathered and lifted her chador when she reached a small puddle in the middle of the road, and held its top corners with her teeth to keep it from slipping down her head and disgracing her. She cussed from under her breath, "May they meet the washer of the dead!" She stopped, turned sideways and made herself as small as possible to avoid any contact with a man passing through. "It's hard enough to walk down the alley without touching the walls. It's so narrow. How is one supposed to stay clean in this place?" She bent her head and added her own spit to the dirty water.

We stopped by the Great Synagogue, put our lips on its heavy wooden doors, make a wish, and kissed it. On my grandmother's request, I ran inside to give the old homeless woman living there a few rials. Her fragile, wrinkled frame was bundled up in a black chador as she sat in a corner of the yard trying to soak up the warmth of the morning sun. "May God give you a good life for remembering this forgotten old woman," she said.

This was a good beginning. My grandmother's face had a glow now that I loved. We stopped by the public water spouts, where she was greeted by women drawing water. "Khebee, khesheen?" They asked of each other's health in Judi, a language spoken only by Shirazi Jews, which I understood but did not speak.

"Shalomalekhem, shalomalekhem," may God be with you everyone said, as if the two words were only one — none knew Hebrew and the words had become an extension of Judi. I watched and listened, invisible. They stood in a tight circle, heads together, whispering secrets, looking like a pyramid of patchwork quilt.

When the women finally tore apart we continued the trip to the deeper sections of the *mahaleh*, places I did not recognise. We stopped and asked for directions many times. I started to wonder if we would ever find the place or make the event in time. We stopped by a pair of small wooden doors in the mazes of alleyways. "Where's the house of Maryam, daughter of Yehuda, the grocer, the wife of Raheem, the carpet man who has a shop by the Karimkhan Bazaar?" my grandmother asked. We were pointed to the direction of another alleyway but were soon lost again in the crossroads of narrow passes. Khanom-bozorg clutched the brass doorknob to another house, but before she could knock, the door opened. She gossiped with the women inside, then asked for directions. Alluding to the event that we were attending, the woman said, "Always good occasions." My grandmother responded, "May happiness come your way too." A little later, Khanom-bozorg stopped by a kiosk crowded with half-filled burlap bags of split yellow beans, short-grain rice, whole turmeric, and odds and ends of the household — charcoal, short home-made brooms, and knick-knacks that were jammed into a small corner of a wall. She asked the shopkeeper where Maryam lived. But she didn't leave without asking for the price of the dried limes and powdered sumac and complaining that they were too expensive. The sugar cone was getting heavier at each stop.

Finally we were there. The house was like most homes in the *mahaleh*, with a small sturdy door opening to a narrow walkway that ended with another set of heavy doors. We entered the house through its courtyard paved with bricks and the usual little pool in the middle, now temporarily covered with a piece of plywood and a kilim on which the musicians were to perform later. Men were busy spreading worn-out Persian carpets on the floor of the yard. I imagined the wedding party, families sitting cross-legged on the carpets, the musicians playing Persian drums and violin, women ululating and singing wedding songs. Like any traditional Iranian home, the living quarters surrounded the courtyard, each section having a basement, a first-floor living area, and an attic. When male members of the family married and had children, they would be entitled to a section if the house had enough rooms. Otherwise, they had to share the space with their parents and other siblings.

I followed my grandmother up the stairs and into a room crowded with women, and surrendered the sugar cone to a woman who seemed to be the bride's mother. We took off our shoes at the door and lined them up by the wall as the etiquette required. A few pillows were piled up

176

on top of a blanket in the far corner of the room. I wondered if we were there to watch someone sleep. Was that possible? I watched the women draped in colourful chadors covering their mouths with a fabric-wrapped hand when listening and uncovering their lips when pouring out words.

I stood in a chair by the exit, watching the women's backs. The mother of the bride entered holding her daughter's elbow, and walked through a path that the women opened for them. The bride had light cocoa skin with a nap of soft black hair on her upper lip and full, connected eyebrows; the *bandandaz* would surely take care of the facial hair. She was unadorned and natural in a modest dress. Her black shoulder-length hair barely moved as she walked. Her feet were bare like those of the rest of us. Her eyes, dark and shy, avoided eye-contact with the spectators. Without a covering, her hair and body were there for everyone to judge.

Women unveiled their mouths slightly and murmured to each other. My grandmother whispered to the other woman next to her, "She is *najeeb*, chaste-looking."

The women answered back, "Poor thing. She is so shy." Khanom-bozorg added, "She is dark, but it's all right. She has 'salt', she has charm." The bride's mother helped her lean against the pillow. A person in the back of the room warned, "Cover the windows, cover the windows!" But someone from the groom's family complained, "There isn't enough light." A woman wearing a light brown chador with pink flowers opened the door a crack and ordered everyone to leave the yard. I couldn't see anything over the head of the women, so I bent down to look through their feet. Two women knelt by the young bride-to-be, took off her panties, spread her legs apart, and leaned down to examine her. One plain dark blue figure said, "Look, here it is."

The voices from the groom's side protested. "Where is it, where? We can't see anything." Finally all the women managed to see whatever there was to see. They dressed

177

the bride, who was shaking too hard to manage the job herself, and began to sing "*Kililili*." Their ululating voices signalled the completion of the task. There was gong to be a wedding. The courtyard filled again with men hurrying about. Someone walked in with trays of sour cherry sherbet. Everyone insisted that the bride should be the first to drink. The bride looked flushed and unsteady on her feet. Her mother consoled her. "Don't worry, dear. It's done!"

The sound of ululation in the small room was deafening. My grandmother pushed me to leave the room, congratulating the two families. "A good fortune," she blessed the bride. Another woman added, "May she be blessed with wealth and happiness."

My grandmother and I left first since we were in the back, put our shoes on, and headed down the stairs. She asked others to point out the groom. Covered in sweat, the groom was helping the other men set up the chairs. He looked old to me. Though he had covered the baldness on top of his head with a long strand of hair from the right side, it had moved to his forehead, leaving the bald spot bare. He had a big smile that showed small yellow teeth. My grandmother blessed the groom, "Don't worry. Everything is fine. May you grow old together." Another woman chimed in, "*Mazal tov*, congratulations! Next year may you have a son in your arms." The groom blushed and bowed in a gesture of gratitude. I had never seen a man turn colour in shyness. Maybe he was going to be a good husband, I thought. The two of us, short and tall, headed for home. I was content. I felt a deep love for my grandmother, who had shared her outing with me, although at the time I was not quite sure what it all meant. I was also pleased not to have the burden of the sugar cone. As we manoeuvered our way through the busy alleyways I felt tired and a bit worried. The image of women gathered by the waterspouts and at the ceremony contrasted sharply with the picture of my mother's lonely figure at home — a picture I had successfully managed to forget for a while. What about you mother? I thought. What about her?

178

Ladislav Grosman

Mea Culpa

Translated from Czech by Sonia Reichmann and George Grosman

I believed Topolovka was the end of the world. It was a pic-
turesque village, situated about five kilometres from the
nearest town. It boasted an old fashioned wooden church.
A gravel road lined with poplar trees led to the village; a
shady, quiet road book-ended by tiny cottages whose red
roofs shone lazily in the light of the fading sun.

There was nothing sad about my assertion that
Topolovka was the end of the world with absolutely nothing beyond it. "Nothing" does not disturb or annoy, not
when one is eight or nine years old! The apprentice said:

"Well, now, right here, this is the end of the world. I've
been down the road, I've seen it with my own eyes. I've
seen nothing beyond the village and so now we can go
back. Anyway, it's late, I'm hungry and we're more than
an hour away from home."

I didn't object but kept turning my head to look back at
the tall, slim poplars, the splendid line of trees which
adorned the road and over which the sun followed its daily
arc till it came to rest at Topolovka, where the world
ended. East of the town, in the magical valley nestled
among the high hills and forests, near the cemetery, the
apprentice had once pointed out to me: "This way is east,
that's where the sun rises and there," he pointed to a
clearing in the forest, "there lie all those who are no longer
among the living, that's where they come to rest." That's
what the apprentice, nicknamed Gechko Hop, told me.

He took me along on walks or for a ride on his bicycle
and it was thanks to him that I knew the four directions of
the world and knew my way around the local roads, all of

which — according to Gechko Hop — ended in the vicinity since the world ends where there are no more roads.

And so it came to pass that for many years I lived at the centre of the world. It was quite enough for me, this small world in which after all we lacked for nothing: there were mountains and animals, rivers and fish, houses and neighbours, those who sowed and those who reaped — in short a perfect little world with the sun shining above to give it light and warmth.

Whence the fear then, the fear inside me which disturbed this intimate harmony? It may be worth noting that it probably started with the volcano. It must have started with the volcanic mountain called Vihorlat. The volcano's majestic beauty dominated the vista of forests and mountains on the south side of the world. There was something inscrutable in the way it hid in the mist, in the clouds, in the winter snow. And that is when the anxiety washed over me, almost a horror at times, as I realised that Gechko Hop might be right.

"The volcano, you know," he began slowly, running his fingers through his close-cropped hair, "the volcano, how can I say this…it's a nuisance. It's like an old, well-trained dog whom everyone, including its master, believes to be completely harmless. How can a toothless dog hurt you? Have you ever seen a toothless dog?"

"Never."

"See? A dead volcano is like a toothless dog. Except that wise men have said: Don't trust volcanoes. Not even dead, inactive volcanoes. That's what I think too! I don't trust Vihorlat," Gechko Hop said darkly and continued: "Truly, have you ever heard of a chimney-sweep in this whole wide world who would climb down a volcano, way down, all the way down to examine its innards, to see if they are still hot and boiling? A sea of flame? No such chimney-sweep exists as far as I know. No one has been to the bottom of the volcano and therefore no one can be certain that it won't ever turn into a fire stuttering demon!"

180

Because of his eloquence, I held Gechko Hop in very high esteem. And Gechko Hop, having been found unfit for military duty, probably needed my esteem. He was glad I took him seriously and listened to what he had to say. My curiosity egged him on to ever-higher flights of fancy. He spoke of rocks being hurled high into the air, huge fiery boulders, clouds of sulphur and fire, sparks and black lava spewing forth from the mouth of the volcano, a sky-rocketing inferno shooting up several hundred metres, then hurtling down and mercilessly burying alive everything in its path.

"But who would do that? Why?" I couldn't understand. I was unable to take on board the indifferent recklessness of a fate that would burn up and destroy everything that was alive and blossoming.

"Who?" Gechko Hop shut his left eye. "Why?" Now he shut his right eye and pointing toward the mountains, he said it all just happened by itself. "A volcano cannot remain inactive forever," he said, "inactivity breeds idleness and idleness breeds thievery. I didn't make that up. That's what your father always says to me!" he said somewhat accusingly. "He keeps harping on it... inactivity breeds idleness and idleness breeds thievery. So there it is, clear as day, right?" he said, perhaps wishing to change the subject. But the volcano story had upset me. "Who needs it if it's so dangerous?"

"How can you ask such a stupid question? Who needs it!! The volcano belongs here just like the hot spring does. The hot spring is useful, the volcano deadly. The hot spring gushes water, mineral water, water with curative powers, fifty metres up in the air. Mind you, once I read that it also springs from the volcano. Who can understand that? Nature strokes you with one hand and slaps you in the face with the other, that's the natural order of things. Lest we become too happy-go-lucky!"

My head was filled with thoughts about volcanic activity. I had dreams about it. I dreamt of a volcano that looked like a giant kettle on top of four devil horns, with the devils' red tongues sticking out. As I awoke, I was sure that was going to be the signal: the devils would rub their palms and the volcano would erupt and bury the town.

I wasn't about to divulge my dream to Gechko Hop or to anyone else for love nor money. The feelings of impending doom and creeping fear remained locked away in my heart, stored as if it were a picture album I might one day wish to peruse.

Gechko hadn't worked for a long time now. There were no apprentice jobs to be found. On his father's advice he tried his luck with the railways. Once I saw Gechko in a train conductor's uniform and felt a twinge of pride, as if I'd had a hand in his railway career.

Gechko's stint in our store came to an end immediately following an experiment that was supposed to prove to me the world was round. It happened on a Sunday afternoon. Neighbours were resting on benches, chatting in the sun or taking a nap but as soon as Gechko began his experiment in the middle of our courtyard, everyone came to life and began to gather round. Children came running. The experiment started inauspiciously. Gechko unravelled some thread, tied it to the handle of a cup and explained: "I will now spin this cup with such force and speed that not a single drop will spill out of it. That proves that the earth moves around its axis. The speed and the force keep the oceans from spilling even the tiniest drop." Then he yelled: "Hop!" and started spinning on his toes.

"I'm dying!!" Some women shrieked. It was my aunt Malvina there to absorb some of Gechko's knowledge. "I'm dead! I'm dying!" she screamed as she was hit in the forehead by the spinning cup. Blood came gushing out and she fainted. As she crumpled to the ground, her hand struck the glasses of the near-sighted bully, Farkash, who started flailing his arms in all directions and moaning: "I'm blind! I can't see!" He squirmed and kicked those who stood near him. A melée ensued, the world was spinning, and it was as if the volcano had exploded.

Fear gripped my heart and pierced it like hot lava piercing the crust of the earth. Yes, it was I who had caused the human volcano to erupt. The neighbours were screaming, fighting, pummelling each other. I was covered in cold sweat, unsteady and nauseous. Yes, it was I who had repeatedly pleaded with Gechko Hop to prove to me that the earth was round.

Henryk Grynberg

Uncle Morris

Translated from Polish by Katarzyna Jerzak

"Where would you rather sleep, here or in my room?" asked Uncle Morris.

"But there is a bed ready for him here, papa!" insisted Rose.

"Why? He can sleep in my room, can't he?"

"What are you talking about, papa," said Rose, her eyes pleading for my understanding.

"But his suitcase and his coat can stay in my room. Let me hang the coat in my closet."

"Please leave it, papa, I'll hang it myself."

"Yeah, yeah, yeah," said Uncle Morris, as he walked away quickly with my things.

Then he moved his chair across from mine, very close, so that his knees touched mine. Staring at me with his narrow, almost Mongolian eyes, he told me where we would go, when, and on what train. He wanted to know whether I liked melon and corn flakes with milk for breakfast and if I drank grape juice or coke with dinner.

"Papa, you'll tire him out! Let him rest, papa!" cried Rose.

"Yeah, yeah, yeah. He'll have plenty of time to rest. What would you like to drink now? Maybe some soda water? Do we have soda water, Rose?"

"Let me check."

"I'll go check," Uncle Morris jumped up.

"Papa, please sit!"

"Yeah, yeah, yeah," he answered and proceeded to the refrigerator. "There is only the empty siphon. Where is my hat?"

"But papa, where are you going?"

"What do you mean, where am I going? To get soda water. You can see there is none, can't you?"

"But papa, that's not necessary, I'll go and get it!"

"Yeah, yeah, yeah," he nodded serially and was gone.

Uncle Morris had retained his Tsar-guard's, pre-First World War stature. Only his chest, once thrown forward like a shield, was now caved in. One could still admire it on a brown photograph of Uncle Morris in a tightly fitting uniform of the elegant New York City restaurant which employed only handsome waiters. The twirled up moustache of a Tsar's guard and his sharp glance were preserved on the photograph as well.

He did not serve long at that restaurant: he could not learn to smile like a waiter. He could not sit long in a sweat-shop, either, because his back hurt from bending over the machine. So he went underground and spent forty years there, opening and closing the doors.

"But the doors have been opening and closing on their own for a long time now."

"Someone has to tell them to open and to close."

"And the incessant noise?"

"Only those who travel once or twice a day hear it. And those who are afraid."

"Afraid of what?"

"That they won't make it."

But he was not afraid. He had the whole day or the whole night. And it never happened that he wouldn't make it. Till the end of the day or the night — under ground it doesn't really matter. He read only at the end-of-the-line stops, but he could think all he wanted. He had emigrated not because there was no longer a Tsar to be guarded and not only because of persecution. He wanted to travel. So he travelled for forty years. And he could go on travelling: he had a free lifetime ticket for the subway.

He kept my suitcase in his room. When I needed something, he would open it for me and then close it again. When I changed a shirt, he would take it away to be washed and I would find it ironed. When I needed

185

anything, he would jump up to get it for me. If I mentioned shopping, he would put on his hat, ready to go with me. Whenever I went out, he would explain how to get there, which way to go, and would offer himself as a guide. "Papa, let it be, papa, don't do that, papa, don't meddle," Rose chided him incessantly. I felt like calling out to her, you stop meddling! I wanted to listen to his directions and instructions, even if the offices, buildings and streets to which he directed me were no longer there. It seemed to me that I would never lose my patience if I had had a father or a grandfather. One who would meddle, correct, give instructions. Perhaps I would not have to feel my way or walk blindly quite so often. I wouldn't wander, I wouldn't blunder into places of no return.

"What are you going back to?! To whom and for what?! Have pity on your youth!" Rose would wring her hands. "Why don't you stay in California with your mother? Why are you going in the wrong direction?" Irving would ask. "Let him be. He knows what he's doing. This may be better for him," intervened Uncle Morris. He alone was not surprised, did not tell me to turn around, did not hold me back, ironed my shirts for the road. "I hope we'll see each other again tomorrow," he'd say before retiring to his room in the evening. When late at night I would go in to take something out of my suitcase, I'd find him sitting in front of a broken television that nobody had bothered to fix over the years, staring into the empty screen.

Uncle Morris was not my uncle. He was the husband of my grandmother's first cousin. I knew her only from photographs which she sent with dollar bills glued underneath. My mother called her her aunt. We did not have any closer relatives and she too treated us as if we were her immediate family because outside of us no one else survived. After her death uncle Morris became our closest relative, one who remembered my grandmother and grandfather. His daughters, who were indeed our blood relatives, did not know anyone in our family. He never said why he supported my plans. Perhaps he

186

thought that it was still possible to make up for what had happened, to save something, to reclaim it. Perhaps he imagined that I was returning in his place. To the place of his youth. And that I would be him there. A guard, guarding memory.

I was his past. And he was — mine. His past was there and mine was here. I rediscovered my past in this pre-war apartment in the Bronx, where there were dark wooden beds and sepia photographs, where silver cups had survived in the chest and even pre-war sets of china were intact. Pale Rose, a good daughter and wife, with a round figure and subtly semitic features, and self-assured, broad-shouldered Irving — suspenders, cigar, the face of a boxer — also survived in a pre-war photograph. In their wedding picture his hair is patted down with brilliantine and parted in the middle, while she has the perm and the make-up from silent movies — emancipated, progressive people who always know what they are doing. Friday nights spent not in the synagogue but at cards, Saturday — movies or the park. Nutritious Jewish food but without kosher restrictions and so all the more nutritious. Too nutritious perhaps. "You do not eat on Yom Kippur, do you?" "We do not eat, we feast!" answered Irving belligerently, even though there was nobody with whom to be belligerent. The past survived here complete with this progressive belligerent spirit.

Rose retained the waist of a woman who had never been pregnant. "Nature did not bless me," she would say with a sigh. But she had an exemplary husband who commuted daily to New Jersey — one hour each way — where he fought as a cutter, then a foreman, and finally — a manager, and each summer he took her to a hotel in the Catskills. Rose's divorced sister Betty was in California with two children, struggling without a husband. The third sister was never mentioned. While Irving was carrying the suitcases, long ready, down to the taxi cab, Rose pressed me to her full bosom and held me there much too long. "After all there is no future for you there," she said.

"Go and see.You'll be back."

They went to the hotel where they stayed every summer for over twenty years, and they left us a full refrigerator and the largest network of underground trains in which Uncle Morris could move with his eyes closed like a mole. "Hey, pops, where can one take a leak here?" asked a middle-aged man as we were coming up from the underground. "Straight and to the left, kid!" answered Uncle Morris and the man saluted him with respect.

With our heads turned up we walked in the city built in the sky. Golden sunrises, sunsets, the blues, and white clouds moved along the glass towers. Very few saw any of that because they all looked straight ahead, toward the goal to which they were rushing. Moreover their eyes were glazed with the fear that they would not make it. They rode under-ground, they walked on the ground, they did not know the city in the sky. Pigeons drank from the fountain in front of the building that stood up against the sky like the ladder in Jacob's dream and the end of the ladder was out of sight. Like in a dream we sped skyward. Once there, Uncle Morris showed me the city like a ship with tall masts, not a ship but a fleet of moored cities. At the entrance to the harbour stood the queen in a radiant crown, holding a sceptre high up. She took in slaves, granted them freedom, took them captive. When we came back down, young people with banners were walking around the fountain.

"Who are they?" I asked.

"Probably Jews," answered Uncle Morris.

"What do they want?"

"More freedom."

"For Jews?"

"No, for Blacks."

We stopped by kosher stores, bakeries selling bagels, and butcher's shops from the other world. Lots of butchers and lots of bakeries, as if they had all been transported here from the world that was no longer. They stood next to one another, all alike but each a little different, with the kinds of breads and meats that could only be suggested by the mystical Jewish imagination. And contrary to others, they were not afraid of competition. Because every Jew had his butcher's and his bakery, like a promised fig tree underneath which he feared nothing, not even competition. "Where are you from?" asked the Jews. "From there?!" "When did you arrive? Only now?!" "What do you intend to do? You're going back?!" — their big eyes would fill with the old fear.

The earthly globe shook in its orbits above the World Exhibition grounds, the contours of continents and seas were flopping. In African bowers covered with straw and in larger tents missionaries showed how to convert primitive villages into oases of salvation by means of faith and money. After each show the missionaries collected money — they had enough faith — and people gave money with the conviction that soon all African, Asian, South American and Central American villages would be saved. In the lay pavilions ambitious plans were uncovered for the salvation of all villages and all cities on all continents. An important role was to be played by the new magical machines for the transmission and multiplication of print. One pressed a button and the machine wrote all by itself, from left to right and from right to left. — "What have I done! What have I done!" Gutenberg held his head. "They will flood us, drown us, stifle us!"

The prophecy fulfilled itself. Books made their way onto grocery store shelves, while bookstores became supermarkets. Secrets of secretaries, revelations of prostitutes, confessions of one's own sons and daughters, lives of famous men written by their ex-wives — all spilled out like hot cakes. Anyone could become an author: a politician, a conman, a charlatan, a spy, a murderer or a thief — as long as he had caused or could cause a scandal. People competed for positions in order to become authors. There were more authors than readers and yet they all made money. All except for the writer who was a drop in the flood of print. Three hundred pages for a dollar and six hundred for nothing. Hard- and soft-bound, with photos and photomontages, in every size and every colour. On every possible and impossible topic: how to make money; how to conquer women; how to achieve everything one wants; how to get rid of guilt (not only for former Nazis); the art of business and bribery; lying in public and the anatomy of power; reincarnation and the eternal now; love and medicine; whom women love and whom they leave; women who love men who hate women who love them too much; how to find happiness; how to achieve intimacy; how to arrive at a flat belly. Shakespeare and pocket Aristotle were drowning. Dolphins, whales and elephants gave place to the ever more numerous and ever more photogenic species of Chryslers, Nissans, Toyotas — in albums as well as all over the world.

The world was in a hurry, the pavilions raced one another. Uncle Morris and I could not keep up with them. The year was already 1964. The 1939 World Exhibition had taken place in the very same spot in Flushing.

Before departure I paid a visit to the queen. She did not have an elevator so Uncle Morris waited on a bench next to a grey-haired lady wearing glasses embedded with rhinestones, while I entered the majestic folds. The queen had no legs but one could climb the stairs into her belly. One could nestle up in her bosom from within. One could get stuck in her throat. Peek in her teeth. Catch her eye. Examine her head. Reach her crown. One could see from up there the city in the sky and in the water and the roads that stood open.

"So how was it?" asked Uncle Morris when I came down.

"I did not know that a symbol of freedom could be empty inside."

"You'll be back to apologise to her!" said the grey-haired lady in rhinestone glasses.

Parting with someone who was eighty years old had to be for ever, but our parting had additional dimensions. We were, for one another, the footbridge toward that part of the world where all the others had all been burnt. We did

190

not have a place of our own. We belonged neither here nor there. Now we were watching that last footbridge go. We were parting not only with each other but with the most important part of ourselves. Standing on deck I photographed him with the queen in the background. Her torch showed the way in all directions. Seen *en face* Uncle Morris appeared as upright as she did. The departure was long and he kept standing there. He stood by her like a bodyguard. So I continued to photograph him even when he could no longer be seen. And I kept him, invisible, on those photographs.

The year was still 1964, I was still young, and the roads stood open. I have time, I thought, I'll see. I had three and a half years of time.

"You see, you went and saw for yourself," said Rose when I came back.

"Yes, I did."

"I told you there was no future there!" Irving was shaking his head.

"Yes, you did."

I did not try to explain that it was all about the past.

Roya Hakakian

The Last Chapter in the Book of Exodus

If there is a Jewish book of exodus, the departure of the Jews from Iran must make up its last chapter. I've often wondered what it was that drove my father to sell our house, his dream home, located in one of Tehran's trendiest neighbourhoods, at #3 Alley of the Distinguished. That house was the monument to his success. The son of a poor, illiterate travelling fabric salesman had made good: left the village, educated himself, and settled in the heart of the capital. Our house was where all the extended family gathered for Passover every year. To honour the ancient Israelites' hasty departure from Egypt, my family hastened, rallying around my mother, to wage our own crusade. Our enemies were not at all alike: the slaves had fought against pharaoh whereas we fought against dirt. We armed ourselves with an arsenal of brooms, rags, mops, scrubs, and sprays. We awoke at dawn, when the "cotton beater" made his yearly visit. He camped in the corner of the courtyard, stripped our quilts and mattresses and removed all the cotton inside. Then squatting among the heap, he brought out a harp-like tool. Holding it amid the heap, he plucked at the coarse strings, till the flattened cotton, caught in the strings, separated and regained their fluffiness.

Inside the house, we got busy. We brought down the curtains, dusted every rod, rolled every rug, and swept underneath everything. Searching our closets, we emptied our wallets and handbags, unrolled our pant cuffs, lined up every jacket and pair of trousers on the clothesline, and turned the pockets inside out. We stretched the corner of a rag over our index finger, traced along the sides of each drawer to the four corners and twirled our fingertip around a few times. The merriment would come later, only when seriousness had been paid its due. And our saviour,

192

our seasonal Moses, our year-round Job, Mother, with an outstretched arm, lamenting her migraine, led us in battle against dirt.

Despite all the work we enjoyed Passover more than any other holiday. Perhaps because it came at the heels of the Iranian New Year, and it felt as part of the same festivity. Or perhaps because all the drama made the holiday feel like a theatrical production. At the Seder, like actors, we recited words which often conjured no immediate bitter memory to the minds of anyone except the few elders. "Bondage," "affliction," and "suffering at the hands of a bad majority," meant little to most of my family. They vowed "Next year in Israel," but knew, even as the words rang in the air, how hollow they were. The family dreamed of the land of milk and honey but wanted to wake up in Tehran. Bondage seemed like a very distant history.

What did truly drive us out of Iran? Was it the Swastika that appeared on the wall across our door on the eve of the 1979 revolution? It terrified us, to be sure. But nothing followed that ugly presence on the wall — no rise in hostility among our neighbours, or friends. If it was meant to galvanise some latent anti-Semitic feeling among the public it failed to do so. Similarly in 1984, that perfectly Orwellian year, an order came for the washroom facilities in schools to be separated by religion. One morning, as my class filed through the schoolyard, we saw men posting signs above the toilets that read: Moslems Only. Above the last two stalls, another sign read: Non-Moslems Only. Like the Swastika, the signs worried us at first. But they, too, failed to mean anything more than a couple of ugly signs. There was an unspoken code among us teenage girls that saw abiding by them an "uncool" thing to do. Everyone ignored it. With the war with Iraq in its fourth year, the Red Alert sirens shrieking through the school corridors on most days, the school officials, even if they wished, were too busy to enforce washroom rules.

So, why did we leave? Not for the reasons that our ancestors left the biblical Egypt. We were rarely singled out to bear great burdens. We didn't leave even for the reasons that Jews left modern-day Iraq or Syria. We left Iran primarily because life under the new circumstances was becoming increasingly intolerable. We left for all the reasons that anyone, Jew or Moslem, was compelled to leave.

This is why Iran is still home to the largest community of Jews outside of Israel in all of the Middle East. Jews arrived in Iran long before Islam had come to exist. And today, nearly 20,000 Jews live in Iran. Along with Christians and Zoroastrians, Jews are considered "people of the book," and are a legitimate religious minority. The community sends its own representative to the Majles. There are synagogues and butcher-shops, even several schools throughout Tehran, though the schools are run by Moslem staff, and are kept open on Saturdays.

Like every year since we arrived in America, my family will sit at this Seder. Someone will make a bitter allusion to the past: *Thank God we left unscathed!* Everyone around the table will second it. All these words will be spoken in Persian. Then, the lavish holiday dinner will be served — bowls of eggplant or parsley stew, colourful trays of saffron, cumin, and berry rice. And as the music of Mahasti, Iran's favourite diva, fills the air, they will compete to tell their stories of the old days.

The Baby Blue BMW

Later that week, drifting in and out of sleep on Farah's bed, I heard her whisper into the phone that Neela and Uncle Ardi's relationship was turning into a smashing romance. Some weeks later, I found snapshots hidden under the same bed, pictures of the couple weathering their first seasons of intimacy: Uncle Ardi's arms around Neela, the two of them standing under the budding plane trees on Elizabeth Boulevard; Uncle Ardi and Neela by the Caspian Sea, their weekend getaway spot. There she was

194

in a one-piece swimsuit in his arms, splayed like an offering he had brought to bestow upon the god of camera. In anther picture, Neela sat on the hood of the BMW while Uncle Ardi, one foot on the tyre, reached to kiss her. Only one photo included other people and that had been taken indoors, in the family's seaside cottage. In it, everyone beamed with joy. Mr Maroof had one hand on Uncle Ardi's back and rested the other affectionately on his chest, like he was receiving him, claiming him as his own. And Mrs Maroof lifted her daughter's hand to show it off to the camera: there was a diamond ring on Neela's finger.

A discovery of Agatha Christie proportions! I had gained the new knowledge by means far more sophisticated than mere osmosis. All on my own, I had pieced together two of the family's greatest secrets: first, the reason for Albert's departure, and now, the engagement of Uncle Ardi. This was a piece of gossip worth a tidal wave of elbowing. But even though I was very excited, I knew I could not tell anyone about it. I, too, was smitten with the couple's grace and the tangible bliss in the pictures and felt compelled to keep quiet. This poignant moment, the sudden exercise of restraint, was an electrifying transformation. And I recognised it as my passage into a glorious new age, into puberty, though the actual physical changes that occurred a year later proved to be terribly anticlimactic.

"Why her?" Farah kept asking her confidantes on the telephone. Her beauty? But every man, she reasoned, was bound to get irritated by a woman his own height, tire of her fashionable slenderness and yearn for womanly plumpness. It would be a matter of days before he saw her nose not as exotic but as deformedly hooked. Was it her hair? Eh, no intelligent man would bank on anything as fickle as hair. Her upbringing and family? Uncle Ardi, so urbane, could not possibly want to associate himself with a mother-in-law so devoutly clad. But that convinced neither Farah nor the listener on the other end. Mrs Maroof's veil was the remnant of an extinct era. A relic from the 1930s: before Reza Shah ordered the mandatory unveiling of all women and sent gendarmes to the streets to pull the veils off women's heads. Her veil was not a symbol of her faith but of human reluctance to rid oneself of something old and familiar. Mrs Maroof had been thrilled by the great reforms of 1962 — "women granted the right to vote!" — and of 1967 — "women granted the right to divorce!" She celebrated the promises that Iran's new future held for her daughters; thus her embrace of an unprecedented fashion: the hot pants and the bikinis on Neela and her sister.

It was Neela's spirit, then, that had captivated Uncle Ardi, Farah concluded after she had reasoned her way out of every other possibility. She paused over the telephone.

Yes, the answer was Neela's spirit, the spirit that was not only hers but theirs. A spirit she and Uncle Ardi shared, one of optimism. At only twenty-three, Neela earned a good living modelling and selling jewellery and Uncle Ardi was already a partner in the Asia Insurance Company. Unlike the disenchanted mascot of *Tafigh*, Coco, they were pleased with the status quo. And since neither had attended university, they read little, knew even less about the little black fishes and the fates of their writers or the constraints of…*shhh*!

They also shared the outlook of a new generation, one that had cast off religion and tradition. Why else would they drive a BMW instead of an Iranian-manufactured Paykan? They accepted no homegrown hero, followed the lead of no guru who was not blond. If they were gong to learn about the power of love, it was not from Rumi but from Roger Moore. If they were going to emulate anyone, in chivalry, for instance, it would not be Imam Ali but John Wayne. If they were to climb anything, it would not be Mount Sinai but the Empire State Building: a mighty couple, with the world's possibilities at their mighty feet.

* * *

At last Grandmother, Aunt Zarrin, and Mother came together to fight Neela. The battle began morbidly, as

196

most events began in Iran. The women, dressed in black, started to make daily visits to Grandfather's grave site. On Saturdays, the men gathered in Grandmother's living room to say prayers of remorse and forgiveness. They arrived unshaved, sat on the chairs, rocked to and fro, recounted the penance the prophets had paid, as if recounting their own, over and over, and stopped only to sip tea, to wet their parched throats, so they could read on.

The kitchen was just as crowded. Herbalists left on the heels of astrologers. The astrologers exited when the palm readers entered. On the stove, miniature pots appeared. Something was always bubbling, steaming. Someone was always stirring, reading a spell. Stirring again, saying the same spell with eyes closed. Stirring some more, repeating the words again, then adding a pinch of this, a dash of that, but never tasting. The ultimate potion, often a dark, viscous liquid, was added to Uncle Ardi's meals. At the kitchen window, Grandmother, leaning out, pleaded with someone: "Do something, I beg you!" I first thought she was speaking to a neighbour but realised later that she was pleading with my dead grandfather not to lose an opportunity to involve God: "May light shower your grave, Isaac! You're the nearest to Him."

Until Uncle Ardi's affair, being a Jew had been a blithe experience for me. It was a licence, unearned, to receive special privileges: an extra day off from school on Saturdays, an additional new year in every new year, endless holidays every season. It was a pass to exceptional places: to the stage as a dancer at the Royal Court of King Xerxes and Queen Esther; in Father's arms to cross a wide canal on our way to the synagogue; in a pool of light at the threshold of the synagogue under elaborate chandeliers; within the range of the rosewater flask of the temple's keeper, who welcomed each congregant with a dash; before a grieving mourner who offered a slice of onion quiche for a blessing; between the men's and the women's aisles, crisscrossing to deliver messages of wives to husbands, secret lovers and their rivals; at the foot of the altar, watching a boy rise, recite a few prayers, and step down a man. Being a Jew was to expect a surprise from the ordinary: like two wooden panels that, once unlocked, revealed a treasure of scrolls draped in layers of crimson velvet and gold-embroidered white lace, melodious with bells atop each; or a single glass that, shattering under a young man's foot, broke the hush of hundreds in a wedding ballroom. Being a Jew was to be a humble number in God's math: adult men, saying kaddish, hid their faces under their prayer shawls and wept like children.

But seeing the family react to Uncle Ardi's affair with Neela, I felt the blitheness waning. I became leery of God, whose love had once come so easily to me. I became wary of my family, its lugubrious underlife, its lugubrious wrath, and the lugubrious practices that had come so easily to them. I examined and reexamined every encounter with the Maroofs. I pondered our day in Darband. The verdant spaces where we had come together with them yellowed in my memory. Had they truly been green? The sounds of nature, the birds, the rapids, the rustle of the poplar leaves — were they there to envelop us equally, bind us equally? The wooden benches. They creaked. The Maroofs sat next to Father, Mother, Aunt Zarrin, and Uncle A.J. and played charades. Mr Maroof pretended to be a baker. Uncle Ardi, his assistant, rolled a make-believe pin over the dough and slapped it against the walls of a make-believe oven. Each performed so well that Grandmother guessed their job in seconds. Was that the real game of charades, or was it the whole of our afternoon, the attempt at shedding our differences to become one? Oh, how we had scrubbed, boiled, combed, brushed, and bleached. We were no less clean, see? Or were we trying to say that we were cleaner?

* * *

198

On a Saturday afternoon, Grandmother's hallway door swung violently open and Uncle Ardi stormed into the kitchen. "Do you think I don't know what you've been up to?" he shouted at Grandmother. He pushed the hair away from his forehead and pointed to it: "Do you see 'idiot' written across here?"

She lowered herself into a chair, repeating, "What in God's name, Ardi?"

Aunt Zarrin rested her arm around Grandmother's shoulder. Mother pleaded with Uncle Ardi to take a seat. He would not. She fetched him a glass of water. It stayed on the table. The kitchen was too small for all of them and the secret that had brewed in it for weeks. The words had to be spoken. The name had to be said. Uncle Ardi said it: "I'm going to marry Neela. This week. And if you try to stop me, I'll just take her hand and go." Without a destination, his threat did not have gravity. So he added, "To Qom."

Qom, as in the Vatican of Iran! No one went to Qom but pilgrims to visit the holy Muslim shrines. No one lived there but clerics. There was nothing to do but study at a seminary. But Uncle Ardi had other business: "I'll have a mullah marry us in Qom." This was his way of saying he would convert if they got in his way.

Aunt Zarrin wobbled a few steps till she steadied herself against the refrigerator. Mother pressed the back of her hand against her forehead. Grandmother rose to her feet. She walked slowly to the utensil drawer. The drawer rattled open. In a world of her own, Grandmother was mumbling to herself, as she did sometimes, looking for a spice container or a missing key. A few more clattering sounds punctuated the silence in the kitchen. "Aha!" she finally exclaimed. The search had ended.

Her best butcher's knife in one hand, she turned to face everyone. Gripping the knife's black handle, her finger appeared whiter than usual. She pressed the point of the knife against her chest, and no longer mumbling, she said, "I'll put this through my heart if you…"

199

The sentence lingered in the air, incomplete. Mother rushed to grab the knife from her. Uncle Ardi stormed out of the kitchen. Aunt Zarrin rushed after him. She called his name. No answer came but doors banging. Then came the sound of an engine. Aunt Zarrin had caught up with Uncle Ardi in the courtyard. Talking through the driver's side-window, she was pleading with him. But we could not hear her words. The car started. Aunt Zarrin kept on talking through the furious roars of the engine. He backed out. She ran alongside the car, still talking. But he sped away. Aunt Zarrin stood at the door, still. She walked to the middle of the block and looked to each end. She was fuming but weakening too. Hunched, her knees half-bent, she stood in the middle of the courtyard. Feeble and disbelieving, she limped back to the street and looked to either side again. Then she shut the door. The hinges clicked into place and she evanesced into the corridor. Only her voice reverberated against the walls: "He'll ruin us. We'll be shamed. He'll speed and kill himself. Or he'll marry Neela. A goy! And make my Farah a spinster for good."

* * *

Two days passed before news of Uncle Ardi came. A call came from the sheriff of a small town near the family cabin by the Caspian Sea. Uncle Ardi was in custody. In his mad drive, he had run over an elderly man who was now in the intensive care unit. Uncle Majid instantly posted bail and a court date was set. But would there be justice, especially if the old man died? A Jew had run over a Muslim, in a small northern town. The incident was likely to transcend the bounds of a traffic case and become a matter of honour for the people of that town. Even as popular and as loved as Uncle Ardi was, he feared standing trial in so remote a place.

Within forty-eight hours, Uncle Ardi was packed for that unimaginable destination, Israel. There was no time for proper good-byes with his fans, friends, colleagues, or even with Neela. He went without fanfare, leaving the family to itself, to its yearning for him. Grandmother's courtyard became a monument to his absence. The BMW sat without its driver. It was all the solidity that was left of that solid, solid man. The family resumed its life again, now that Neela was no longer a threat. More than anyone else, Aunt Zarrin credited herself for the break between the couple. She believed that her last plea with Uncle Ardi in the courtyard, just before he drove away, had made all the difference. Through the driver's side-window, she had begged him before he took off, "Don't do it. Not because of me, Mother, or anyone else. Not even because you'd make Father's soul uneasy in his grave for all eternity. Do it for Farah. No decent Jew would ever marry a girl whose uncle has married a Muslim."

Vesna Domany Hardy

Sharon and Seth

For Batia

"I am depressed and I am reading *The Myth of Sisyphus* because I believe it might help me," said Sharon in one breath, over the phone.

I didn't voice them, but I had my doubts about finding the solution to depression in the Sisyphus Myths. I recalled how the war in Algeria forced Camus to leave his country and come to France where, as a *pied noir*, he remained an outsider for the rest of his life, never completely accepted by his foster motherland. Maybe Camus attracted Sharon because she, too, had escaped from her beleaguered country — the cause of her frequently dark moods. She sometimes told me about her warrior lovers, killers constantly confronting their own deaths. There was no peace to be found with any one of them, for they slept in fits and starts, haunted by apparitions of fallen friends, or enemies killed, or their countrymen burning in napalm flames.

While her country was at war, Sharon scratched a meagre existence as an artist in Milan. In her spacious studio on the Canal Pavese, where she lived and worked, she glued plump cupids, cut out of paper and painted white, on to black satin canvasses. She prepared her black satin canvasses by sewing layers of cloth on a sewing machine, each layer of cloth first cut in a different shape or pattern. She modelled the cupids on the putti of the old masters, particularly Leonardo's. In the Louvre there is a 16th century copy of a painting, supposedly by Leonardo, of Leda with her children by swan/Zeus, at the moment that two pairs of twins hatch out of their eggs. Sharon often told me that these putti, these two pairs of mythological twins, represented for her something most erotic in art. Interpreting them in her own way, she painted them on a very large scale. When fixed on the background of black satin, they seemed to really come to life.

I must admit that the effect of her putti was not at all calming, as observing someone's newly born baby can be. Something very anxious exuded from her works. Sometimes this feeling of anxiety was so strong that it woke me up in the middle of the night. An Italian art collector told me that such force in art is something very precious, and when a work of art has such an effect on him he returns to buy it without hesitation.

Sharon achieved the depth and relief-like dimensionality of her canvasses by cutting into the layers of satin. She used scissors to cut out the flaps, which she would turn over in the desired direction and then glue to the background. In this way she achieved the depth as well as the effect of chiaroscuro.

In spite of her creativity, Sharon always suffered from a feeling of guilt, because while she was preoccupied with art, her lovers, real or imagined, were killing their Arab enemies on the Golan Heights, or in the South of Lebanon. Every time we met, she would repeat the same story. "Killing for them is a question of survival. If they do not kill, they risk being killed themselves." She would tell me how angry they were with her, because while their country was at war, she acted the role of "la belle dame de gauche", living in Italy, exposed only to the hardships of her Bohemian life.

It was not easy to maintain a friendship with Sharon. Since I first met her, she had gradually aggravated many people. Of course amongst wealthy Milanese, some of it was due to her poverty. She was also not interested in anything outside the field of art. To top it all, she told me that her own creativity didn't make her happy, and that she didn't even like what she was making. It was an inner force that made her do it, like a command that had to be obeyed. Sometimes I envied her that uncompromising drive, even though it was difficult to get used to her creations, the anxiety of which always struck me anew. And she herself never ceased to surprise me. Often when I rushed to her studio after a call of despair, almost from the edge of suicide, I found her painting, refreshed and content, dressed in some never-before-seen combination of clothes and colours, which she had pulled out from God knows where.

Her dress sense was exquisite. She looked comfortable and attractive in whatever she wore and her every movement radiated a sense of freedom. She was like a phoenix, forever re-emerging from that deep depression caused by loneliness, poverty, or not being fully accepted in the Milan art world. I admired her ability to cure herself with her creativity, which seemed to emerge from the bitterness of her existence. But when we met we mostly talked about the world of art and ideas, current exhibitions, or the latest gossip from those circles. Most of all I loved to hear the bizarre stories of her impoverished childhood in Israel, where she grew up on a farm amidst equally poor Palestinian neighbours. In art, as in life, her model was Ljubov Goncharova, a Russian avant-garde artist from the time of the October Revolution, about whose work Sharon knew everything that could be known.

* * *

Seth came to Milan one night in January. Prior to his arrival Sharon had never met him. For a long time he was only an unknown soldier, writing letters to her from the front, inserting in each one a fifty dollar bill to help her out. She never used that money, even though it would have helped her pay the bills. Instead she framed each individual note in a used Polaroid picture box, and hung them side by side on one of the studio walls.

The evening before his arrival she called me late, informing me that she was going to meet him at Linate airport. By her tone of voice I sensed a request to accompany her, but as she didn't ask directly, I could choose not to understand.

Instead, I called her two days later. Merrily she chatted about his arrival, adding that he did not excel at all in physical beauty. I had no idea how to comment on this, so in order to interrupt the silence that followed her unusual observation, I asked her what sort of man he was. At that she laughed contentedly, adding: "Wonderful!". Still, I wondered at her brief embarrassment and told her that she had gone native, for most everywhere else the contents were considered more valuable than the packaging. Again she giggled contentedly. I suggested they come for lunch one of the following days.

"Only with you!" she answered, "you are the only one I could introduce him to."

We agreed that they would come for lunch the following Wednesday.

On that day I prepared lunch early, leaving myself some time to finish a radio report I was working on. Then around lunchtime I phoned her to check. She was surprised I had remembered, asking me again if I was sure I wanted them to come, repeating that he was not very beautiful to look at. Intrigued by her apparent embarrassment I repeated my invitation.

* * *

Seth was obviously a man of open spaces; he looked like a farmer or a fisherman. His face was sunburnt with sharp features carved by winds. His body structure was compact, almost square, leaving the impression of a rock, and although not tall, he exuded obvious physical force. One does not see such types anymore in the cities of Western Europe, where I have lived for many years. Comfortable living has made us city folk ever more beautiful, as we engage in various activities to help us get rid of surplus energy and fat. We jog, ride bicycles amidst traffic fumes, pay expensive memberships to mushrooming health clubs

205

where we submit ourselves to various sufferings so we can keep in shape. It seemed that the very idea of a health club would be anathema to Seth, whose face looked much older than his thirty-five years.

"He has survived five wars!" announced Sharon from the door, and all through lunch she continued to speak about him in the third person, as if he was not there. Of languages, Sharon told me, Seth only spoke Hebrew, which I did not speak. Naturally, it made any direct communication between us impossible. My gaze would stray to his rough, strong hands. The knife and fork appeared insignificant in them, while Sharon went on talking about him, how he was of Bulgarian origin but could not speak Bulgarian, because he was born in Tel Aviv. How he was also of Sephardic descent.

I was asking the usual conventional questions, easy for Sharon to translate. His answers were long and torrential. Not being able to understand, or judge his choice of words, I listened to the sound of his speech, guttural and hard. From the torrents of his words Sharon would translate only a few. After several of his tirades I asked her why she was censoring him so?

"He talks very picturesquely, as if sitting by a camp fire with the whole night in front of us to waste!"…

Sensing her irritability I offered a way out: "You mean he expresses himself in an epic way?"

"Exactly!" she took it readily and we continued with lunch and Seth's occasional un-translated tirade.

I asked him, through Sharon, if he had seen anything of Italy yet. Since his arrival they had hardly been out of her studio, so both of them gladly accepted my offer to drive them out of Milan the next day for an outing, perhaps to one of the neighbouring historic towns.

As soon as they left I regretted my offer. I understood that I had let myself in for something I did not understand and did not have time for, unwilling to act as a tour guide for my friend's lover. During the night my anxiety grew while my brain kept inventing plausible excuses for calling the next day's trip off. I had just finished reading Le Carré's *Little Drummer Girl*, about secret Mossad agents infiltrating Arab terrorist cells, and although I thought it one of his weaker novels, its traumas now fed my imagination with suspicions that Seth was here on some sort of mission and that it would be wiser to keep a distance. Newspaper headlines swam before my eyes, "Mother of Two Dies in Traffic Collision with Unknown Terrorists!" and so forth — scenes rooted in the abundance of media that fills our lives. Still, to my husband I said nothing. He had his own nightmares to contend with, mostly fearing that some important exhibition from the British Museum, or suchlike, might get lost on account of bureaucratic negligence, or impossible customs formalities. As his nightmares were partly rooted in his experience and partly in his inborn anxiousness I thought it would be best not to tell him about my own. So in the morning, as soon as our children left for school, I drove to the Canal Pavese to fetch Sharon and Seth.

* * *

Sharon's modest belongings were neatly distributed around her spacious and light studio. Two iron beds were put close together under the north wall of the studio. The back side of one of her paintings was used as a screen, while another painting was suspended from the ceiling above the beds, as a canopy, to shelter them from the window high up on the wall. Not used to such orderliness in her studio, I would have guessed at a military presence, even had I not known Seth's profession.

Because she had warned me that he had no warm clothes for the sharp Milanese winter, I brought with me a pair of my son's overgrown snowboots and an embarrassingly bright orange skiing anorak.

We left immediately and in no time were circling the town on its endless eastern orbital in the direction of the Venice motorway. Driving through the greyness of Milan's industrial landscape I became anxious again, and Sharon soon sensed it. I thought she must be totally mad, for how else to explain her invitation to a completely unknown soldier to spend a month of his leave with her. Perhaps it was a combination of her generosity of spirit and somewhat guilty patriotism. Besides him being a stranger, she hardly had enough money for food for herself, or for her studio bills.

"What I have, we share!" She interrupted my thoughts as if reading them. I continued my inner monologue, thinking how several centuries earlier she might have been burnt as a witch. Then I recalled that I had had the same thoughts already, when she had asked me before his arrival to lend her some spare bedding. I could not understand then how she could invite a soldier, a legalised killer, to live and sleep with her. But my own conventional way of thinking shook me, and I decided that worse than her imprudence was my being judgmental about something I did not understand.

Be that as it may, my initial anxiety about him had only increased. As a man he was the complete opposite to Sharon's oft proclaimed feminist principles. I asked myself how she could have transformed herself so quickly into a Nietschean model of a woman, whose role was only to function as a warrior's repose. In stark contrast to his rough manliness, she had become so vulnerably feminine, a little woman in the self-denial championships.

"I like it!" she again interrupted, as if I were talking out loud. "And I like being under him!" she laughed. I felt hurt by her vulgar candour. To stop her from further reading my thoughts I began telling her about what I had planned for our outing. I suggested that we first walk around the old upper town of Bergamo and afterward take a walk in the hills beyond, where we could lunch in a simple tavern, a place I had sometimes visited with my children during the occasional Sunday walk.

She translated the plan to Seth and he naturally approved. I wondered if the dignified beauty of old

Bergamo town would impress him. I parked the car immediately within the city walls and then took my guests through the cobbled streets of the beautiful old town to its central Piazza.

Bergamo's Piazza Vechia was one of the most beautiful squares I knew, and I was always glad to share its beauty with my friends. Only a few days earlier I had been pleased to read that the great architect of the Modern period, Le Courbusier, was of the same opinion. Besides its great beauty and harmony, the Piazza had many pleasant associations for me, for I had spent many hours there in the company of an old friend and her painter husband, as they had proudly introduced me to the beauty of their beloved town.

Spacious, harmonious and artistically paved, the Piazza was different from any other. The town lodge was placed over a planet measuring device executed in the marble floor. The lodge cut the piazza diagonally in two unequal parts. In the bigger part there was a porphyry fountain. Four white Carrara marble lions stood at each corner, connected with heavy chains to form an enclosure around it. Right next to the lodge was a very old but well-preserved stairwell with a wooden canopy over it, leading to the municipal offices. Academia Carrara closed the Piazza from the south side. One the other side of the lodge was the Cathedral with its richly decorated façade in different shades of pink marble. In the left corner of the Piazza stood a statue of Bergamo's famous poet, Torquato Tasso, and next to him the café/bar "Tasso". As the Christmas period was not long behind us, Tasso still held an empty champagne bottle under his armpit, presumably a present from some joker.

As we passed under the lodge to the smaller side of the Piazza we were almost blinded by the strength of the January sunlight shining over the Coleone Chapel, the façade of the Cathedral and the baptistery next to it.

I suggested we go into the Cathedral. Seth was perplexed. Visiting Christian churches in Italy seemed to him a strange habit, a definite waste of time, even worse in the cold winter weather. But as we were in the majority, we overcame his doubts. I had hoped it would be possible to see Lorenzo Lotto's inlay panels. We were lucky as the sacristan was in the Cathedral. Usually it was necessary to charm him to make him want to unlock and show the six panels protected by six covers, also executed in wood inlay work, each with a different cabalistic symbol on it.

The sacristan was mopping the floor and he told us he would show us the panels once he had finished the entire Cathedral. It took time, and he had probably hoped we would give up, bored by the long wait. But we waited, even though our feet were getting frozen standing on that cold stone floor.

Sharon used the waiting time to show her soldier friend 14th century frescos on the Old Testament theme. More than by the story depicted in them, he was intrigued by the fresco making method, of using the earth pigments on wet cement plaster. When she was on her terrain, Sharon could be fascinating, capable of captivating anybody's attention.

Finally the sacristan came armed with a big lamp and a bunch of keys. One after the other he slowly removed the covers off the panels. When all six panels shone in their full beauty we went silent.

The inlay work was executed in four different types of wood. The first panel represented the besieged town of Boetia and the enemy camp outside its walls at the moment of first dawn. The streets of the besieged town coming to life; people opening their houses and shops, an equal liveliness in the camp outside its walls. On a raised position, above the others, stood a tent with regal markings and a crown. A girl in a long skirt and many tresses on her head was emerging from the tent. In one hand she held a severed male head and in the other a sword. The sacristan broke our silence by explaining that it was Judith, who had just chopped off Holofoerno's head. On our soldier's face we could see the first signs of an interest

210

awakening up. People in the camp were still unaware of what had taken place, going around performing their morning ablutions completely carefree, some pissing in the direction of the besieged city, others buttoning their breeches up, or performing their morning toilette. The 16th century artist must have been quite a joker.

Even the gloomy sacristan's face expanded into a smile at Sharon's interpretation of the scene. She explained that his contemporaries considered Lorenzo Lotto a queer man, an eccentric. When she told the story of the panel in Hebrew we could see Seth's interest showing clearly on his face. A true work of art enables so many layers of possible explanations and reaches so deep. Lotto had masterly intertwined different colours and tissues of different kinds of wood, achieving a relief-style plasticity and a feeling that everything was in movement.

The sacristan started performing his old trick of quickly changing the direction of the light beam over the panels. The wind swayed the boughs of the trees while the people inside began to walk about, but by then our feet had become numb with cold. Sharon told me that Seth had pains in both his legs from old war wounds and that he would not be able to go for a walk in the hills. So we left the Cathedral for the warmth of the "Tasso" bar.

* * *

Outside it was beautifully sunny but freezing cold. The Piazza was always cool even in the hottest summer heat. The old town was high above the plain, already one foot in Bergamo's Alps. High peaks in the distance were shining white in the sun of the cold clear January day. Encircled by such brilliance it was difficult to imagine the greyness of Milan left behind us, only 40 km to the west.

After having warmed up in the bar we returned to the car and were soon heading through the town gate. I was driving in the direction of the mountains, north of Bergamo, on the St. Vigilio road. The hill road for *Croce dei Morti* was in a bad state, evidently not repaired since last year's snows. Because of the steep hill, or the cold, the engine suddenly stalled. I started the movements of a hill start, when Seth suddenly surprised me by giving me instructions for what to do in perfect English.

I was speechless. I looked at Sharon who seemed equally surprised. With a commanding tone of voice, giving orders to be obeyed, he told me to: "Put the gear stick in a neutral position! Ignite the engine! Use the hand break!" and so on and so forth, without making so much as a single mistake. My surprise was bigger than my pride so I forgot to tell him that I could have managed anyway. Instead I complimented him on his English. Suddenly, as if becoming aware of what he was doing, he went silent. I tried to analyse his sudden outburst of spoken English, and thought about all possible analagous situations, trying to suppress the anxiety that had returned to torture me.

Throughout lunch and during the whole drive back, Seth did not address me any more, although I could see that he appreciated the warm atmosphere of the tavern and the simple but good meal they served us. We took coffee in front of the open fire. The fireplace was so big that it had benches inside it, on which some local people were sitting. I suggested we return to avoid the afternoon rush hour. On the way back they were engaged in conversation with each other. Out of politeness, Sharon would translate an occasional sentence of their conversation. As I dropped them off at the door to the studio, Seth offered me his hand and we said "Shalom!" to each other. It was to be expected that after that Sharon would not call me, while he was in town.

* * *

Although Sharon expressed herself through her art, I knew that the hardest thing to bear in her Milan exile was the isolation from her mother tongue. Even though she was fluent in English and Italian, spoke some French and

Bulgarian, there was no one to speak Hebrew with. Knowing other languages cannot substitute for communication in the language we grew up in, the language we start to perceive the world with. With her life as an exile, particularly in the loneliness of her bohemian existence, it must have been some relief to have someone to speak with in her own tongue.

* * *

She called me a week after Seth's departure. She sounded desperate; it was as if her voice touched the very bottom of depression. I invited her over. As soon as she came she attacked the fridge as if she had not had any food for a long time. Besides food she longed to hear any news of our usual Milan circle of acquaintances, artists and their admirers. During the month of Seth's stay, they had hardly emerged from her studio. I noticed soon that she did not pay attention to the answers to her questions. She was tense and obviously nervous. Then she started crying and asked me to hug her. I gave her a homeopathic calmer which seemed to have an immediate effect, the tension in her face loosening up along with the pain it had been causing.

"It's because of Seth," she said, "all during his stay we fought; he would beat me up when I tried to explain that life has more value than all the killings in this war."

It was clear that I had to hear her out without comment and that for her it was more important to justify Seth than to talk about her own feelings. But the real importance was active listening; I learned much later working with children traumatised by war.

At that time we thought that Seth belonged to the world of death which had formed him. Considering his horrific war experience it would be long, if ever, for peace to make any sense to him. After any war, veterans find normal human activities and routines a waste of time. They are used to expecting their next meeting with death, hoping

213

that once again they will be lucky enough to trick it. The importance of everything else fades away in comparison.

"We spent many nights during which I tried to explain to him what you just said in a few words. Do you think there is any hope for him?"

How could I know? Not to sound negative, I said that maybe he would find a solution working the land. Then I realised I was bullshitting, that my thoughts were bookish, that I had simply adopted Tolstoy's romantic idea of an idolised Levin. To a city dweller it seems only logical that nature and working the land could give life its lost sense.

"How about philosophy? Does it provide any solutions?" she asked.

"Philosophy cannot provide solutions, but can perhaps enable us to find our own. There is no system that gives a ready recipe, except some religions to their naïve followers."

"What about Camus's philosophy of the absurd?" Sharon went on.

"Depending which problem you talk about. Camus ends his *Myth of Sysiphus* almost optimistically. But for me it is hard to accept his conclusion that although punished to push that heavy stone uphill forever, he was happy to have that heavy stone to push!"

And then I suddenly I realised I was lecturing, while there was really nothing to say, and we both went silent until the children came back from school.

Naim Kattan

The Neighbour

Translated from French by Judith Madley

I used to see him several times a week, a brown briefcase under his arm. We lived in a building on Durocher Street and his apartment was next to mine. I never heard him, no visitors or music. He was small, thin, alert and bright-eyed, with a high-pitched Asian voice. Was he Vietnamese? Chinese? Burmese? I didn't dare ask, nor did I feel the need to know. It often used to happen that we would be going up or down the stairway together. He would greet me briefly with a nod and a barely perceptible smile. We crossed paths by either speeding up or slowing down. We always avoided speaking to each other. Were we afraid to break the silence and, in so doing, destroy an intimacy we were obviously determined to protect?

One rainy morning I called a taxi. I was getting in when I saw my neighbour taking his umbrella out of its case. He was about to brave the downpour. Without thinking, I invited him to share my cab. He accepted impassively, without showing any annoyance or relief.

He was going to St James Street, not far from my office.

"Mr Young," he said, holding out a hand and indicating with the other that he meant himself.

I introduced myself and added, "Mr Young, that's a very English name."

"No," he said without a smile, "it's a Chinese name. I'm Chinese."

"So you work at the bank," I said.

"Yes, for the past ten years."

He didn't ask me any questions. We were embarrassed. How could we go back to being silent, sitting next to each other like that, our knees touching at every sharp turn and sudden stop?

"Quite a downpour!" I said.

"Oh, yes," he agreed.

What did he do at the bank? He would find that a prying question and it would encourage him to question me. I looked out of the window of the cab door; a stream of water was enclosing us on all sides and rushing down on us like a cataract.

When we parted he took my hand discretely and thanked me without any warmth.

After that our paths crossed now and then at the entrance to the building, in the halls or on the stairs. In the morning Mr Young always wore a white shirt and a plain brown or green tie, and under his arm, the brown briefcase. Sometimes I used to see him going out in the late afternoon or early evening. Then he would be wearing a chequered sports shirt without a tie, and, under his arm, a briefcase similar to his morning one, only black.

At the end of the summer the outbreak of a fire on the first floor made all the tenants run out into the street half clothed. The firemen were there, busy doing their job. "It's not serious," they told us calmly to reassure us.

Mr Young and I found ourselves at the entrance. We greeted each other in the usual way, embarrassed by our reticence.

"It's shocking," I said.

"Yes."

"It doesn't seem to be too serious."

"No." He looked me in the eye, smiling slightly.

"Are you still at the bank?"

"Yes, of course."

I thought I detected a shadow of dread on his face. "Still the same job?" I asked mechanically.

"No," he said. "I'm not on the elevator anymore. Messenger, I'm a messenger."

"Then you have the chance to get out, to move around, to go for a walk," I said after a slight hesitation. A forced laugh followed each of my words.

216

"No, I never go out."

"Of course, it's better. You avoid the snow, rain and heat."

The alarm was over and we returned to our homes. I was on the verge of inviting Mr Young in for coffee or a drink, but he already had his door open. A strong cooking smell filled the air. So he made his own meals too. Did he live alone? I was convinced that he did.

I never heard any sound through the wall separating us. I even wondered if he had a television set. So I was quite astonished when one evening, returning from a film, I heard clamorous, incomprehensible voices coming from my neighbour's place. Were they arguing or were they expressing their joy at being reunited? They were Chinese; there was no doubt of that. Then all of a sudden — silence.

The following day Mr Young was wearing his fixed smile. Neither of us referred to the incident. After all, it was his home and he had a perfect right to entertain his friends.

"Do you speak Chinese?" I asked him several weeks later when we were going up to our floor together.

"Yes, of course," he replied.

In November a colleague from the office took me along to a lecture given at the university by Malcolm Muggeridge, the British writer. To my surprise, I saw Mr Young sitting in the first row with a notebook on his knee and a pencil in his hand, taking notes.

Several weeks later, at a meeting on the government's urban policy, I saw him again, with his notebook and pencil. We nodded to each other. Mr Young was engrossed in his work and I didn't dare disturb him.

That evening I heard a female voice through the partition. I couldn't determine whether she was laughing or crying.

I saw Mr Young again two weeks before the election, at the meeting for the member of parliament for our riding. He was carefully taking down our representative's words. I meant to meet him when it was over, but when the time came he had disappeared into the crowd.

The following Monday I found a notice in my mailbox for a meeting. A well-known lecturer from the United States was to speak on pollution. Spontaneously, I rang my neighbour's bell. He was already wearing his chequered shirt and he greeted me without surprise. I showed him the notice.

"Yes, I know, I received one too."

"We could go together if you like," I said.

"No, I'm sorry but I've decided to go to a feminist meeting. If it's over early enough I will meet you there."

"Oh, don't bother. I think I'll just spend a quiet evening at home."

Two or three months later, when I met Mr Young at the entrance to the building, I realised that I hadn't even noticed his absence. "You disappeared," I said, putting on a show of good humour.

"I've been here all along," he said.

"Oh!" I was somewhat disconcerted. "I haven't seen you."

At the end of the winter I took two weeks' vacation. I wondered if Mr Young had been away as well. When I returned there wasn't a sound from his place. But that was only normal.

A week later I saw him climbing the stairs. "I was away on vacation," I said.

He looked at me impassively, nodding his approval.

"How about you?" I asked.

"I've been sick. I only went back to work yesterday."

"What was the matter?"

"Nothing in particular. It must have been fatigue."

"Did you see a doctor, at least?"

"Yes, but it was no use. He didn't know either. He said to wait."

I was about to answer but he was already inside his apartment, closing the door while nodding to me.

For five or six years we greeted each other. Mr Young left each morning with his brown briefcase and white shirt, and each evening with the black briefcase and chequered shirt. We had tacitly agreed to stick to our customary trivialities. I was always glad to see him on the stairs. Life was following its immutable course. The embarrassment had vanished from our relationship. We were neighbours, perfectly courteous at all times.

One Saturday afternoon Mr Young rang my doorbell. "May I come in?" he asked casually. He was already in the hall.

"Of course."

He sat down on a chair in the living room. "Can I get you some coffee, a glass of wine or some cognac perhaps?"

"No, thank you, but I'll take tea if you have it."

"Yes, of course."

I busied myself in the kitchen, avoiding asking myself any questions.

"I have come to say goodbye," he said, slowly placing his cup in the saucer.

"Goodbye? You're going away?"

"Yes, I'm leaving Canada."

"For long? A holiday perhaps?"

"No, permanently. I'm going home to China, to Peking."

"So you're leaving Canada," I stammered.

"Yes."

"You made the decision, just like that, all of a sudden?"

"No," he smiled, "I decided to return home twenty years ago. When we left China I was very young, a child. My father said to me, 'We are leaving but who knows, perhaps you will return.' We spent fifteen years in England. I left London when my father died. My father always sought out the most precious thing a country can offer — knowledge. 'Never cease to pursue it,' he told me. 'Learn, never stop learning. There's always more to learn.'"

"So you always knew you'd leave," I said, disappointed.

"The trip is a long one and very expensive. I didn't have much of a job here and it took a long time to put enough money aside. I need a little money to live on over there."

"What will you do?" I asked with a touch of irritation. I

219

had a vague feeling he had deceived me.

"I have accumulated notes during my twenty-three-year stay in Canada. I haven't missed a single conference, meeting or lecture. My treasure is a large suitcase full of notes. I didn't always understand the lectures but I recorded them. I knew that one day I would have ample leisure time. I have often been told that Peking has the same climate as Montreal, but less snow and less cold in the winter. I want to see it again. I must find out for myself. Someone told me the sky is the same colour as it is here, but I don't believe it. You can never know the colour of the sky from far away…"

As he spoke endlessly, I watched his thin face, the tiny eyes lost in colourless cheekbones. His intonation didn't change, there was no emotion. I followed his high-pitched voice like a sound in the distance, a taut thread that suddenly becomes loose and falls to dust.

"Don't you like Canada?" I asked.

"Oh, yes. Canada is a marvellous country, and what a mine of knowledge! Never a single night without a lecture or a meeting. I've kept everything. I'm taking all my notes with me. I'll need ten or fifteen years in which to consult them, to put them in order, to assimilate them and to absorb this treasure. It's all there in my suitcase."

"I will miss having you next door."

"And I will miss you. You have been an excellent neighbour."

Albert Memmi

From *Le Mirliton du Ciel*

Translated from French by Jennifer Langer

The Wish
Among the flat gravestones
of the ancient cemetery
next to the mausoleum
lies the greatest of our saints
Si Fradji el Fassi
(blessed be his memory!)
I prayed the way you should.
Then I distributed
fistfuls of raisins,
pine seeds and almonds
to all the bystanders
without of course forgetting
a glass of boukha.
At last all was done
mouth against stone
I murmured my wish
I entreated the Saint
to make Guedj die
he had dared to show lack
of respect for my sister.

The Succah
In the Succah of palms
and of hispid reeds
hung with dazzling white curtains
and silk scarves
my mother had suspended
fruits of the season
my brother Menachem

had made lamps
in waste-oil cups
my sister Nin sways
foolishly on one foot
I eat fried bread
with honey and I wait for God
he will come presently
my father promised us that.

Forgiveness
This new season
vast crowds
besiege the courtyards
of the miniscule synagogues
to beseech of God
their annual forgiveness.
The recalcitrant summer
is adorned with blue down
the rim of the night.
Girls stroll
their cheeks of white satin
discretely rouged.
Striped blacks of exile
or mauves of hope
gird the loins of men
clothed in wild silk
holy strips
on brows and in hands.
Women since dawn
have grilled chickens
for the twelve meals
wisely laid out
now they rest
on beds of painted wood.
Everyone smiles at everyone else
as all are convinced
of a triumphant judgement
for the sake of the next world

beside the Eternal One
the most compassionate
I come again to you
to implore forgiveness
Whoever is not pardoned
in the eyes of the dearly-beloved
will be struck out
from the great book of the sky

At Dermech

At Dermech you gorge yourself
on the morning of sun
after having swum
with the bearded gods
intoxicated by the siesta
amongst the orange trees
you become aware
of the flowers between your fingers
at night you rave
head in the sky
where millions of stars
start to dance
against this tornado
nothing can be done
except to embrace the earth
and crawl to bed

Sami Michael

Ge'ula*: The first day in Israel

Translated from Hebrew by Judy Weiner

The dual-engined plane pierced the heavy spring clouds
and staggered between violent gusts of stormy wind. We
were about forty Iraqi refugees, squashed into a narrow
space, confused and exhausted feeling that any time soon
we would vomit out our guts. For all of us this was our
first flight. A few hours earlier in Iran we had broken off
contact with Mother Earth, in the same way that Iraq had
turned against us after a stay of 2500 years. Iran did not
hide the fact that we were unwanted guests when we
arrived as persecuted refugees from the Iraq who had
taken revenge upon her Jews because of the defeat of its
army in Israel.

There were no old people on the plane. However, deep
down we all felt the despair of the elderly who realised
that the pillars of their existence had been shattered to
their very foundations.

As the flight was unofficial, for reasons of secrecy, we
were informed, as were the Iranian authorities, that the
plane's destination was Paris. Mentally, Israel was
never far from me when I was in Baghdad. To me, it
resembled a branch of a psychiatric hospital for incur-
able patients. I felt that those who had cultivated the
dream of establishing a strong, safe home in this crazy
region were like birds insistent on nurturing a nest of
fledglings on the back of an unruly shark. I believed
then that the Middle East was the homeland of lies and
deception. And so when the tired plane struggled
through the turbulent winds, I wasn't lulled into rose
tinted dreams. I felt that I was passing from a department devised to murder me between its walls, to

another temporary department where a loaf of bread would always be soaked in blood.

I held my little bundle of clothes close to my stomach, on top of the luxurious winter coat that had protected me from the Persian cold, and sealed my ears to the sounds of retching vomit around me. I closed my eyes, seeking refuge from the boredom of the wall of cloud that the plane persisted in finding its way through. I was twenty-two and at that age one doesn't recoil from the rush of adventure. But this flight wasn't just an adventure. Every kilometre that the plane swallowed, formed a one way tunnel for me. The flight was a separation from painful love.

When I opened my eyes, I imagined that I was observing a strange nightmare vision of everything I had known in the past but also I was experiencing new feelings of the bitterness of betrayal. Outside the window, a fan of sunlight rose and cleared the sky until it gleamed like a shining crystal. Below, beneath the plane, lay white houses like a chorus of herons on a mountain slope, its peak decorated with green woods and its feet dipped in glistening water. A magic city like an innocent girl who reclines naked in the bosom of a monster. Happy is the person who finds a home in this magic hallucinatory city. Like an act of wizardry, the plane circled above the shivering sea, and landed at the small airport of Haifa.

Paris evaporated in the air, I muttered to myself and in the same breath added: it's not possible! A strict underground movement and education had taught me to control my emotions, not to get carried away. But the north of Israel at the beginning of April is like erotic fur in hundreds of shades, a blue dome with a caressing wind blowing through it. The earth breathes with a thousand curves giving off the scent of perfume. I had an attack of dizziness that grew from deep inside me. I was a virgin then and I told myself that this is exactly what the first girl, on whose gentle nakedness I would feast my eyes, would look like. I had grown up in historic Iraq, had lived in a Persia haunted by history and assumed I would reach

225

an Israel shackled by the handcuffs of history. And here, the first piece of ground that I land on is fresh, pure and young and bereft of any enslaving history.

I loved Haifa then and for over half a century I have faithfully retained this love. But at the start of my first day in Israel there weren't extra moments to dedicate to love. Like a flock of birds stunned by a long journey, my companions and I climbed into the back of a polluting truck for the journey to the New Immigrants' House in Krayot. This was a run-down British army camp whose barracks were packed to overflowing with a motley multitude of humanity wearing the expression of creatures who had lost their sense of direction. For the first time in my life, I found myself in a restricted area enclosed by a barbed wire fence. Holocaust survivors moved like shadows of burnt paper, words engraved on their foreheads but mouths sealed. Babies screamed and this was the only language understood by all the inhabitants of the immigration house. Elderly people shamelessly demanded food and bedding. Girls and boys teeming with burning hormones, shed the boundaries of embarrassment and shocked fathers sniped at them.

I felt that I had been dropped into a noisy suffocating human crater, in which man has withdrawn to his basic needs. The sky was still clear as crystal above us, but the scent of spring evaporated in the giant human whirlpool, that screamed and shouted, ran back and forth and wept or converged on dark corners with the frozen look of Holocaust survivors. Haifa quivered on the southern horizon, pure, clear and unattainable.

Like a drowning man I struggled out of the boiling pot, moved to the open gate and stood close to the wire fence. I didn't know Hebrew and was like a poor tramp. Therefore it was pointless walking through the gate to the beautiful flowers — out to starvation and shortages. Behind me, in the old army camp I lost my individuality. I became a name with an identification number. The simplest physical act became vile and bestial. When I went to the toilet I found a carousel with holes and above each hole squatted a half naked character secreting the remnants of his shame.

As I stood in my tailored suit near the gate, I realised that my luxurious coat was missing. I had also forgotten the number of my hut even though I had put the mattress and sheets given to me on one of the beds there. With horror, I realised that my expensive Parker pen was in the pocket of the lost coat. Before entering the plane I had been required to tear up and burn anything I had written in Iran, proof that the flight was managed in "underground" conditions. For me the Parker was the strongest thread linking me to the spirituality that allowed me to rise up above the stinking carousel.

At the gate a tall Israeli entered, it was difficult to ascertain whether woman or girl, although she was heavily pregnant. She turned to me, chattering in Hebrew and I shook my head in sorrow because she was very pretty. She carried about her something of the spring freshness beyond the wire fence. "A new immigrant?"

I nodded my head silently, attempting to defend my honour with my silence in the eyes of the beautiful girl. Silence is preferable to stammering. I told her we could talk in English. She stuttered a lot in English, but she wasn't the shy kind. She informed me that she had heard that a surprise "delivery" of Iraqis had arrived, and that she was married to a young man of Iraqi descent, who was still an enigma in her mind. He was serving, as were most men, in the army that had just ended the war and she had come to the new immigrant house out of deep curiosity to see and talk with the fresh Iraqi "delivery".

I told her that I myself was part of the "delivery" and her eyes lit up. She felt, it seemed, that her belly represented a barrier for misunderstandings and she touched the fabric of my suit. "Where are you travelling to?" Touching me seemed to gratify her.

I looked behind me at the medley of humanity that articulated its wretchedness in tens of languages, to the men

227

and women moving around, dwarfed by creatures and dependent on what came out of the mouths of diligent officials. I felt like a drop of pus secreted from an open wound. I told her that I didn't have anywhere to go to and that I had lost an expensive coat at the airport together with a Parker pen, which was very important to me. I didn't tell her that in my pocket, I had just two liras and nine cigarettes that I had guarded with my life because of the craving fed by my despair. "I'll take you to the airport." I stared at her with suspicion. I had come from the Third World where if you lost a coat in a public place there was nothing left for it but to mourn over it. From China to Turkey there was no such department as Lost Property.

My smile didn't please her. "We will find your coat!" Her certainty annoyed me. She was younger than me by at least four years, and she led me off as if she were my kindergarten teacher. When she was informed that I had no family, not even friends, and that I was a stranger and alone in the country like a fallen leaf, she linked her arm into mine and pulled me to the main road. I had only seen a man and woman strolling arm in arm along the street, in films, and here I was, led through a public area on the arm of a beautiful woman. I squirmed, I blushed, I sweated. I gently extracted my arm from hers as we got near the bus stop. At the airport the coat was waiting for me in all its splendour. I looked at the beautiful woman with astonishment, as if she herself had performed the miracle. My fingers clawed the pockets, but emerged defeated. "They stole the Parker," she whispered in hoarse indignation.

I don't know if she understood the depth of my disappointment. There was something symbolic in the loss of my pen as if an empty space had formed in my brain and nothing familiar would have sufficient strength to fill it. I had lost the written word around which every creator builds his spiritual world. "Are you coming back to the camp?" In her voice there was a loathing as if she had spoken about a repulsive tendency that stuck to me.

I was silent. We walked, again arms linked, on the asphalt because spring with its flowers and vivacity had taken over the kerb. She said that her name was Ge'ula and for a long time she tried to explain to me in her faltering English, the significance of her name. I didn't understand. I just stared from above at the solid, impudent belly like the flowering of spring that had taken over the road.

"And the laundry?" she inquired. "Do you have something to change into?" I didn't know how to repel this abundance of generosity that threatened to engulf me as if the human crater in the New Immigrant house wished to drown me in its midst. I had not yet had a relationship with a woman and therefore I misread twisted hints into her pure intentions. I rejected her invitation to come and shower in her house. I also told her that I would wash my clothes myself. When night came, I crawled into the bed that had been allocated to me in one of the huts. I did not sleep a wink.

The silent Holocaust survivors arose for resurrection in the dark. The minute sleep overtook them the window of nightmares opened. There is nothing more piercing than the wailing of adults in their sleep.

The following morning I was so happy to see Ge'ula's belly bursting through the gate. She immediately located the nightmarish shack that had swallowed me up in the escape of embarrassment the night before.

Translator's note: *Ge'ula* means redemption and is also a woman's name.

229

Gina Nahai

Moonlight on the Avenue of Faith

There was no sound, only the touch of a cool hand, a brisk motion sliding me through the sheets and pulling me upwards to a sitting position. Someone was putting shoes on my feet, a coat on my back. I smelled the sea and opened my eyes. Roxanna smiled at me in the dark.

"Shhhhh!" she whispered, almost mouthing the words. "Don't talk."

She picked me up off the bed and walked towards the window. She was barefoot, carrying her shoes in her coat pocket. Her feet were so light, they sounded like raindrops against the stone floor. At the window she stopped and looked into the yard.

"We're gong to go down the ladder," she said, her lips grazing my hair. "You must hold on to me and not let go. When we get to the ground, I'll take your hand and we'll run."

She put me on her back and wrapped my arms around her. Five years old, I was almost too heavy to be carried anymore, but Roxanna moved around as if she did not feel my weight.

When she climbed onto the windowsill, I buried my face in the space between her neck and shoulder, and did not look down.

The outside shell of our house was made of yellow bricks and white stone. Roxanna was going to climb down two storeys — from my bedroom to the yard — using a built-in ladder that served only repairmen and chimney sweeps.

"What about the dogs?" I asked.

"They're dead." Roxanna sighed with relief. "The Sponge Woman poisoned them."

It was early November. Morad the Mercury was still in America with Sohrab and Teymur. I had started kindergarten, but Roxanna was still confined to home, guarded by Fraulein Claude, allowed no freedom.

"Fraulein Claude is asleep," she told me. "We'll be back before she wakes up."

The night air was cool and light and startling. Roxanna breathed it in, trying to contain her excitement, and when she exhaled, she was like a child with no sorrows.

I had always imagined that the world outside our house was as silent after dark as my bedroom. Now I stood on the sidewalk, holding Roxanna's hand, and for the first time, watched the night bloom before me into a thousand buds of light. Men strolled past us in work suits, chatting as they smoked. Beggars wrapped in torn blankets called from every corner, and cursed when Roxanna did not give them money. Children with scabbed faces and bare feet pulled at my coat sleeve, shoving boxes of gum, packs of red Marlboros, folds of lottery tickets in my face.

Music spilled out of the open windows of passing cars and washed over me like water. An old man wrapped in newspapers for warmth held a monkey on a leash and searched for a spot to put his animal on display. The monkey wore a satin vest, sequins on the edges of his shorts, a fur hat. When the old man called him, the monkey turned around and looked at his owner with disdain.

A flower vendor, her arms wrapped around a bunch of garden roses, bumped into the old man inadvertently. The roses fell out of her arms, loose petals paving the sidewalk.

"Look!" Roxanna yanked my hand.

A woman was crossing the street. Her white chador billowed in the wind to reveal her long, lean legs. She wore no stockings — only a pair of red patent-leather boots that reached up over her knees. Her appearance confused the drivers on the street. Cars screeched to a stop, sliding on the icy road, honking furiously as they tried to avoid her. The women threw her head back, the chador slipping down to her shoulders, and laughed a clear, resonant laugh that echoed through the street and dimmed every other sound. This was Pari-with-the-Boots, Roxanna told

231

me, Tehran's celebrated prostitute, known for her beautiful long legs and her preference for wearing only boots.

A taxi stopped an inch from Pari's feet. It was packed with passengers — seven people in a tiny orange car — but the driver stepped out and insisted that they must leave. The passengers protested, demanding to be taken to their destination. The driver was adamant.

"Pari Khanum here needs a ride," he told his passengers, referring to Pari with the reverence due to a lady. Around them traffic had become gnarled and furious. People left their cars to scream at the taxi driver that he must pull aside so they could pass. Pari-with-the-Boots just stood with her chador down on her shoulders, black hair shiny and soft, bare legs showing no sign of being cold, and laughed. Even from the distance, I could smell her perfume, the tobacco that had made her young fingertips yellow, the cold, dry steam that blew out of her mouth every time she laughed.

We walked to the next street, Roxanna tried to call a taxi, but in vain: they were all full, carrying many people to different spots along the same route. In the end, Roxanna opted for one of the passenger cars that operated illegally as taxis.

"If anyone asks," she warned me, "don't tell them our name. Everyone in this town knows your grandfather. They may tell Fraulein Claude they saw us."

Only then did I realise that I was still in my pyjamas, my coat covering them to my knees.

We drive along a wide and crowded street, northbound in a car full of strangers, and it was all I could do to keep my eyes to the ground and my heart from bursting out of my chest with excitement. When the car finally stopped, Roxanna pulled me onto a sidewalk full of people and music. Red and blue and orange lights flashed in my eyes.

"This fair is here all year round," Roxanna told me. "It's open every night and often I have wanted to bring you here, and to come myself."

232

The man in the ticket booth had a blind eye that was completely white, with no pupil.

"You shouldn't be on the street without a man," he said as he handed Roxanna our tickets.

We stood in the Ferris wheel line. When we sat in the chair, Roxanna squeezed my hand and smiled. I watched as the ground pulled away from us, the people getting smaller, the music sinking away, then coming back, drawing away, and back again. Roxanna took my chin in her hand and tilted my head upwards.

"Look *up*," she said. The sky washed over me like water.

"I flew there once," Roxanna said. "I was six years old, still living with my mother. One night, I grew wings and flew."

She saw the stunned look in my face.

"I don't know how it happened." She shrugged. "Maybe I only dreamt it. Maybe I'm different in that way.

"But from that time on, I could never stand the feel of my feet on the ground anymore."

The Women

My French Catholic grandmother, independent spirit that she was, married a man she barely knew and, in the years between the two world wars, followed him to Iran as the second of his two wives.

The first wife, a kosher Jew from the city of Kashan, kept the meat and dairy separate, and spoke to her seventeen brothers in a language no one else in the house could understand: the dialect of the Jewish ghetto where they were born. She allowed the Frenchwoman into her house (she was infertile, and my grandfather wanted an heir), but not into her husband's heart. In vain, she tried to impose on her the ways of Eastern wives: obedience, subservience, forbearance.

The Frenchwoman realised she had made a mistake even before she had set foot in the country. In Paris where

233

he had courted her briefly, my grandfather had seemed gentle, amusing, even exotic. He was importing French cigarettes into Iran; she was the boss's secretary at the cigarette factory. To marry him and leave Paris, she had thought, would be a great adventure — a chance to see the Orient up close. She had already accepted his proposal when he told her he had a wife, and yet she went ahead with the wedding, married him on a rainy autumn day when they stood alone before a civil judge who had been presented a fake passport — one in which there was no trace of the first wife. Her parents, opposed to the marriage, had refused to attend. She went home afterward and packed her things, said her goodbyes for what turned out to be the last time.

It was still raining when they boarded the train that would take them from France to Turkey and then to Tehran. She wore a red dress and red lipstick, silk stockings, a hat. The moment they had crossed the border into Iran, my grandfather reached into a bag and gave his new wife a black scarf. "Put this on," he said, and his voice was already loaded and stern, "and wipe the paint off your mouth."

* * *

The French woman asked for a divorce soon after she had arrived — give me a passport and a train ticket — but was told this was impossible. She attempted to find a way to leave on her own, and found there was none: women in Iran did not — still do not — have a right to a passport. To leave the country, to even travel from one city to another, my grandmother needed written permission from her husband.

She stayed a month, and another. Bitterly and against her own judgment, she bore two daughters, then a son. She spent her days fighting her husband and his Iranian wife. She fought their relatives and friends, the servants, the night sentry who stood guard in the alley outside her

234

bedroom. My grandmother had married a Jew but remained fiercely Catholic, let her children be raised Jewish but told me that Jews were Christ killers. She wanted to send her son — my father — to university in America, but her husband would not allow it. My father was married off at an early age and instructed to produce a son; he went on to have three daughters. My grandfather, who had wanted nothing more in the world than for a succession of male heirs to perpetuate the family name, would die bitter and disappointed, convinced he had been short-changed by God.

* * *

And so we lived, my multi-cultural family and their many-layered sorrows, seven Jews and one Catholic in a country that was 97% Shi'ite Muslim, at a time when the West cast a shadow nearly as strong as our own history over every Iranian's consciousness. My mother, offspring of a Russian Lubavicher rabbi and of his Iraqi wife, had internalised the discipline and the sense of duty they had taught their children. But she was also a freedom-loving soul who dreamt of doing significant things she knew were beyond her reach. She wanted to go to university, but was not allowed to because she was married; wanted to have a career, but had children instead. She was outspoken in a place where women were expected to be silent, restless when she had no choice but to stay put.

By age twenty, my mother had arrived at the conclusion that being a woman was the worst thing that could happen to a person. She said this to my sisters and I, then told us we had a duty to find a way out: we had been born in Iran's golden era, when Jews were liberated from the tyranny of the mullahs and when women were beginning to have rights. We had access to a real education, and, more importantly, permission to believe in possibility. Unlike our mothers before us, we were allowed — within reason — to question authority, to challenge the conventional wisdom that had long ago determined a woman's best option to be a well-placed marriage. My sisters and I were allowed to have expectations: that our parents would value their daughters — not as much as they did their sons, but value them nevertheless; that our husbands would treat us, if not with respect, at least with kindness; that our elders — male and female — would not deny us happiness merely because it had been denied them.

A paltry sum, to be sure — this permission to *want*, without any guarantee that you would *get* — and yet it was so much more than any woman in our history had been allowed, so much more than most of them would have dared imagine. It implied a responsibility that was made clear to us early on and that we are expected to fulfill to this day: to be dutiful and correct as our mothers had been, and to find happiness so great, it will undo all their heartache.

"Study hard," my mother said. "Get a job. Never depend on a man for your livelihood."

"Be patient with your husband," the kosher grandmother whispered. "Give him what he wants. A woman without a man is like a queen without a crown."

"Expect the worst," the French grandmother advised. "Arm yourself against the world and you won't be disappointed."

My sisters and I celebrated every Jewish holiday, went to church with my French grandmother, memorised the text of the Muslim *namaz* for school. We were an odd and solitary bunch, forever caught on the border of things — of faith and culture and personal identity — at once lured and repelled by all the elements that constitute, for most people, the cornerstones of belief. With the battle forever raging around us we could not take one side without betraying someone else we loved and so we opted, without knowing it at first, for the neverland of in-betweens.

Hard as we might — and did — try we would never be able to carry on our grandfather's name, never mend the heart of the Jewish wife who had been denied children and also lost her husband, or release our French grandmother

236

from the adventure that became her prison. We could not compensate our mother for the injury done to her because she was born a woman in a world that was defined and dominated by men, could not please our Jewish relatives who thought us "not Jewish enough" or our Muslim friends who told us we were "different" because we were Jewish.

So we sat in the house, through long summer days when the heat struck the flies dead in the air and melted the silver shell off the life-sized statues of Persian princes that stood guard in every corner of the yard — and listened to our two grandmothers talk about how each had destroyed the other's life. We came home from school, in the winter when snow piled knee deep on the ground and cars skidded like toys on the ice-bound surface of Tehran's wide boulevards — to find our mother looking pale and disappointed, cooking dinner and talking about the day she was told, by her high school principal, that she couldn't return to get her diploma because she was engaged to be married. We watched the men who oppressed the women, watched the women who were at once our role models and the very examples of what we knew we should not become. We could see that the men were disappointed; that the women were too; that, instead of reaching out to one another, they each stood on a solitary shore surrounded by an ocean that we — the girls of the new generation — were told we could cross.

But to sail from any one shore toward another would mean abandoning the others; to stay would mean squandering the chance we were given to leave; to do nothing would be to bury everyone's dream.

What do you do, mother, when personal happiness is, in itself, a loss?

* * *

I think now that it was this same ambivalence, the eternal ticking of this clock that reminds me of my sins against the

237

others — I think it was this torment of the runner who is forever in a race she knows she'll never win that became the driving force in my later life: a sense of profound and unrequited guilt for having failed, even before I had started, at the task for which I had been brought to life.

I studied hard, taught myself to be patient, learned to expect the worst. I aimed to achieve knowing I had already failed, learned to persevere, to distrust.

And I made my peace with guilt.

* * *

Early in their marriage, my parents had resolved to leave Iran for good. My father could not bear the tyranny of a monarch who ruled by edict and who held the nation at his whim; my mother wanted a fresh start, in a place where the ghosts of heartaches past would not haunt her and her children. Long before the Islamic Revolution sent waves of Iranian immigrants to the West, my parents shipped my older sister and I to boarding school in Europe, then bought a house in America and moved here with my younger sister. I went home to Iran one summer from boarding school and said goodbye, then flew to Los Angeles to go to UCLA. It was the farthest I had ever gone from Iran, the first time I had enough perspective to look back.

I drove to school, in the morning when the fog sat low on the hills above Sunset Boulevard and sleep veiled the eyes of my American classmates whose lives were so vastly different from my own — drove to school and walked with books in my arms toward the hollow auditoriums where the echo of others' voices spilled like rain over the silence and the loneliness that defined me in those early years, watched the young people around me and wondered what it was that made me so different from them, that made them so much more present, more confident, more able to bet on the future.

I stayed home on weekends and watched my mother cook for the American neighbours she invited to dinner —

older couples with stiff hair and shiny Cadillacs, who arrived on time and left early, sat straight-backed at the table and feigned interest in the conversation only to mask the obvious truth of how little they had in common with their hosts, how little they wanted to know about anything that did not have to do with America.

Through college and graduate school, I reflected on my childhood in Iran, and tried to understand the dynamics that had set our lives spinning as they had. I studied Iran's history and traced the Jews' presence within it, spoke to the Iranians who had come to America to escape Khomeini's mullahs and tried to find the dominant themes among them. I learned about the Jews' suffering under Shi'ite Islam, the pogroms and persecution, the ghettos and the forced conversions that our grandparents had endured but rarely mentioned — that they had wanted to forget because it was painful, or deny because it shamed them.

And I saw something else as well — something I had thought was particular to me but which I learned was common enough: I saw a hierarchy of pain *within* the Jewish Iranian society itself — generations of women gripped by an eternal sense of loss that transcended class and family, that made real change, even here, in a new country, seem impossible — that trapped even blue-eyed foreigners who rode a train one rainy day in a red dress and silk stockings.

I watched these women with awe and astonishment, wondering at the courage they had displayed throughout their lives, and at their resilience, but wondering also about this pattern that repeated itself every time, this weight, above and beyond that which was exerted from the outside, that pressed at all their hearts: so many of the Iranian Jewish women I came to know in America, I learned, had suffered at each other's hands back in Iran, been shunned and persecuted by other women for the smallest infraction. So many had showed little or no tolerance of anyone who dared question or defy the rules that

239

oppressed them all. So many had been punished for their courage, ambition, honesty.

I saw an oppressed people who in turn oppressed each other. I could not tell the victim from the perpetrator, could not be content with having escaped, albeit not unscathed, the fate of the others.

I asked questions and pieced together the memories; asked questions and tried to understand; asked questions and began to write.

It's a strange and inevitable consequence of writing that any story, no matter how alien to the writer at first, will be transformed, through the act of creation, into an experience as personal and intimate as any she has known. Every story we write is about ourselves; every truth we record is our own natural truth. Without it — without the ability to draw on our deepest and more urgent passions, we can mouth the words but not create the sound, tell what happened but not make it resonate with the reader.

The stories I wrote about other Iranians became my own. The women whose lives I had begun to record were replaced by the characters that populated my books — ethereal beings that followed me everywhere I went; relentless creatures whose voice rose from my pages and who told of wasted lives and pointless anguish and the hopelessness of a thousand generations who had lived and died under the same murky sky.

I knew, even as I wrote each tale, that mine wasn't the only truth worth telling, that what I had observed, what any one person can observe, was only a sliver of a greater picture. I knew that my truth would offend as many of my Iranian readers as would relieve them, that it would con- stitute, to so many, yet another form of betrayal: to portray my people in a light that wasn't always favourable, to show their scars, their shame — not just to themselves but to strangers the world over. I was about to tell the story of a people who had existed for nearly three thou- sand years in solitude — quiet and self-effacing and able to

240

survive the mullahs' rage only if they became invisible. I was about to present them to Westerners who didn't always understand, to Americans who might rush to judgment, who might hold this knowledge against the new immigrants among them.

Had she known, years ago in the vast living room of our house in Iran, that Friday afternoon when she sat in the green velvet armchair with the wooden handles that were carved in the shape of angry lions — mouths gaping open, teeth ready to tear, tongues scratched and coated with dust — had my French grandmother known that the story she told me then would one day be read by strangers?

All her life, her father had forbidden her to cut her hair short. The day she turned eighteen, she went to the barber and had him chop the hair off at the nape of her neck. Then she brushed the mane and laid it out in a long flower box, brought it to her father like a dozen roses. Here it is, she said, *you* can have it if you want. I'm my own person now and I don't take orders.

He had kept the box, like a coffin, under his bed. It remained there after she had married my grandfather and left to spend her life fighting other orders.

I did realise — yes — that the very act of speaking would constitute a transgression in many ways; that it would split open, for so many, wounds they had stitched closed; that it would imply that I had, once again, opted for the border. I did not wish to transgress, to hurt, or to betray with my stories. And yet, like the dust that used to settle at the bottom of hundred-year-old wine bottles buried in our basement in Iran, my sense of the importance of ending the silence remained painful and troublesome, but ineluctable.

The sins my two grandmothers had accused each other of, I wanted to say, that they had accused their husbands of; the sins my mother had blamed on nature, that women I had grown up with had blamed on men; all those wrongs that my two sisters and I were charged to undo with our own joyful lives, that we were supposed to set right but

241

instead wanted to atone for — those transgressions for which I felt such guilt were not mine alone. They were *ours*, and *theirs*. They sprang from intolerance, from the particular brand of cruelty that is so common among the afflicted, from our desire to protect the community even at the expense of the individual.

I knew a thousand stories of injustice and pain. I could not change the plot or the ending, so I chose the only other option possible: I tried to bear witness.

* * *

My Iranian Jewish grandmother came to Los Angeles in the summer before the fall of the Shah, and never went back.

The Frenchwoman, who had the chance to do the same, refused to move: she had gambled on one adventure and lost; she wasn't about to risk another.

My parents, who had shown enormous courage in leaving their country when they didn't have to, went on to fight, and sometimes to win, even bigger battles. My two sisters have indeed "made something" of themselves. My fellow Iranians — Jews and Muslims, Christians and Bahais and Zoroastrians alike — have turned exile into triumph, managed to safeguard, outside Iran, all the precious gifts of a culture that is under attack at home.

And I, who know well the consequences of my words, who carry my guilt still like a shadow, I look through the landscape of events and characters I have painted around myself at their real life counterparts — at all the women whose lives became my stories, at their children and grandchildren who are scattered now across five continents — I look at them and am only too aware that they remain, for all the witness I might have borne, forever untouched by mercy.

242

Samir Naqqash

The World of the Odd People

Translated from Arabic by Saddok Masliyah

Here I am at last on the mountain top. My gasping competes with the beating of my heart, my fatigue bordering unconsciousness. I do not know whether I am alive or dead, but I know that I am safe from them and will not be followed. Soon I will ride the golden boat inlaid with turquoise and gems and sail on the waves of the sky, rowing with diamond oars among millions of glittering stars, up or down toward the mist of truth surrounded by halos of darkness extending millions of light years. Then when I reach the infinite sun of eternity and understand the truth, only then will the remnants of my existence disintegrate and disappear in the open space of eternity.

At every step, eyes agog with amazement stared at me. My mind repeatedly crashed against the rocks of astonishment. I swear that I did not grow up on this earth. I was definitely scooped up from a garden beyond this universe and was tossed into this world. If I were truly of this world, I would not have named it "the world of the odd people." Logic conforms to what we are accustomed because our judgment is an outcome of our beliefs and criteria. There is something intangible in me that contests the criteria of this world. The donkeys of this world roar, but something profound in me senses they should bray. The lions here are the ones that bray but they should roar. Everything here is contrary to my instincts because the owls sing, the nightingales croak, and the snakes walk on feet while the centipede crawls on its belly. Here, people wake up in the intense blackness of the night and lie down for a deep sleep in broad daylight. The true heroes here are honoured with wreaths of thorns while criminals and evildoers are stoned with myrtle and bouquets of flowers. Everything here is contrary. Perhaps the world from which I originated took a diametrically opposed position teaching me that its stance was the true one. But when was this and who were my teachers? Whenever I interrogated myself, my memory descended into a whirlpool of ambiguity and my mind filled with a thousand entangled and intertwined strings. There must be buried origins of whose source I am ignorant. It is possible that I lost my memory or abandoned this memory of mine in that unknown universe from whence I came.

I recall numerous words unfamiliar to the inhabitants of this world without a trace in their value system. What is good and what is evil? What is honour and what is immorality? What is justice and what is inequity? What is conscience and what's corruption of conscience? What is manliness and what is indifference? What is to care? What is to co-operate? What is...? What is...? They ask me in amazement. "Are you crazy? From where did you originate with these strange words?" They know, however, that the word "freedom" is a universal concept — a world apart. Dictionaries define it: "Freedom is when man does what he pleases without reservation." This word is supported and supplemented by another phrase, namely, motive and reason. It is the steering wheel of freedom. This other word is the "ego," of the nucleus surrounded by the glittering halo of the worshippers. I!...I! am armed to the teeth with the deliciously wonderful weapon of seclusion — the infinite universe, the stars and the suns, the galaxies and the nebulas. I?

I used to see corpses dumped in the streets and smell the stench of the stink. I was arraigned for days in the cellars of the security police merely because I wished to assist a dying man on the open road, or attempted to bury a man who had died on the street. The charge is intervention in others' affairs. They question me, "Who permitted you to remove yourself from your halo and penetrate the halos of others?" Then I would set out to defend myself and explain the faint call of the distant past that unsettled me and emanated from the depths of my lost memory. These were halos that had died out, their innards having meta-morphosed into the big "ego" somewhere in the desolate regions of existence, or had been transformed into the vast void beyond the universe. They insisted that it was time for these motionless, innocent, free bodies, heavy as lead, to be deposited in a deep well in the desert, and that all the rocks of the Himalayas should be thrown at them...! I am assailed by utter confusion until I leave prison and see the corpses, some decomposed, some merely skeletons. Now I flee far away to save my skin. The concepts of my world are distant and unknown here. I comprehend that normally wreaths of thorn are not bestowed to express love, appreciation or friendship, that criminals are not punished by stoning with roses and flowers, and that all the innate values from my distant, unknown world have become unbalanced and that opposing ones hold sway in the world of the odd people.

The voices of resurrection released me from my dreadful seclusion in the apartment overlooking the square. The noise tore through the layers of spiders' webs lingering on the curtain. I drew it back and a scene from the Day of Resurrection met my eyes. The square was crammed with corpses and skeletons. Dressed in threadbare garments, they were all standing on their worn-out palm leaf feet, arms raised, waving with their spider and crab hands, making a whistling sound, as if exhaled by a storm penetrating the upper floors of a building like the wailing of a ghost. The blood of the furious demonstrators boiled in its temporal veins as if the square were stained with the red liquid. How numerous are nightmares in this world. Despite all this, woe to these ambiguous calls emanating from the depths as if originating from different incarnations, from previous animals, from worlds unfamiliar with consciousness, fear and mercy, or mercy and fear! Then the rusty peel that isolates the heart disintegrates and the heart contracts freely, seized by

245

twitching pains, The heart continues to beat until it jumps out of the rib cage, rushing into space like a frightened pigeon.

The scene lured me back, I hesitated but curiosity and concern overcame me and drew me back to the open window. When I closed my eyes, my ears were filled with a dreadful whistling sound, but I soon discovered that it was the voice of one of the dead demonstrators. He explained his tragedy with bitterness: "Three months ago a car ran over me. I fell on the spot, suffering from fractures and injuries. I bled continuously for two days writhing in pain. My aches reached heaven and the earth drank my blood, or more probably, I swam in a pool of this blood until I drowned and departed from life."

Before I could comprehend this nightmare, another sharp whistle, piercing as a pin, struck my ears. I immediately realised that it had emerged from the cavities of a skull attempting to enunciate the words as clearly as possible: "Hunger crushed me for over a year. All avenues to a livelihood were closed to me until my sense of honour faded away and I stretched out my hand to beg. No one saw me. I believed I had donned the skullcap of concealment. I lifted my hand to feel my head and it felt like a piece of a rag, weakened. My tongue hung down. My voice dried out. My body and veins dried up, My blood fled from me. My soul flew off. My corpse gradually rotted on the spot over the course of more than a year. I stayed in my place, no one noticed me, and no one smelled the stench of my corpse."

The third dead person was whistling like the wailing wind, jabbering: "Months ago I was struck by a heart attack while walking on a crowded pavement. I hung onto an electricity pole. All the pedestrians were blind and deaf. Nobody noticed me. I collapsed. The passers-by stepped on me until my soul departed from me, I died in the spring of my life. Had they helped me, I would have been walking in the street among the blind and the deaf people."

In the square, darkness had almost descended, but the

246

storm of the dead continued whistling and exhaling stench and fear. The bones stuck together in strange protest ceremonies of resurrection, in a noisy resurrection where bones did not wear their flesh, but tried to rid it off the odd people's bones. Suddenly there appeared a rotten skeleton whose shape indicated that it was one of the homeless people from the streets that generations of worms had eaten following which they suffered indigestion. It climbed onto the shoulders of its demonstrating dead friends and screamed in its most ear-piercing whistle: "We demand to be buried and covered with dust!" Everyone responded, "We demand to be buried and be covered with dust!" He whistled again, "We demand to rest in our graves peacefully!" The dead mob repeated his call.

I was oblivious to what was happening as if I were wading in legendary swamps where filthy water at the bottom concealed old shattered worlds whose splinters pierced my bare feet. Then the forgetful eagle revived me and tossed me to the window, oblivious to what was happening. And here were the policemen who surrounded the square, releasing their savage, starved mice that meowed as if confronting barking cats, convulsed with hunger, and advancing towards the heaps of demonstrating bones. Then in a collective movement, seized by a great wailing of fear and seeing the ghosts swimming in a fire of earthy hell, the mice, having sharpened their teeth, together with the human mobs attacked and surrounded the heaps of angry bones. As a result, like a decorated bow, the human ring became compressed and the crowd of living humans devoured the heaps of skeletons. In a moment all of them returned, smacking their lips with pleasure, burping out of satisfaction and scrubbing their teeth. The square was entirely devoid of the dead bodies with no corpses or skeletons remaining to show what had happened.

I observed all this and was torn between pleasure and pain. I was confused about the truth while in this world. I did not know how to be sure of it, what was true and what was not, what should happen and what should not, but soon the street was once more crowded with corpses.

The anonymous root of my being controlled my behaviour and I had a tendency to search for anything overlooked. Then suddenly I found myself involved in a grinding, fierce war in which I was defeated in every round. I was besieged by a boycott universally imposed on me. I faced three options: to separate my soul from my body, quash my thoughts and alter my nature to conform to that of this world, to join the masses of discarded bodies in the streets, or to hide in my secluded hole and be inspired by the memories of bygone worlds. In this manner, sweet dreams multiplied in my sleep and nightmares and ambiguous memories blasted my consciousness and increased my awareness.

One night the inner voice spoke of an ideal city that had existed but had fallen into complete oblivion. Later it recounted, "The foreheads of the city people were bright and light radiated from their faces. The doors of their houses were open day and night for the hungry, the needy and the stranger to enter. They feared neither thieves nor robbers because theft and other crimes were alien to them. If a stranger entered to burgle a house, they would be generous to him, give him what he desired and let him go free. People in that city competed to support those who faltered and soothed those struck by ill fate. If a shopkeeper made a profit in the morning he would command his customers, 'Go to the next shop. I have sold and earned enough while my neighbour has not yet sold and earned anything.' It is also said that 'good fortune birds' used to perch fearless on the heads of men of the city and that sparrows would land on people's outstretched palms to peck at the grain. Other wild birds would roam between pedestrians' legs, unafraid of being stepped on, because every citizen had an internal guardian comparable to a warning siren, instantly alerting him when he was on the verge of committing an unintentional

248

evil deed. If there was an unavoidable occurrence and the siren was inadvertently delayed leading to someone perpetrating a misdemeanour against another, he would impose self-punishment and partake of neither food nor drink, neither sleep nor awareness. He would not experience peace of mind until the two wounds were healed: the wound of the offender and the wound of the victim. A fusion existed with each person oblivious of his own needs, doing his best for others. Altruism and sacrifice motivate every individual in the city and therefore everyone derives joy from the happiness of others and shares the misery of others. The light of the halos woven from sunrays crown their heads while necklaces formed by the reflection of the moonlight decorate their chests. Love, virtue and reason prevail in the city. One day no trace of the ideal city and its people was found. It is said that a king from the other worlds used to look through his telescope to discover the universe and the worlds. It happened that he saw the ideal city. He watched it continuously, observed its people and was fascinated by their merits and happiness. As this king desired to annex this ideal city to his kingdom, he ordered his men to attack and uproot it from the earth together with its inhabitants and to bring it up to him. They did so, leaving in the city a huge trench that still exists, where the odd people toss the losers in their ongoing evil, dirty wars."

When I observe the deeds of the odd people, the distant past reveals everything of the evil city. The call whispers from the depths of my memory that the deeds of the inhabitants were recorded in the books of the antecedents. It is said that they were rude giants, ugly and ill-natured. Their eyelids resembled those of a camel, their ears were those of an elephant, their noses continuously ran and their eyes were red and oozed blood instead of tears. They had horns like those of devils and their faces bore marks. They always displayed and stuck out their teeth which resembled those of animals. Their complexion evolved into

249

the colour of dust and layers of filth covered their bodies. Their hair and nails grew long because they avoided cleanliness and drank from impure sources. Their doors were always locked and their city was barren and lifeless with no greenery or water visible. Birds and animals avoided the city travelling to distant places, so that no singing bird or tame animal was ever seen. At night, when they sought shelter in their homes, the city sky swarmed with bats and devilish night creatures competing to commit sins. One would let his brother fall and celebrate the fall. If one of them frowned at a stranger entering their city, all the inhabitants, without exception, would encircle him and one by one would attack him from the rear until he capitulated. Then they would tear him to pieces, divide his parts and take them to their homes to cook and to heartily consume the tasty meat in a banquet. If the stranger was less fortunate and did not die following the attack, they would escort him to one of their homes. If he was tall, they would let him sleep in a short bed and cut off his head and legs so that his height equated to the length of the bed. If he was short, they would stretch him on a long bed and pull him from his head and feet until his joints tore and he died.

They regard a good deed as a crime, and woe betide him who dares to feed a hungry man, assist a man in trouble, help a bungling person, or host a guest. They would take this "criminal" to a city square, light a fire, fill a pot of lead and place it on the fire until the lead melted and overflowed like ashes. Then they would pour the lead into his body cavities so that his soul would depart from his body before all the cavities were filled in. In the event of his soul not fleeing the body, the city people would tear and share the parts three days later. During those three days they would publicly expose the body, to deter those tempted by the devil to commit the "crime" of doing a good deed.

The inhabitants of the city continued to be sinful. They developed and refined their methods of evil-doing and excelled in inventing means of torture to the extent that the black smoke of their disobedience reached a gigantic being in the heavens. It is said that this being desired to establish justice in the rest of the universe, was angry at what it saw and wished to punish the evil city. This being had aides and servants created by it from flames of fire, so it gathered and informed them about its intention. As a result the fiery hearts of the aides took pity and asked their master, "Will you destroy a whole city when there may be good people among the inhabitants?" He answered, "If it had ten good men I would forgive it." They also asked, "And if there are five?"

"I will forgive it too," he replied,

"And if there were three good men in the city?" some of his aides asked. The patience of the great being was exhausted, and he said, "I'll forgive the city if you find one good man in it."

It is said that the great being was much-forgiving, compassionate and zealous for justice and that it supported the deprived and punished the offender. To ascertain the situation in the city the great being sent three of his senior servants. The three reached the city at night when the sky was teeming with bats and owls. The silence of the city was broken by croaking, cawing and wailing. Each of the three knocked on one of the closed doors, but wished they had not done so because they speedily awoke the dormant evil. All the doors opened suddenly and the people emerged. Their eyeballs shot out of their sockets in amazement, circling the globe before settling in place again. Men and women crowded around the three like ants. Since the bodies of the men and women were made of the element of fire, the genitals of the men and vulvas of the women burned. They poured the containers of urine and jugs of filthy water onto the three messengers to turn them into charcoal for use in boiling their human victims. The three messengers, however, were not perturbed by the filthiness of the impure water and the urine. Rather, they glared, glittered, and burned

251

more because of the surprise and anger that struck them. Through their sensors they penetrated the inner selves of the city people but were unable to locate a spot untouched by sin, crime or ill-deeds. They soared, immediately returning to their great being, the master, declaring repeatedly, "Destroy the city; it is the shame of the entire universe!"

The great being inflicted on the evil city burnt offerings, extermination and destruction, such that it was wiped out and obliterated and the filthy spot was erased from the surface of the universe in very strange circumstances. In the course of time the great being entered a huge, black hole and was lost in its unknown tracks and paths. The voice completed his story about the evil city and the great being that destroyed it and whispered in the depths of consciousness; "in this manner after the great being disappeared into the bottom of the huge hole he returned generations later to unsettle everything again, to violate nature and disguise evil deeds."

The voice became silent and suddenly I found myself colliding with waves at the meeting place of the two seas: the sea of grief and the sea of fright.

Alicia Partnoy

Alicia Portnoy was imprisoned by the military regime in Argentina from 1977 for almost three years, three and a half months of which were spent in "The Little School" where she was blindfolded with hands bound, was on starvation rations, was not allowed to speak or move and was tortured. Many of the other prisoners were amongst "the disappeared".

Rosa, I Disowned You

To all my sisters who are still silent.

The story I was going to write today, before my daughter called and told me of her horrible dream, was supposed to start with the image of my husband's back. I could not see it in the darkness of our bedroom. His voice I did hear, through his tears and mine, *"Soy una mierda!"* he screamed. "I'm a piece of shit! Twenty years living with you and I just realise that you don't know it. You were raped! *Por dios, Flaca*, you were raped!"

But then, this morning my big kid called and she told me that in her dream blood came out of my mouth. She warned me, "Be careful with what you eat." "Or maybe with what I say?" I retorted. But since she did not know about the story I was going to tell you here, she just repeated, "No, mom, seriously, mind what you eat." And I answered, *"Gracias brujita*, invoice me for the reading," and we both laughed and that was that.

Still, at the airport, dutifully in line at some security check-point, my mind could not stop pondering the story. "What good will the telling do? Whom will it help? After all, it was not a simple rape. I would have recognised a simple rape and I would have reported it already, like I did with the torture, the killings of my friends, the birth of

Graciela's child at that concentration camp back in 1977."

And later I stood waiting for my turn at the Frontier Airlines check-in counter still trying to organise my thoughts, when this man I had hardly noticed pointed to a red, shiny, fat drop of blood on the floor between us. "Just what one needs to see before boarding a plane, these days," he said. "Or before writing these kind of confessions," I thought, but I just answered, "Oops," and smiled, and got lost again in my thoughts, trying to figure out whose blood that might have been, and remembering some Andersen or Grimm tales I used to read as a child, where drops of blood talked to children.

And since I do not know what this drop is telling me, and the flier is already out, and the women from the seminar will for sure come tomorrow to listen to my story, "Rosa, I Disowned You," I cannot be such a coward. A few blood signs can't scare me. Why is this man in front of me freaking out, then? And if it is true that I was raped, who is going to benefit from my telling? Who is going to be hurt besides my reputation as a witness, and my parents, and my children?

"That was not consensual, you were blindfolded, helpless, you were a kid, he took advantage of you," says my husband. He tells me these things in Spanish. We speak Spanish at home, but I'm only talking about this in English so you do not take over my bedroom. Now he is mumbling some nonsense and I don't want to pay attention any more. I barely touch his back, while he stays there, sitting on our bed, and I am far away loving him because for a second I can see. The pain is no longer a dull sensation muffled by guilt.

But then, again, I should listen to my daughter's dream and its reminder that greeted me from the airport floor. After all, this story owes itself to dreams: the dreams of a better world that I had when I was twenty, the dreams that have been masking these memories for twenty-five years, the dreams that made room for this tale in my nights for the past week, allowing it to take shape without disturbing my busy days. How could a dream kill it? And what about a dream and a drop of blood?

Rosa was not afraid of blood. She had joined the resistance movement. The challenge, should she be caught by the Army, was to give her blood in lieu of names, information about the others. Rosa was arrested and I think of her now while I watch Nenita's documentary. On the screen the woman listens to the radio and furiously writes her name, her pencil tears the paper. While the newscaster tells of testimonies by women forced into sexual slavery during the Japanese occupation, the Filipino woman on the screen is lost in her memories. They parade in front of the audience. It pains me to watch the teenage girl raped over and over, the line of soldiers outside her dirty cubicle; the tortured bodies of those who try to escape, the tormented eyes of the woman in the kitchen.

But I am not the woman in the kitchen, and Rosa was not like these young victims of World War II either. She was not enslaved by force. She shed neither her blood nor the information that the enemy demanded. However, imprisoned and deeply humiliated, she wanted to believe that by pleasing the guards she would get information, food to share with her friends, time without her blindfold, a chance to talk without being hit with the rubber stick, access to the bathroom when needed, a shower more than the one monthly allotted to her, unlimited contact with water while doing the dishes. She wanted to believe that instead of a prisoner, a slave, she was a sort of Mata Hari, that her body did not make her vulnerable but allowed her to control the situation. Later, Rosa fell in love, or at least that was what she wanted to believe.

This guard would protect her from the others. He had even told her his name and had offered to hide her in his mother's home if she was released. "They are killing the prisoners they let go," he had confided. He spoke with affection about two of Rosa's close friends who had already been "transferred", presumably to their death. He told her stories about them and his own life during the endless

255

nights in which she waited, blindfolded on her dirty mattress, to be killed.

One night after Rosa asked to see his I.D., he had said, "Here," and had placed something that felt like a tiny address book on the palm of her hand. "Can I look?" she had asked, ready to check for his name and confirm that he did not lie when offering refuge. "Of course," was his answer, but when she lifted her blindfold and looked down, her hand was holding a chocolate bar.

The girls in Nenita's movie were not talked to, nor were they offered chocolate. True, they were allowed to sit under the sun, eat without a blindfold, and they were "only" killed by diseases, sadism or if they attempted to run away. The documentary is about to end and the woman in the kitchen frantically repeats, "Ninotchka, my name is Ninotchka," but I hear, "Alicia, my name is Alicia."

Now, on the plane, I am a civilised traveller who writes on her yellow pad. I cannot scratch it with violence like the Filipino woman whose face in tears I barely see through the steam of her boiling pots. Her radio blasts the news, and she whispers something that to me sounds like "Rosa, I disowned you."

My husband knows that Rosa loves him. As for those of you who have been listening to this story, I just beg you to let me know that to tell it was not in vain, that somebody's soul will breathe better because of it, that my daughter's dream is not taking place, that blood is not coming out of my mouth.

Mauricio Rosencof

The Letters that Never Came

Translated from Spanish by Louise B. Popkin

*Mauricio Rosencof spent thirteen years in prison,
eleven and a half in solitary confinement.*

Days Beyond Time

What I don't remember is the word. It was a single word and
I don't remember it. But when I first woke up, I did. When
I woke up, my head was still full of those syllables I had
never heard, spoken in some undreamed of, extinct tongue
— a dead language, from antiquity maybe. It could have
been Chaldean or Aramaic, one of those desert tongues that
died out with the mouths that used them. I wonder what
they talked about that last time. Those "last Mohicans" of
Chaldea, on the run, maybe, in a tent or down by the spring,
what did they say to each other, those survivors of chaos,
and plagues, and wars, until some inexplicable meltdown
came along, a drought, smallpox, a drop in glacier temperature, and *ciao,* they were gone. I might have asked them
about that word they left behind, but there are no contacts,
no clues, no handy 900 number to call for an answer, what's
the meaning of this word, look it up in the dictionary, will
you? It would be a simple matter, really, nothing complicated, to invent it, to reinvent it, something strange-
sounding like the language of Ray Bradbury's Martians. But
I won't do that. Because this is a true story I'm about to tell,
it's history, not literature, although I'm in no way obliged,
compelled or bound to stick to the facts which in any case,
generally get changed around some in the telling.

Now, mind you, I do know what that word meant to me.
I never doubted its meaning, or gave it a second thought,

or said what the fuck is this. No, I caught on immediately and I spoke it, a whole sentence, a fairly lengthy one — that work in Chaldean was an "Open Sesame" for the part of my brain that got put in charge of thinking, when they divided the work up rationally: "OK, now," something or someone told it, "you do the thinking, got that?"

There's no doubt either, Papa, that the word was spoken by you. In a voice that made it sound like part question, part exclamation, and part command.

Then I woke up, and I realised it wasn't a dream. I never actually spoke the word, but I did speak its meaning, its translation, that sentence.

It was brief, I'd venture to say two syllables — Chaldean has no proparoxytones — but I had no place to write it down and in any case, I'm not sure I would have.

And that's what I was up to, when someone kicked at the door, and I leapt to my feet, stood at attention, pulled on my hood. Time to pee.

* * *

Home, as a person recalls it, isn't that big a place. Home is always more than you remember. Memory shrinks it. But the shrinkage isn't systematic, what you come up with isn't just a scaled-down model. Let's see, how to explain this? Here, I'll give it a try. Say, on Sundays, you went to soccer games at the Stadium. Ten Sundays, or twenty, or a hundred. And the Olympic Grandstand is right here, the Amsterdam is over there, here's the lawn, there's the Tower and so on. Look at any photo in any newspaper, with the goalie on the floor, the melon in the net, the centre forward whooping it up over his goal, some bleachers in the background, and there's no doubt that what you're seeing is the Stadium, with its seating capacity of eighty thousand — it's all there, on record, you never dreamed a few brain cells could hold that much. But what's "all there on record" isn't really there at all. It's not like it's filmed or photographed, it's something else. If I told you to draw the

258

Stadium, you'd draw it. But not each step, or each floodlight or the loudspeaker, or the sideline, or the penalty spot. No, you'd draw a few parts — let's say the tower, or something like it, maybe the curved outline of the Olympic Grandstand. And that's all. But it's still the Stadium.

And with everything else, including home, it's exactly the same. At least for me, it is. Home, my parents' house, isn't as huge as it was when Mama had to clean it. It had four rooms, with very high ceilings and an old wooden floor that always needed fixing, the long floorboards kept rotting away and we had to patch them with hammer, saw, and nails. Underneath was a basement that only the mice still used occasionally and sometimes, to Mama's horror, they burrowed their way upstairs and Papa and Zapi had to go after them with a broom. For the cobwebs, we had a feather duster in two parts, it was grey, an ostrich at the end of a stick that you had to attach to another stick to reach them. And there was the patio. That patio was our green space, home to Mama's forty plants that she watered religiously every morning, pinching off the dead leaves, greeting them one by one, commenting aloud on their condition, she knew them stem by stem, the face on each leaf, the joy of each bud, each flower. And her prize plant, the "ocean spray fern," sat in the centre of the table, curly like the crest of a wave, over a floor of large black and white tiles — like a checkerboard — that was much easier to clean than the other floor, a quick sweep, a once-over with a mop, and it would shine. That patio, Mama, was the only park you ever went to. You, who never went anywhere except the grocer's, or to the cemetery on the anniversary of Leon's death, had your own little park right there at home.

And with you, Mama, it's the same with the house. I can't think of that patio without thinking of you, seeing you there. You were that patio. The patio and the kitchen, with the Primus that was forever clogging up, and you'd yell for Papa — "Is-a-ac!" — and he'd come running with that little tin gadget of his with the needle on top, and soon everything would be back to normal, the nipple unstopped, the pot in its rightful place on the burner. Papa in his shop and you, Mama, with your eye on the pot roast so it wouldn't burn. That patio and the kitchen were your kingdom, Mama.

In my memory, you're the smell of tomato sauce and the scent of geraniums, home is you, Mama, how could they not have realised that you and that house were inseparable, that throwing you out of there was like throwing all that away? How? And yet, they sent you off to the Home.

I found out abut that, Mama, during a visit. The two of you told me during one of your visits, because "it was something I had to know," I was in a barrack on the border, gaunt, filthy, unshaven, and that's where you told me: forced to move ...kicked out... home for the elderly.

Then I came back to my dungeon, to my endless three feet by six, and that's when my conversations with Papa began.

* * *

Thoughts bounce off the walls in here. The words in your thoughts come bouncing off the walls. Because saying them, actually speaking them, isn't allowed. Nothing, not even a scream. In this territory, silence reigns supreme, such absolute silence that when the voices die down outside, after taps, after the bugle sounds (just think, all that noise to call for silence!), if you pay attention, you can even hear the spiders at work. When they spin their webs, I pick up the squeak of their noisy little needles and if they happen to catch a fly, you wouldn't believe the racket, the fly puts up a squawk, the guard goes over to put a stop to it (don't you know it's after taps?), and that's when she pounces and applies her pentothal — charge, daddy longlegs, here comes the herd, let's get on with the slaughter! Hey, how come they don't use arachnid pentothal as anaesthesia? I guess they prefer the other kind, that gas that puts you out before you can count to three, or if you want you can get it by injection from the arachnids of

260

medicine at that Swiss, or Swiss-German, or German lab... And once she has him under her feet, Juanita (that's her name) sucks him right off the wall, swallows him up, digests him like a miniature Dracula. Anyhow, I hear all that, everything, it keeps me up at night. They keep me up at night with their screwing, first the male spider stalks his prey, scurrying back and forth on the walls of the dungeon, always along the same path, at a speed that (allowing for size) would rival Jesse Owens's, then he grinds to a halt in the spiders' corner, and the two of them eyeball each other, she's huge, much bigger than he is, and they keep that up, it's a come-on, until they parallel park and the bed creaks. In the silence, noises take over. The clatter of millipedes on the cement floor (every so often, I catch one to munch on) is like a subtle, rhythmical drumbeat, the ideal accompaniment for a *bolero*. But the noisiest thing in here is yours truly. My lungs make a racket. So does my ticker. My jeans don't rustle, they creak, every night they get louder, I sleep in them, live in them, we're growing old together and they creak, they're always complaining. And when there are mosquitoes around, forget it! The sound of their propellers is a constant threat, you really have to concentrate so you'll hear them turn off when they land, helicopters, coleopters, who the fuck knows, and after they touch down you slap at them, and when you're on target you see the blood, and the waves from that slap bounce off the walls, just like everything else, it's three feet by six in here, a real bargain, hey, you can have it cheap, in fact you can have it for free — wanna swap? — look, everything bounces. Everything bounces in here, *Viejo*, and I'm writing to you mentally, begging you to hang on, I know you can give me lessons when it comes to that, Papa, there's nothing about hanging on that you don't already know, but I'm arguing the point anyway, harping on it, insisting, laying it all our for both of us — for your sake, *Viejo*, so you'll know I'm in you and you're here with me, and for me, because I need to feel that as much as you do. And this whole thing is so

261

charged, Papa, it's all so powerful, that it catapulted me out to where you were and you into here and every so often you'd come back again and I know I'm out there with you, because I heard you and you saw me. And no one believes that, no one understands, and I talk about it or I don't, hardly ever, just to a few people, and I can't get myself to write it down, because they'll think it's all in my head, some tall tale I dreamed up. Well, they can think whatever they want to, you and I know better and that's that. I've said enough.

* * *

One thing that's missing in here, Papa, is children. There are no children. The world isn't liveable without them, and my world, *Viejo*, has no children. So when they take me to the crapper, I try to bring some back. They make you wipe your ass with old newspapers, Papa, just like we did at home (Way to go, *Unzer Fraint*!). In here it's *El Pais*, but the same routine, a torn-up paper, dumped in a corner of the latrine (hey, it rhymes!) and I scope it out, and if I'm lucky when I wipe my ass I get to tear off a little piece with a kid on it. I've got two of them now. Not many, but what can you do? Anyhow, there are two of them, both little boys. I've got them inside my shoe, they keep me company on my walks, one two three half-turn, and I take them everywhere — to soccer games galore and even horseback riding! But why the fuck am I saying this, I'm getting sidetracked... Come on *Viejo*, let's talk about us. We can take turns.

* * *

They've sent you back into exile, Papa. This is just another exile, you can take it. Actually, you've always lived in exile. In your little Polish village, you were just a transient. There was always a pogrom or two (usually, two) to remind you of that, you and your parents, and your

262

brothers and sisters and nieces and nephews, all of you, you're not from here, you're not one of us, you don't belong here, that's that. And your parents knew it, *Viejo*, and so did your brothers and sisters, you all did, that's why you held on to your language; you were Polish, you all knew Polish, spoke it almost like natives, but you never let go of Yiddish, like you, Papa, you spoke Yiddish, you could read and write it, and you knew a little Talmud and Sholem Aleichem. And you took all that with you into exile, when you left Mama in the village with Leon, a tiny baby, and came looking for a country without pogroms, you weren't looking to make it big in America the way others had, all you wanted was a place to settle down, where noisy Poles with torches and vodka wouldn't be shooting at the shacks where Jews lived and setting fire to them. And first you went to Sao Paolo, but you didn't like it there because it rained all the time, so then they brought you here, not to a country called Uruguay, but to a shop and as soon as you were off the boat, before you even took off your cap or put down your bag, they taught you to say *"Boinos dias"*, and told you, "OK, you go there." And there you whipped out your needle, Papa, and donned your thimble and a stitch at a time — hundreds, thousands, millions of stitches — you built that little path across the ocean to bring your family over, Mama and Leon, you'd lower your head in earnest over your lapels and stitch away like mad, happy to be with those comrades from the shop who were forever laughing and joking and drinking grappa and teaching you how to say "door" or "button". And you'd be crooning some old Yiddish song, softly under your breath, the way I'm always singing tangos to myself, they help me play tricks on my stomach and take me home again, to our house, our house, the one they booted you out of, *Viejo*, with Mama, when you were both so old and so frail.

263

Matyas Sarkozi

And Now in Amsterdam

Twenty-one years have passed since I first came to Amsterdam and made it my home. From where I sit, I can see the canal and the huge trees. Our home is said to be three hundred years old, and it is as massive as a rock. I need the indestructibility of thick walls.

This new home of mine resembles the old one in many ways. Even the tall plane tree in front of the window reminds me of the one in Budapest, although that was dustier. And Amsterdam has no sparrows.

Of course the view is altogether different; I see the wide ribbon of water with barges floating down it, and further away there is a bridge which opens every now and then, making a rasping noise. The cyclists stop and wait at the side as they flock out from the laundry. In October, an autumn mist shrouds the canal: in Budapest this kind of dampness is unknown.

My marriage to Ivan lasted twelve months. He died twenty years ago. He loved me very much, and I got used to him: we were more or less happy to have each other. He was already elderly when he came back on a visit to Budapest. We met, and shortly afterwards the wedding was arranged. It happened all too quickly, and the following week we came back to Holland. Of course his way of life was rather enviable, a respectable businessman's life in the civilised sense. No interruptions. Ivan left Hungary in good time, and in Amsterdam no one knew about his race or religion. He was able to avoid persecution, his nose was quite straight. A dull, honest, pink face, with greying temples.

When he came to Budapest, at the end of the war, the purpose of his journey was to look for a suitable wife. I was introduced to him, and at first he didn't like me. I wondered why. I was young and full of life. Although the shops were empty I tried to dress well, and I always followed the fashions. Probably he was afraid of my mother. But he found out pretty soon that there was no danger of my mother following me to Amsterdam, because by this time she had become an invalid. She was bedridden, but even between the sheets she remained a frighteningly large and domineering woman. Her back propped up, she sat there always irritable, noisy and red-faced. Of course she was charming to Ivan. She said: "You know, dear, our Daisy has a beautiful body. But how should people know? They don't know. This is a real handicap with my daughter."

From this, I presume that she must have known that some men found my large, oriental-type mouth, the black shadow over my lips and largish nose repulsive. But I did have a good body, and my skin was unusually white. I could admire myself, standing in front of the large bedroom mirror. Locking the door, I would take off my clothes and admire myself. Rushing off to school, after a bath, I often moved about the flat stark naked, so my mother knew my body. I had been brought up fatherless. My mother was widowed almost as soon after her marriage as I was after mine. Our husbands died in very similar circumstances. Ivan had his stroke on the ferry crossing the harbour. He was still alive when they took him to the first-aid room. A nurse tried to telephone me but I was out shopping and by the time I arrived at the hospital to which Ivan had been taken, he was dead. He was peaceful, his eyes remained slightly open and this made his face somewhat strange. For the first time and the last time in my adult life I burst into tears.

My father's death was slightly different. Mother told me the story over and over again of how his grotesque and sudden stroke happened. He came home from the office nervous and irritable. Why was he so restless? We never knew. Dinner was late and this annoyed him even more. At such times it was better not to talk to him; anyway he hated small talk at meals. My mother used to place titbits

265

next to his plate to stave off his hunger, like radishes on a piece of cheese.

He refused his soup and asked for the main course. Mother could describe that veal escalope in every detail. It was cooked with a lemon and sour cream sauce; in our family we called this à la Auntie Schmidek.

"How he loved that piquant sauce!" my mother used to say. "How he loved that piquant sauce!"

My father had finished about half his escalope when he had his seizure. He couldn't raise his right hand. Although the right side of his body had been almost paralysed by the stroke, with enormous will-power he grabbed his fork with this left hand and finished the meal. But a second stroke killed him and, dropping his head on the table, he died. He loved food. Death could not take his escalope away just like that. He put up a brave fight.

Mother described the scene to me a hundred times. Often it was too much for her to bear; she broke down and cried. She had become such a young widow! When she was telling me how I lost my father she used to play either the role of a martyr or of a master-cook. In her sentimental moods the story became a lament of loneliness, and she related in detail what a struggle it had been to bring me up without a father. But at other times the tragedy would not affect her so much, and the story would continue with a detailed description of the proper way to cook veal escalope à la Schmidek.

It is true that she had a difficult task in bringing me up. She tried to be the ideal mother. Much effort was put into my education. Thanks to this I was always an outstanding student, and when I left school she wanted me to travel round Europe for a year. During this time I was supposed to make up my mind whether I wanted to go to university or take up an interesting job. But this later proved to be more than a dream; the German Occupation of Hungary destroyed it all.

My mother tried to grasp the new situation, but events followed in much too rapid succession. Her rhythm of life couldn't keep pace with what was going on; she was completely bewildered. After all, she was the daughter of a high-ranking civil servant and the widow of a war hero. Yet, my father had volunteered to serve at the frontline; he had lied about his age. He was wounded four times and returned with a chestful of decorations.

We were respected by everybody, the shopkeepers came to their doors to greet us. Physically my mother was quite different from me. I am not so young, now, I've put on a little weight, but I can never become as strong as my mother was. Her body was not fat, but her breasts were rather large. She was tall and upright, so her large bosom was not so noticeable. All sorts of corsets kept her in shape. From her breasts, a soft line fell to the tip of her shoes, particularly as she wore very long dresses even in the 1940s. As a child I could never sit properly in her lap; her only way to keep me from falling was to press me gently between her body and the edge of the table.

The yellow star, which all Jews had to wear after the German Occupation, didn't go well with her exclusively tailored dresses. So she went around without the star. No one dared to report her to the police.

Then we had to part with our maid and cook, and what was even worse, our landlord personally disliked my mother and he made sure pretty quickly that we were moved to a so-called Yellow Star House, a place where Jews were prepared for deportation. Fortunately, Uncle Aurel's enormous six-storey house became one of these Yellow Star places and we were installed in a comfortable flat. But the building became more and more crowded and gradually even the halls and the corridors were filled with odd bits of furniture. I could never understand why people moved in with such gigantic wardrobes and such huge, weighty dressers. On top of the bundles, cases and boxes, dozens of noisy children played and chased each other.

Finally, one of our rooms was taken away from us and an Orthodox family moved in, headed by a bearded bookseller. We knew him vaguely, he specialised in religious literature. His two sons nosed around the other flats and occasionally ventured out into the street. So Mrs Auspitz ran to the corridor forty times a day, leaned over the railings and yelled across the yard: "Heymlouser!"

The cry had something in common with the frightening, ominous sound of an owl's hoot in a dark forest. During these tense, tragic and unbelievable times these cries for Chaim and Eliezer became part of our everyday life in the Yellow Star House. The cries interrupted the constant murmur of old men and women gossiping down in the yard. We heard them as we were quietly reading or sewing in our rooms.

We never cared for gossip, and we didn't go down to the yard to hear shocking stories about certain country towns from which all the Jews had been deported to Germany in sealed freight trains. But after a few weeks even we were able to sense the rapid deterioration in the situation. Although my mother knew that history was behaving very unfairly and further humiliation was to come, she was simply unable to do anything. I think she expected some kind of joint action from the "better classes", action that one could support — with certain reservations, of course. But to anticipate as an individual seemed completely wrong to her. She didn't want to evade the axe by means of any cunning trick. I suppose it must have been affluence that killed any healthy Jewish self-preservation in my mother.

But not in me. The atmosphere of the Yellow Star House became so unbearable that I couldn't sleep at all and I thought of only one thing all this time: how to escape. The huge apartment house depressed me more and more as time went by. It frightened me to see how defenceless and exposed we were. The crowd used to be most alarming during the air raids. When the sirens began to wail, hoards of people ran towards the shelters, jostling and scuffling, in absolute panic. There was disorder in the shelters too; children cried, and some grown-ups angrily demanded silence.

One day I could bear it no more. The sirens were howling again and the big rush started. It was forbidden to carry lights across the yard, and only a few blue painted bulbs lit the staircase. Mother was quick as a squirrel. She flung her coat over her shoulder and grabbed the case with our valuables in it.

Something must have happened to the sirens that day; they kept howling endlessly. Stepping out into the outside corridor I saw Uncle Auriel rushing towards the staircase holding up an umbrella to shelter Aunt Lolka from the rain. What would happen if a bomb were to fall right in the middle of this crowd? What umbrella could save Aunt Lolka from being blown to pieces?

"I'm staying in the flat," I said to Mother

"You take this case and come down at once!"

"No!" I stamped my foot.

The sirens had gone quite mad.

"Alright, do what you like."

She picked up the case, turned and hurried down the stairs. For a while I sat in the dark. The old alabaster clock kept ticking bravely. A cupboard creaked. Strange hollow sounds came from the central heating system.

I suddenly decided to leave. It took a few minutes to find my coat and gloves in the dark. As I ran downstairs an inexplicable gaiety seized me and I felt like whistling.

The street was deserted. I thought up all sorts of silly plans; to go down to the square, to sit on a bench, walk a little, feel the coarse bark of the old trees.

It was a cool night, dark and friendly. When the sirens stopped at last, an unbelievable quiet descended on the town. From above the clouds the very distant murmur of enemy bombers could be heard. I kept near the houses, walked slowly towards the square and breathed in great quantities of darkness. At the Roses Square a single gas lamp was still working, its light dimmed by a clumsy black shade. Further down the square I knew a wooden bench; years ago an old soldier used to sit there, a veteran of the 1849 War of Independence; opposite was a small building,

269

a mere shack, where they used to sell excellent lemonade. Sitting in the dark, listening to the patter of the raindrops falling from the bare branches on to the tin roof of the lemonade stall, I more or less sensed its mass in the dark and suddenly a sharp taste of lemonade tingled on my tongue again.

The next moment a small gang of Arrow Cross boys appeared at the other side of the square. I think they wanted to sit down on the benches. They came towards me. When I jumped to my feet I clumsily tried to hide behind the trees, but I already knew that it was too late. A heavily built tram conductor pulled me by the arm and they shone their torches right into my face. My captor yelled at me:

"Are you Jewish?"

I lost my voice completely.

"She is. Of course she is," said one of the boys in an extraordinarily high-pitched voice. "You only have to look at her."

They grabbed me from both sides and started running. Down some unknown side streets we ran, my feet often not touching the ground at all. Our mad rush soon slowed down to a fast march. Finally we stopped in front of some sort of cellar, with steps leading down from the street to the basement. The tram conductor pushed me down the stairs and I fell against a wall.

"Here's another one!" he yelled triumphantly.

A middle-aged man came out. I remember his long, crackly leather coat, his military-looking ski hat, his ski boots with shiny brass clips. He had an intelligent face. Grabbing me by the hair he looked straight into my eyes.

"Are you from the country?" he asked.

I gave no answer.

"Don't you come from Szombathely?"

His voice was almost kind. But at the same time he was pulling my hair so hard that I almost fell on to my knees. He left me kneeling. The others pushed me down into the cellar where I found twenty or twenty-five people sitting on the floor. I didn't know any of them. They were mostly women, including an extremely fat market-woman type, wearing a knitted sweater and a peasant scarf.

The leader came into the room with a tiny pistol in his hand. "Stand up," he said quietly. "Stand up and raise your hands above your heads."

They surrounded us and in a disorganised group we staggered out into the street. The rain started to pour, and in no time we were soaking wet. Walking for about fifteen minutes, we reached the Danube. The group was led through a hole in a wire fence and we came to a halt at a warehouse.

"Come on everybody," yelled the young man with the eunuch's voice, taking a soldier's hat out of his pocket. "Let's have all your watches, jewellery, fountain-pens and lighters!"

I said goodbye to my watch but with trembling hands, managed to pull off my diamond ring and hide it quickly in my pocket.

We were lined up at the river bank. The leader called his men together; they were all armed. The fat woman started to yell: "What do you want? I know you, Laci Patak! I'm a widow with six children…"

Bang! A gun was fired, and the enormous body fell into the river with a great splash. There was a little panic then and I felt very faint. I heard a salvo of shots and a sharp pain seized my stomach. Throwing my arms backwards to the sky, I fell.

The current swept me away with enormous force. It made me go under, my lungs were gasping for air. My shoes came off and at one point I was spun round like a feather. I still don't know how I grabbed a metal ladder that was hanging from the side of a warehouse. For minutes I hung on to it, twisting my fingers around the iron bars, crying. I had only one thing in my mind: "I shall lose so much blood that my strength will leave me and I'll fall back into the water and drown." I examined my body. Not a scratch. They had missed me. Shivering with cold, I staggered through a yard. At the other side I found a night-watchman's hut. When I knocked on the door a dog started to bark hysterically inside. The door opened a little and an old man peered out. He must have known that this late caller, dripping with water and wearing no shoes, must be in grave trouble. But he opened the door to me.

By midnight all my clothes were dry, thanks to an over-heated little stove. The old man got me a pair of torn carpet slippers. We didn't exchange more than twenty words. His hands were trembling all the time and his dog sensed the old man's nervousness, refused to sit and just kept looking at me with an unfriendly gaze. Had I found a wise old man? Or did he think that I had tried to commit suicide and failed? I found a silver five pengo piece in my pocket for him.

At five in the morning I got back to the Yellow Star House. The Danube was my guide and I ran from door to door. The wider streets were the most dangerous; I crossed them as fast as I could, still anxious to evade suspicion. Once one of my slippers fell off right in the middle of the road and I had to rush back to pick it up. But the streets were deserted.

My mother was fast asleep on top of her bed, fully clothed. Her head was slanting sideways a bit, her mouth was half-open, she was breathing heavily. She was wearing a black dress with a white lace collar and a green cardigan on top. There was a crumpled handkerchief in her limp fingers, about to fall.

As I switched on the bedside lamp, she woke suddenly. She sat up quickly. A pin fell from her hair.

"Where have you been all night?"

"I went out of the house," I said quietly.

"Where did you go?"

"I almost died…"

One of her eyelids started to twitch nervously.

"What?"

I explained in a few words what had happened. By then she was sitting on the edge of the bed. I started again:

"They took us to the Danube. We were lined up and an old woman began to yell…"

I had got this far when my mother became very red in the face. Half-standing, half-sitting, she leaned forward and slapped my face quite hard. She wanted to give me another but I stepped back and her palm passed in front of my face.

"You're lying!" she whispered. "You're a liar!"

Perhaps it is rather unfeeling of me that this incident was the first thing that came to my mind when I received the letter from home. I had very little in common with her, but I would hate to be cynical. The funeral must be taking place now. Very far from my trees and canals in Holland.

Max Sawdayee

All Waiting to be Hanged

Monday September 23, 1968

For myself, I'm totally nonchalant to all that's going around. I'm astonishingly quiet and aloof, still desperately persevering in my plan to escape. Living in Iraq becomes to me like living "the last days of Pompeii", with the only difference that, adhering to the sacred values of life, I'm determined to live and not to succumb to the diabolical methods of destruction which the fiends in power are employing. It's of paramount importance now that some-body, someone, flees the country illegally, so that others may follow. Somebody has got to reach Iran alive. If I'm caught and killed, well, that'll be no more than a stroke of bad luck. So much the worse. Yet nothing counts for me than to reach Iran alive. That's my only goal at this moment.

Living rather in a world of my own, sometimes I pity myself, sometimes I suddenly feel scared of what I'm attempting to do. But that doesn't matter any more. I'm resolved to go on with my plan till the end.

Tuesday June 9, 1970

At three o'clock in the morning, we're all up. The four of us. It's our D-Day!

Wife prepares a quick breakfast, the children help each other dress, while I, having washed and dressed, lock the suitcases upstairs and add some finishing touches to the house to leave it in good order.

The spirit in the house, to tell you the truth, is quite low. It's rendered turbid not only by apprehension and

274

worry, but also by last minute questions, most of which are petty. Wife is nervous and taking everything to heart. Elder daughter, now nearly seven, keeps asking whether it's today that we take her to her aunt Violet in Iran, and how. Belinda, still sleepy, asks why we've packed her clothes and her big doll Chenile. And so on. And so forth.

I, in an extremely bad mood, and deeply concerned, choose to hum very old Arabic songs and tunes to busy my mind and mouth while carrying the suitcases down. Wife listens to me humming and thinks that I'm really delighted! She snaps out: "What makes you so glad and so confident?" "Human weakness, and people's lack of talent to guess rightly and quickly or let's call it lapses of human stupidity, my dear. That and only that may save us from getting caught on our journey to Iran!" I answer and resume humming my tunes!

At last! Four a.m. The taxi arrives at the door. The children's ex-nanny, a nice Christian from the north, who stayed with us the night, and who knows all about our intended escape, locks the door while we all get into the taxi, and goes home.

All along the road, seated beside the driver, I try to assess what's liable to happen if the government finds out that we reached Iran safely. I think they'll have to choose between two alternatives: they'll feel awfully ashamed of themselves that my escape went "smoothly", say nothing, and consider the matter closed, in which case many other Jews will follow my example in one way or another; or they'll make lots of trouble, probably also kill a number of innocent people in order to frighten the rest and quench a little their thirst for blood. These two alternatives have a fifty-fifty rating.

I also try to assess and sum up the whole situation in Iraq as I see it now, prior to my departure from the country. I can see no prospect for the Iraqi people to live decently and develop peacefully until the present government and the Ba'ath Party of Iraq are ousted. Some other power should elect a responsible body, by democratic means, to replace the present butchers, give this miserable Iraqi nation a chance to progress in freedom, and put an end to the oppressive terror from which it has been suffering for about two years. If no such change comes, Iraq is sure to settle, most unluckily, into a very dark age.

The road to the north is not devoid of huge problems and fears, and sometimes also fun. The most troublesome item among our personal effects is of course, my diary, written in English, which I bundle tightly and hide in a small leather bag carried by my little daughter Belinda. Smuggling my diary is more than a problem. It's a life-and-death issue. But I rationalise that in the first small section of our journey, which is the road to the north, it may be less dangerous than I think, as any search on this road may not be rigidly thorough. Moreover, I can always manage to dispose of it one way or another in case it becomes too dangerous. As for the second part of the journey, viz, from the north to Iran, and that's the tougher and knottier part — well, if I get caught without succeeding to dispose of it, the outcome will not be basically different. I'm escaping illegally, and that will provide the basic charge. I may be tortured a little more before the final scene of my tragedy: death by hanging. That's all. In that case it's worthwhile taking my diary along!

At a checkpoint near Kirkuk, the old policeman, learning that we're going to the north on vacation, and recognising a Jewess in my wife, naively exclaims: "I was unaware that Jews are already permitted to travel to the north on vacation! God bless our government! They are treating you well! Now, pass on!"

Near Arbil an army patrol stops us to search the car and baggage, from end to end and from top to bottom. Little daughter Belinda, seeing one of them open all the suit-cases, innocently hands over to him the one she is carrying, where the diary is hidden! I can hardly keep my tranquil demeanour! The man takes it, laughs and puts it aside, to open it or probably not. But Belinda begins to cry!

She wants it back! It's her favourite bag! Seeing her crying for her bag, the man laughs again and hands it back to her. "Here, here, don't cry, little girl! No need to open your small personal bag!"

We arrive at Salah El-Din in the northern mountains at ten in the morning, and instantly contact Daoud in his tobacco shop. He sends us to a very small, completely empty house he had arranged to evacuate beforehand, not very far from his shop. There we find the rest of our bags, which he has already brought with him personally.

Wife feels happy that we arrive here safely, and looks forward to seeing the rest of the journey accomplished without much worry or danger. "Well," she joyfully points out, "we've already covered some fifteen per cent of the road! Let's hope that the rest is not very risky!" I'm glad she's looking forward with optimism, but I'm afraid that the rest of our journey is full of dangers. In any case, we're alright so far.

Following Daoud's instructions, we empty all our suitcases into the jute bags, have the children eat a little, and wait for him to come with fresh instructions while contemplating the beautiful mountains from our little window.

A knock on the door. It isn't Daoud's voice calling us to open! Doubt! Suspense! The Kurdish tribal leader calls on us to collect the rest of his money and say goodbye. I insert the money, which has been kept hidden with my wife, into his pocket. Composed and very solemn, he says: "Remember, from now on your name is Ahmed. You're an ex-officer of the Iraqi army wishing to reach the Iranian frontier with your family. Your wife's name is Leila. You only say you're a Jew when you get to the first police station in Iran, and not before then. Listen to me again. Not before then. As for the rest of the instructions, Daoud will keep you informed." "Yes, Agha," wife answers, using the Kurdish word for "sir". The Kurd goes on: "The men, the three Kurdish guides who will accompany you all the way to Iran, are gentle people, but only one of them will know

277

that you're Jews. He is my agent-guide Hamid, leader of the caravan. As soon as you reach Iran we will contact your friends in Baghdad to help them escape too. Now goodbye and God bless you! Your people in Baghdad will be happy to learn later on that you bask in freedom in Iran! Don't ever fail them! Be patient, tough and sure of yourselves. Otherwise you will not reach your destination safely!" "Thank you, Agha, we will do our best. Goodbye!" wife answers. The Kurd glances at me, smiles and with a wink hands me a dagger. "It's a present. You'd better fasten it in your belt. It may help you on the road!" he says and leaves the house.

Later on wife decides that all along the road to Iran, and for reasons of caution and security, we call our elder daughter Wifaq and the younger one Wafa, two Arabic names. Yes, that's better. I welcome the idea.

At one in the afternoon Daoud comes in with the leader-guide Hamid and a taxi driver. The three put our jute bags in the cab, and we all leave in a hurry. Wife, the children and I sit in the rear. Driving at full speed up and down the wonderful mountains we arrive at Harir, a nice Kurdish village still in Iraqi hands (i.e. not occupied by hostile Kurds), and situated in a little plain between two mountains. The time is three-thirty. We have a delicious cup of tea, have some rest and buy cigarettes. We leave Harir and again at full speed travel east and arrive at Gali Ali Begh at about five. Here we sit near one of the most gigantic and fascinating of all waterfalls in the north of Iraq, while Daoud and Hamid take the taxi far away with the driver to remove the jute bags, putting them in another taxi in which Hamid hastens northwards.

Small, beautiful Gali Ali Begh village is also in Iraqi government hands still. Being a strategic military site, it is full of Iraqi army officer and heavily armed soldiers, roaming the serpentine mountain streets and passes, going and coming near us in groups of ten, twelve or more. Some of them keep looking at my wife and children in a suspicious manner. I begin to worry. For about an hour we don't

278

move. We're seated on the ground and staring like statues at the wonderful waterfall. We're inviting so much attention and suspicion that we can't move an inch, just can't.

At six in the evening, when all of us get almost completely wet from the tiny drops of water reaching us from the big waterfall, Daoud comes and takes us in the taxi again, amid stupefied soldiers and officers, who look at us with eyes wide open. We're fortunate none of them thinks to ask us even one question. We could face real trouble.

It is not yet dark when we encounter the first army control, just after the village we've left. A young Iraqi officer, standing near an armoured car at the head of a narrow wooden bridge, orders us to halt and asks for papers. Daoud and the taxi driver show theirs, while I say nothing. I only smoke. The officer looks keenly at everybody for a few seconds, then gives the signal to cross. Wife and I are so scared that we find it difficult to utter a single word for some time.

For a little less than half an hour, army cars pass by driving at full speed through these narrow mountain roads, not without difficulty cutting their way along. Others coming from the opposite direction slow down to get safely through. At the same time everybody looks at us astonished. Wife and I deliberately keep dead silent and hardly turn our faces to each other.

We continue heading north, instead of the usual way east. At six-thirty Daoud says "Be careful, please. Here it'll be very serious. We're arriving at Diana army camp. You children, don't utter a word, do you hear me? Not a word!" Wife and I have difficulty breathing. We're both white! I sweat abundantly. But I endeavour to preserve a measure of self-control.

"Stop! Diana Iraqi Army Camp. Control" — the sign reads. Wife instantly snatches the diary bundle out of daughter's small bag and throws it deep inside her own clothes, while I take a handkerchief and quickly dry the sweat from my face and forehead and throw the dagger to the driver.

279

Two soldiers start searching the car thoroughly, while Daoud engages them in conversation on all sorts of things so as to divert their attention. When the search is finished and we get back into the car one of the soldiers demands to see our papers. Just when Daoud and the driver show theirs, and the moment one of the soldiers comes closer to me at the rear, undoubtedly to demand mine too, a big, fat captain appears from nowhere, comes too close and pushes his entire head and neck inside the car. The soldiers step behind in respect and discipline. With his dark face, big, black, wide eyes and long and thick moustache, looking all round inside the car for more than sixty seconds, I don't exaggerate if I say that I feel our journey will end right here and now!

"Where are you going at this hour?" asks the officer.

"To visit friends in Diana village behind the camp," Daoud answers, as coolly as he can manage.

"Where do you come from?" asks the officer.

"From Salah El-Din, where I live and run a tobacco shop," replies Daoud, emphasising that he works there.

The officer looks at all of us again; says nothing. I turn my head to the left and see, to my utter astonishment and good luck, that the two soldiers are busy searching a small car that has just arrived.

The officer goes on: "I wonder if I didn't see you in Salah El-Din before? Anyway, is everything here in order? Papers, car, everything?"

"I believe so, sir," Daoud answers calmly, while the driver switches the starter on.

"Alright, move off. Let's help the soldiers search the next car behind you," says the officer. The driver starts slowly, but after some twenty feet employs the maximum speed he can mobilise. My wife and I exchange silent looks. Each of us knows what our eyes have to suggest. Wife, feeling better after those moments are gone, holds both children tight to her head and kisses them.

"That was our last official Iraqi check point on the road," Daoud, turning to us, says smilingly. "From now on it's the mules that'll do the job! I've had enough myself, by God!" he adds jokingly, and with no little satisfaction.

Along the camp road on our way to Diana village, seconds before the dark night takes over, I can see army armoured cars, trucks, light guns, all lying in rows, along the way to the end of the camp.

We're now at Rendezvous Café in Diana village; a small, shabby, deserted café, where Hamid is supposed to turn up with the two other Kurdish guides, our jute bags and, of course, the mules. It's dark. Daoud is tense. He would like to see Hamid take over and relieve him of all this troublesome business. He would like to go somewhere in the village to spend the night, with the driver, before returning to his village of Salah El-Din tomorrow morning.

At about eight we hear the tapping of hoofs approaching. The mules appear. At last! We've been waiting for them. The experience of riding a mule has in it a particular element of pleasure, and whether it's time to think about it all in such a situation as ours is doubtful, but I won't conceal my joy in looking forward to it. The sight of the five astonishingly big mules coming towards us makes me smile. "So that's it. I'm to quit the country, my Iraq, my former cherished home! And in what manner? I'm fleeing. On mules! Does one escape from a person or thing that one loves? Unfortunately, they compel me to do it. They reject my loyalty. They offer me no alternative."

With wife and children, and with only one hundred dinars left in my pocket, and only a limited change of clothes, I'm going out of the country after having bidden a hearty farewell to Baghdad, my home town.

Jamal and Salman, the other two Kurdish guides, both armed with small pistols dangling from their sides in their leather holsters, get down from the mules to swallow some hot tea before we move, while Daoud and the taxi driver leave in a hurry. Hamid, our Kurdish leader and guide, delivers to my wife and children, and to me too, Kurdish clothes to wear all along the road as a necessary disguise.

Dressed exactly like Kurds, we take our second and last cup of tea. I laugh over how I'm to ride a mule for the first time in my life! Wife, looking pretty in her Kurdish dress, with eyes full of emotion at the start of a tedious and fateful journey to freedom, keeps asking me if everything is alright with the children and me. And now we try to get astride our big mules, not without difficulty of course. Wife decides to take younger daughter Belinda with her, while Cordia joins Hamid. Just before we move, Hamid comes close to my wife and asks whether she would like to entrust him with her valuables, if any. Wife gladly does; keeping only the diary bundle hidden in her clothes. Hamid appears decent and responsible.

The first thing that comes to my mind when I'm installed on my mule is to give it a name. I decide to call it Mabrook, which in Arabic means "blessed". It'd be most suitable for my new friend and companion on such a hard, dangerous journey.

At nine in the evening, when it is pitch black and a little chilly, Hamid gives the signal to start. In a deeply touching, pathetic mood, the freedom-bound caravan, no less equal to its task, obediently follows the leader onward.

Bracha Serri

Jerusalem and San'a

Translated from the Hebrew by Yaffa Berkovits

Jerusalem on high
And San'a down below
Are one.
One is my city
A patchwork of colour,
A Babel of sounds
And smells.
The same openness
The same majesty.
An old woman's blessing
Like a neighbour's.
The same yearnings
The same prayers.
God has moved
To Jerusalem the capital.
Old Jerusalem
Not the young one.
I longed to kiss
These strangers,
Our "enemies",
To whisper my thanks
That they exist
As in days gone by
Never to return.

I become a hovering dream
In the lanes of the Old City
A tiny spirit
From Yemen
Which is no more.

Intoxicated by the scents
Tipsy with the sounds
The perfumes, the spices.
Aromatic coffee
Dried figs and almonds
Assorted raisins
Saffron and myrrh
Sweet incense
Souvenirs
From the Temple.

Dish

Translated from the Hebrew by Yaffa Berkovits

Mother cooked meat in the pot,
A tasty dish
To make you healthy.
They cooked me
In a song
— alive —
To make you happy.

Someone slaughtered me
A ritual slaughter!
— make no mistake —
He cut me to pieces,
Threw salt on the wounds
To draw the blood.
Oh, he kept strictly
To the rites!
Immersed me in water,
Waited the set time,
Someone else came, put the water to boil,
Castigated my flesh.
Someone roasted me over a fire,
Someone fried me in hot oil,
And added pungent spices.

May my spirit rise,
Sweet incense
In your nostrils,
To awaken your body's
Senses.

Ruth Knafo Setton

I Wore White

I wore white
And he wore white too.

I followed the road to the sea.
My wedding? His funeral?

Walked behind him six paces
as if I were veiled, and not he.

My husband, let me see your face,
He didn't turn, walked faster.

The muezzin called the faithful,
but I am faithless, she of no faith

that when he turns, he will restore
the garden: gold pears and silver

wet figs that dropped, one
by one, blooming breasts

into his waiting hand,

In the Blue Room

I slide sharp Kashkeval cheese in honey
    and bite before I see you, squeeze
glass-green grapes down my throat, suck
    persimmon to the skin before I come
to you: blue man in your blue room.
    A bear ate my brother, you tell me.
I mouth couscous from my palm, lick
    semolina grains bleached from the sun,
before I stare into your eyes, blue
    as the woods. Your nipples shiver
under blue light: across the street,
    Mickey changes the reel.
They scream and laugh
    as if we are the movie.
You wind my shirt
    around your head, a turban,
then gnaw at my neck, chew
    deep into my belly. Before,
before I come to you, I swallow
    figs from King Solomon's garden whole:
juice stains my thighs, I move towards
    you on slow desert feet. Outside
they watch the kiss against the stone
    wall. My father sailed the seas, searching
for the blue line that sliced
    the world. After, you tell me,
I smell my finger all night
    and faint from you. After,
after, I bare my teeth
    and taste only my palm.

Gillian Slovo

Every Secret Thing

The air hostess with her blonde hair was a living example
of someone with a normal carefree life. In my imagination
the thing that caused her to worry was whether her lipstick matched her nail varnish not when the police would
next come calling. Somewhere deep inside of me, I lusted
for that kind of normality. I had built a wall of defiance
around myself, placing my dazzling parents at its invul-
nerable centre. Only in the darkest night, alone in the
middle of South Africa could I allow myself a twinkling of
desire for ordinary life.

I think of my mother then, of her French perfume and
her carefully straightened hair and I wonder whether it
was like that for her as well. She was, to a stranger's eye,
a defiant communist, quirky enough to care about her
appearance but willing to break every one of society's con-
ventions. And yet when I look at her in the photos of those
days, with her neat suits and her carefully constrained
hair I see a women whose secret ambition might have been
to be Jackie Onassis.

From mother to daughter and down again. Tilly transformed herself from a Yiddish-speaking child into a
fearless dowager whose English accent was crystal cut. My
mother was utterly defiant and yet struggled almost her
whole adult life to disown her unruly Jewish frizz. And I,
her growing daughter, lay beside a sixties Barbie doll pretending to despise what my heart desired.

Back to Johannesburg to normal life. I was in my last
year of primary school and the starting gun had just been
fired on the competition for the end of year prize. In my
own way I continued passing for white, pretending that
my life and my school friends' lives were on par. It was
easy to pretend. I knew how different were our realities

but they did not. Their days were played out in an immutable childish paradise, insulated from harsh reality. The history they learned started in the seventeenth century with the arrival of Jan van Riebeech and ended in a white victory over the savage hordes. The black people they met emptied their garbage, made their beds, mowed their lawns and cuddled them when they were sick, and all of this with a smile. The anger that was brewing in the country couldn't really touch them. They must have seen the occasional picture of a policeman peering at the remains of a blown-up phone box, but all this was so very far away. Big brother, their government, was watching; it would take care of them.

We three children of Joe and Ruth pretended, for as long as we possibly could, to be like them. We listened, as we always had, to radio plays and afterwards, we'd creep down the corridor to our bedrooms, keeping our backs to the wall, because, for some reasons we never analysed, we were scared someone might stab us from behind. The front door would go, it would be one or other of our parents returning from a mysterious outing which we all pretended hadn't really happened. The next day the lowered voices and the soft clicking of the front door, would disappear from our memories. In the brightness of each new morning we ate our breakfast and were driven to school. With Shawn already at secondary school, Robyn and I turned up brightly in our short-sleeved blue and white gingham dresses, surreptitiously donning our reviled white panama hats as we moved through the school gates, ill-matching brown shoes polished to a gleam by our Elsie at home.

I learned fractions that year, taught by Mrs Bowskill with her ring of pearls resting on her fluffy pink bosom, her thick black-rimmed glasses and her sheer white hair. She was a teacher who had the light of knowledge shining from within, instantly believable, especially when she spoke of God. That was the year that, for a few months at least, I turned to her God, a Christian one who would watch over everything we did and, we hoped, over our parents as well. In the bedroom we shared, I forced Robyn down on her knees beside me and I told her how to pray to Him for forgiveness. Mrs Bowskill's God was stern but fair. We were sure that He would understand why we could not tell our parents about our religious conversion. They had their secrets — well, now we had ours.

1963: it was the year when disaster struck my parents' political movement and we were at the centre of a storm. Our teachers must have got a hint, even in the early months, of what was coming. Nothing was said but when Ruth came to pick us up they smiled meaningfully at her in a way I always thought was friendly.

How little I knew of what was going on in those adult heads. Many years later, in 1989, my publishers forwarded a letter which was post-marked South Africa. When I slit open the airmail envelope, a wad of densely written A5 pages slid out. The prose started affectionately enough with the information that my correspondent, who had just finished reading one of my detective novels, had taught me at school. She put in a few fond memories of what I'd been like as a child — shy, clever, polite — and said how hard that last year must have been for me.

But when I had finished one page and went on to the next, I did a double take. The letter was no longer friendly, it was vicious. In one long uninterrupted breath, my old teacher wrote that she had heard about my mother's death, that she was sorry for me but that the pity she felt was savage: she felt sorry, she wrote because my parents were both terrorists whose hands were stained by the blood of innocents. And that wasn't all: my father, she continued, had killed my mother and the South African police had proof of it. Not that the writer objected: she was glad Ruth was dead, and glad that they would soon get my father too.

My vision tripped over words which crawled angrily one on top of the other, making the last few pages almost indecipherable. I, though, didn't want to know. I crumpled up the letter and chucked it away.

In 1963 we kept on smiling although our life was in the process of splintering into pieces. It started innocuously enough with Joe leaving town. He told us he was going on a short trip and that he'd be back soon and then he drove, illegally, across the border.

At the time he wasn't lying. He expected to be back. He had gone to organise the training of MK recruits throughout Africa, and to plead for guns and arms from sympathetic states. When that was accomplished, he was due to return: to operate underground.

Many years later, I asked him how he could ever have believed that the plan could possibly pan out. Mandela had gone underground and had been caught. "How long," is what I asked Joe, "did you think you'd last?"

He answered with a slight, ironic smile and a question, "It does seem crazy now, doesn't it?"

Crazy, because even the newspapers were following his every move. In June they reported that Joe and fellow communist J.B. Marks had gone to Southern Rhodesia where they'd both been arrested. Two days later the same newspapers spotted the two men at liberty in the neighbouring Bechuanaland capital of Francistown, staying in a local hotel. On 8 June the *Cape Times* informed its readership that Joe had, the night before, telephoned his wife.

The furrows on Ruth's face grew deeper. One day she packed us in the car and drove us through the Johannesburg suburbs. We sat in the back seat, licking our fingers for the last taste of the hamburgers in baskets we'd bought from the Charcoal Oven and singing songs. The Beatles were a faint whisper from the mysterious "overseas"; we stuck to local products, singing that early sixties jokey, whiney, favourite "*Ag* (pronounced gutturally as in the German Achg) *pleez daddy*". We sang out gustily:

Ag pleez daddy, won't you take us to the drive-in,
All six seven of us eight, nine, ten.

291

We wanna see a flick about Tarzan and the Apemen,
And when the show's over, you can bring us back again.

Ag pleez daddy, we sang, pretending that our father was
like the others, out at work, earning money to buy us our
hearts' desires, not somewhere in Africa, bargaining for
guns. We loved the song's words, the demands of insa-
tiable childhood for zoos and aquariums and South African
boxers who would "donner" Yankees to the floor. But best
of all, we loved the chorus. We belted it out:

Popcorn, chewing-gum, peanuts and bubble gum
Ice-cream, candy floss and Eskimo pie
Ag daddy, how we miss nigger balls and liquorice
Pepsi-cola, ginger beer and Canada Dry.

If our mother, usually so fast to pick up on racial insults,
noticed our shouting out the word nigger, the knuckles on
her steering-wheel did not visibly tighten. Or perhaps I
just didn't notice. They were already almost translucent
with tension as she steered the car through the northern
suburbs of Johannesburg to the Liliesleaf farm in Rivonia.
At a farm gate she peeped the horn and a black man
appeared. He peered in the car, smiled in recognition and
opened up.

A gabled mansion stood at the end of the driveway, its
front half opening up on to a rolling lawn. But when my
mother stopped the car and we all got out she led us away
from the house past the garage and to a set of low concrete
buildings, the servants' quarters.

I climbed two low steps up to a concrete platform from
which the bare rooms ran off. It was dark inside and each
room seemed to be crowded with serious African men. The
low mumble of their various meetings was drowned out by
the endless background clatter of a duplicating machine.
My mother's special friend, and our family favourite,
Walter Sisulu came out and hugged us and then he took
Ruth to one side and started talking urgently in her ear.

And all the time we hung about, unable to understand a word of the conversations going on around us, only sensing that our fates were tangled up in that makeshift place.

For many years I nursed an embarrassing secret. I had no idea what I was doing on the day President John Kennedy was assassinated. It seemed almost impossible: every member of my generation was supposed to know so why didn't I? It wasn't as if other world events passed me by. I can remember driving with my mother through Jo'burg during the Cuban missile crisis, for example, convinced that the gas-works we passed was about to blow up. But the impact of Kennedy's killing and the aftershocks that remained firmly lodged in most living memories, were lost forever in mine.

Only now, in hindsight, can I find an explanation. For on the day, 22 November 1963, when Kennedy was shot, my mother was enduring her 106th successive day of solitary detention. Nothing else mattered to me then.

I remember almost every minute, frame by frame, of that 9 August when they picked my mother up. I was eleven years old and on a constant weekly round of visits to orthodontists and opticians. I remember a ninth-floor office with lime green blackout blinds. I sat on a high-backed chair in the dark, cold, iron frames, wedged against my nose, struggling to answer the insistent questioning as to which of two sets of circles — red or green — was the clearest. Each time I blinked the focus would change. I could feel the eye doctor's exasperation rising at my indecision, which only made me hesitate more. But finally the ordeal was pronounced over. I walked out there as I always did, clutching the spectacles that I refused to wear, sure that it wasn't the optician's halitosis but my failure to give him what he wanted that had made things end so badly.

My grandfather was waiting in the entrance hall. Mild-mannered, unassertive gentle Julius. As a child, I adored him, this one member of our adult world who seemed content to stay calmly in the background. As an adult, I marvel at how little of himself he left behind. There's a passport, a plaque commemorating his eighty communist years and a handful of black and white snapshots. In many of the photos, Julius seems frozen by the camera. He stares out, unblinking, at an unlikeable world — like a man from a strange unknowable culture trapped in the photographer's unfriendly gaze.

On that day, however, in the optician's foyer, Julius was his usual, calm, silent self. We went out to his car to join my waiting sisters.

He drove us through Johannesburg's business centre and into the suburbs, an ordinary route on an ordinary day. Even today, if I concentrate carefully I can hear a faint echo of my sisters' voices as they ganged up on me, rhyming "gully" with "silly", "Jill" with "ill" and "pill" in one endlessly unchanging lilting poem. I was almost lulled into sleep by its monotony when Julius suddenly stamped his foot down hard on the brake. By the time I looked up he was already out of the car. He was such a careful man yet he left us skewed at an angle to the pavement, the engine ticking over, while he strode across the road to a corner café. I can guess now what must have caught his attention — a newspaper billboard with my mother's name on it. At the time, however, I didn't spot the head-line. I just knew that there was something wrong.

Julius emerged soon after that. Clutching a newspaper, he walked towards us and got back into the car. I remem-ber clearly the sound of Shawn and Robyn teasing each other. Julius folded the paper and threw it near my foot. I wanted to pick it up, to read what it was that had turned his face so white. Julius started the car. I left the paper where it lay and looked at him. He didn't seem to notice. Staring straight ahead, he pulled out and drove faster then he ever had, to our home in Mendelssohn Road.

When we got home we found the iron garden gate was open and, in the driveway, a stranger's car. The front door was also open and there was a stranger waiting there.

Silently, we walked towards him. I don't remember Julius with us. Perhaps he wasn't there: perhaps he'd dropped us off and fled.

Inside the house every drawer and cupboard, every nook and cranny, was being turned over by policemen. I saw my grandmother and our nanny, Elsie, hovering in the background, their hands hanging uselessly by their sides. My two sisters and I walked down the corridor, conscious of alien faces watching with expressions we couldn't fathom. I held my chin high and felt an illicit childish thrill at the attention.

Ruth was in her bedroom, packing. A man, leaning nonchalantly against a wall, was watching her every move. She greeted us, her face immobile: almost everything she did showed her iron control. I remember her tapered fingers, painstakingly folding each piece of clothing and laying it carefully on top of the one that went before. Halfway through, she fetched a book from the dressing table — Stendhal's *The Charterhouse of Parme* — and put it in the suitcase. As I watched it going in, I heard the policeman snort. My mother heard him too. She turned to look at him, her eyes blazing. He couldn't hold her gaze. He pretended to relax, folded one arm into the other and leaned heavily back against the wall.

The suitcase closed with a final click. My mother picked it up and started walking. Men went with her to the door. I followed them. They put her in the car, in the front seat, one on either side of her. Three jovial burly men squeezed themselves into the back seat. My mother looked at me, almost as if she didn't know who I was. I stood, waiting for her to say something. Finally her eyes seemed to focus on me and, leaning closer, she tossed a few loving reassuring words my way, topping them up with one last injunction. "Look after Robyn," she said.

The man beside her pulled the car door shut. The driver on her other side turned on the engine and started down the drive. I didn't wait while they reversed carefully out into the sharp bend at the bottom of our drive and then drove off. Instead, I went inside the house in search of Robyn.

I found her in the kitchen, standing close to Elsie who used to wake us, feed us, dress us and paint mercurochrome across our cuts and bruises. Shawn was in the garden and my grandmother kept walking in and out, opening her mouth to say things that had no meaning. I stood by Robyn in the kitchen, helping her make apple fritters.

Ronny Someck

On a Girl Whose Parachute Has Not Yet Opened

Translated from Hebrew by Vivian Eden

Tonight I gathered feathers from the angel's shoulders,
   yours,
And I dreamt of the moment of the thud
On Earth.
It's too bad I'm not a soul plumber,
With a flashlight that makes light
Even of the sun, and a hand that cleans rust
Off the dream pipe, a moment before
It crumbles a wall that imprisoned
The word
Mother
In your mouth.
From the window, I can see the baiting smile
Of other women , hooked on a line cast
To fish words from the children's mouths.
Carry on, I want to tell them. Wave flags
In honour of every syllable
But also think of the flags folded in the chambers of the
   bodies
Of the silent.
Wait quietly for the parade of the first word,
The drums of the hand that will caress,
The wind that will pluck the strings of the parachute
That has not yet opened.

Shoes

Translated from Hebrew by Hanni Dimitstein

The shoes that she hides under the bed
dream at night of the animal skin they were torn from.
They learned to tame her legs the way I learned to walk in
her body,
sole after sole in the forsaken zone where
fox's eyes froze in her eyes
and the roes' run was engraved in the slumbering skin
of her feet.

Baghdad, February 1991

Along these bombed-out streets
I was pushed in a baby carriage.
Babylonian girls pinched my cheeks
and waved palm fronds
over my blond down.
What's left from then become very black
like Baghdad
and the baby carriage we removed from the shelter
the days we waited for another war
Oh Tigris, Oh Euphrates, pet snakes
in the first map of my life,
how you shed your skin and became vipers.

Ilan Stavans

The Disappearance

"Honest Gentleman, I know not your breeding."
—*Henry IV*, Part II, Act V

For Verónica Albin

I wonder if stomach cancer is one of the prices one might pay for gluttony, for that is what killed Maarten Soetendrop at the age of seventy-one. It was my old friend, Yosee Strigler, who wrote informing me of the death of the corpulent, legendary actor in the heart of the Belgian *pays noir*. It was in Charleroi, the city named after a bewitched, dull, Spanish king, where Soetendrop lost his footing. And it was there that he made his final exit from the stage, too.

Yosee sent me a long, poignant letter, along with a clipping of the obituary published in *De Telegraf*, where Soetendrop's disappearance — in Brussels it made headlines and was dubbed *De verdwijning* — is recorded in detail. I read what he had sent me about the life, and the death, and the deceit, and I put it away. There Yosee's style is succinct, affable, yet also agonising, a reflection not only of the way his mind works but of the debates we used to have. He believed Belgian Jews were at risk. They never felt fully at home. The number of Muslims was rapidly growing. He sensed a suffocating, unstable future.

I've reread what Yosee sent me attentively. That he decided, after all these years, to mail these things to me — I've changed addresses seven times since we last saw each other — might show that friendship triumphs over passing disagreements. But it is also proof that the sparring has not ended, that, clandestinely, Yosee remains eager to prove his point. Or has he finally capitulated and accepted mine?

Yosee and I met for the first time more than two decades ago on a hike in the Sinai desert — shortly before the Israeli army invaded Lebanon. He worked in a kibbutz near Lake Kineret; I was enrolled at Hebrew University. I believe the next time we saw each other was in Tel-Aviv, at a play by Ephraim Kishon. After the show we found a cosy café on Dizengoff Street and talked for hours about the challenges of the Jewish Diaspora since Auschwitz. That he was from Charleroi (although his family moved to Brussels when he was twelve) and I from Mexico City allowed for humorous exchanges. Neither of us was fully comfortable in Hebrew, his Spanish was a path filled with puddles and I could make myself understood in Dutch with the help of a *heymish* Yiddish, but only after a couple of beers. Our common ground was an invented language that sounded like Edmund Wilson translating *Eugene Onegin* back into Russian from Vladimir Nabokov's literal English rendition. Later Yosee and I travelled together to Massada, then went for a swim in the Dead Sea. During that trip was when he mentioned wanting to return to Belgium, selling his belongings, and coming back to Israel to make *aliyah*. "Only in Israel is the Jew safe from adversity," I remember him saying.

When I left Jerusalem after my first year as a student, Yosee happened to be on the same flight to Munich. We spent the time talking about the works of art the Nazis had stolen from collectors and shipped to Prague, which they hoped to turn into a museum of the "lost Jewish race." We parted, I backpacked around Europe on my own, and some months later I visited him and his family in Brussels, where I stayed in an apartment that belonged to a school pal of his a few blocks from Rue Royale, within walking distance from the Gare du Nord. At some point during my week-long stay Yosee took me to see a performance of *The Misanthrope* with Soetendrop in the lead role. My friend told me he knew Soetendrop, one of the best actors in Belgium, according to my friend. The two had met in Jerusalem. Tour guides fluent in Dutch, the neutral tongue of the majority of Belgian visitors, were difficult to find in those days, and Yosee not only spoke the language, but was also passionate about Biblical archaeology, so while still in the kibbutz, he had been hired by an agency to moonlight as a guide for a group from Belgium and Holland.

Soetendrop, Yosee said, was a powerful presence in the group, not because of his temperament — he could be at once charming and abrasive — but as a result of his fame. "Everyone has seen the movie *Doktor Travistok*! at least twice," my friend claimed, then categorically stated, "He's outstanding as the absent-minded scientist." The Old City was a natural rendezvous that brought people together and it seemed to nurture a relationship between Yosee and Soetendrop. Back in Brussels, the actor invited my friend to his residence in Deventer, where he met Soetendrop's wife Natalie. That same year they celebrated Hanukah together and was served a meal Yosee described as a "bacchanal," with *latkes* the size of a salmon, Spanish cheeses, an asparagus soup, a soufflé, a salad with boysenberries. Soetendrop's portions, Yosee believed, were nothing short of gargantuan. "Jews and food — eternal companions. At one point Maarten looked like a Rembrandt creation." As it turns out, it was the last time my friend saw the actor in person.

As Molière's Alceste, I found Soetendrop extravagant. He played the role on mannerisms. His corpulence was stressed through hirsute clothes, before engaging in a dialogue he oscillated the neck like a hyena devouring her prey, and he improvised a slight stutter around the letter *t*. Maybe because my friend had recounted their adventures in Jerusalem, off stage I imagined him to be loud, even obnoxious. "As I get to know him better, he appears to me to be uncomfortable with himself in *real life*, as if body and soul refused to match." Yosee underscored the two words as if for Maarten Soetendrop the border between this world and the imaginary one had already been blurred. I remember thinking to myself: Do all actors suffer from a similar sense of unreality? In any case, the fact that my friend knew Soetendrop in person made Molière palatable. After the performance, Yosee asked me if I was ready to greet the actor in his dressing room. I declined: unless I'm paid to represent them, I never quite know what to say to celebrities.

It seems that Soetendrop's fading act was methodically planned over several weeks. His obesity doesn't appear to have been an obstacle. His movements were agile, even when at the hospital after his ordeal. He was a master of make-believe. Did he ever doubt his talent to conjure a parallel truth, to make people think he, the most revered of thespians in Belgium, had been mistreated by a horde of hooligans? Only if one is convinced he knew the distinction between truth and lies. "It is Maarten's sense of morality that is in need of urgent revaluation," Yosee believes.

The basic facts are uncontestable. On the frigid Thursday evening of December 3rd, 1987, the police commissioner of the industrial city of Charleroi, in a hastily-orchestrated press conference, announced that Soetendrop on tour as Sir John Falstaff in *The Merry Wives of Windsor*, had not arrived at his usual 6.30 p.m. call before that evening's performance. Thirty-five minutes later, the floor manager alerted the theatre producer who, aware of the actor's tempestuous personality — yet conscious of his unrivaled punctuality — asked for patience. The hotel in which the actor was staying was put on alert. Repeated calls were made to his room. With the producer's permission, the room was searched. A bar and a restaurant Soetendrop frequented were contacted. At 8:15 p.m. the evening performance was cancelled and, soon after, a search was announced. Since the police commissioner didn't want the media to find out *avant la lettre*, he himself let the word out: "Maarten Soetendrop is a distinguished star. It is too early in the investigation to draw conclusions. We're hoping for the actor's safe and speedy return." A free-lance reporter dismissed the police

302

commissioner's search as premature. "When a Muslim goes missing near a mine in Bois du Cazier, do the police bother?" Any misgivings were swiftly put to rest the following morning the minute the mailman delivered an envelope to the office of Rabbi Awraham Frydman, some fifty-five miles north of the city. A single-line, carelessly-typed note claimed Maarten Soetendrop to be under the control of the Flemish Fascist Youth Front.

News of the disappearance touched a nerve in Belgium. The Saturday newspapers offered profiles of the actor's life and career, reflected on the ideology of the previously-unknown neo-Nazi group, pondered its whereabouts, and speculated about its chances of assassinating the famous Flemish actor. In the following days a series of equally muddled notes arrived at the homes of other Jewish leaders, a TV anchor, some members of the Chamber of Representatives, and Natalie Soetendrop. (In one note a quote in French from the Constitution [Title II, Act 20] was added: "*Nul ne peut être contraint de concourir d'une manière quelconque aux actes et aux cérémonies d'un culte, ni d'en observer les jours de repos.*") After she received the note, Natalie Soetendrop begged the kidnappers for mercy. She urged the Belgian government to act immediately yet responsibly.

"During World War II, Belgium engaged in a silence that turned us into accomplices," Yosee writes in his letter. "This time around, people were eager to shout."

In a display of solidarity, a demonstration took place in the Netherlands, at a church in Amsterdam, on Saturday, December 12th, more than a week after Soetendrop's exit in Charleroi. It attracted politicians and celebrities. The Speaker of the Belgian Parliament described the fascist group as "rats coming out of a hole." Soon after, the Justice Minister spoke about appointing a special prosecutor to investigate neo-Nazi activities.

With a voracious appetite for beef, Chilean wine, and attention, Maarten Soetendrop had turned fifty-two on the day of his last performance in Charleroi as Falstaff. In three more days he was scheduled to travel along with the theatre company to the cities of Liège, Antwerp, and Ghent. As an actor, he had an esteemed reputation as much for his thespian technique — he was a loyalist of "The Method" — as for his choice of roles. Audiences knew him not only for *Doktor Travistok*! But for films like *The Messy Self*, *Valpurgis* and *The Night of the Birds*. There were reports he was under contract to be in *Amsterdamn*. Plus, Soetendrop was the impresario behind *Aunt Julie*, a successful season of a lesser-known Pirandello play, and the musical *Anatevka*, based on Sholem Aleichem's Yiddish novel *Tevye the Dairyman*. His favourite playwright was Chekhov.

The obituary in *De Telegraf* describes Soetendrop as the product of "a mixed background": a Jewish father, also an actor; and a Christian mother. "The embodiment of a divided spirit," Yosee states. In 1940, when Soetendrop was five and his brother Hugo almost three, their mother abandoned the family abruptly. She had been having an affair with a married man for quite some time, a Nazi collaborator called Siegbert Himmelstrup. Soon after she filed for divorce and married her lover in 1944. The brothers were separated; Hugo stayed in Brussels where he lived with his mother, stepfather, and his three children. Maarten was sent to a farm near Leeuwarden, in northern Holland. For almost two years he was hidden from the Germans by a family. According to Yosee, the episode became a source of shame. "In his eyes, Judaism was about secrecy. His was a servant's mentality. He was hidden because he was inferior." After the war, he lived in Antwerp with a paternal uncle for two-and-a-half years. Eventually Soetendrop was sent to a boarding school in Bordeaux. In the sixties, he sought out his father in order to talk about his half-Jewish self. His infatuation with drama, he trusted, came from being an outsider — a foreigner — in Belgian culture. He needed his father's approval to remain on the edges, to peek in, to be aloof yet have the gravitas needed to impersonate other characters, not only himself. The father welcomed him, but chose not to answer Soetendrop's questions about the past. "Silence... Is it right to define it as the absence of sound? Isn't it an existential condition?"

The obituary mentions a rather pallid, unforthcoming autobiographical essay Soetendrop published in an obscure theatre journal in 1991 called "*Wertewelt des Judentums.*" According to Yosee, in it Soetendrop mentions that in 1979, already as a promising actor in the Brussels theatre scene, he underwent a religious conversion on the eve of Yom Kippur. At that time Soetendrop was still single, for although he had expressed his love to several women, he had never proposed marriage to any of them. Later on he surveyed an existential vacuum inside himself. "I had lost touch with the inner voice," Yosee quotes him. Soetendrop found out that the Jewish holidays were about to take place. Formally dressed, with tennis shoes appropriate for the occasion, the actor entered a synagogue in the working-class Anderlecht district, which brewed with Muslim immigrants. Never in his life had he been exposed to prayer and the *Kol Nidré* melody sweetened his heart. A few months later he visited Jerusalem with Yosee as his guide. A friend gave him a copy of *The Star of Redemption*, by German philosopher Franz Rosenzweig, which he read with difficulty but admiration. He started therapy with a psychoanalyst called Hermann Musaph. Unexpectedly, the sessions ratified his faith.

In 1987, in the early days of winter, Soetendrop was in a state of stupor. In an interview, Natalie Soetendrop portrayed him as "taciturn, under duress," yet when pressed by reporters, she refused to be more specific. The reticence turned out to be a strike of luck. His Falstaff was universally applauded by critics all over Belgium and tickets quickly sold out. The same day he disappeared, a lengthy encomium appeared in the magazine *Dag Allemaal.*

What transpired while Soetendrop was purportedly a hostage of the FFYF is still the subject of conjecture and

305

gossip. The Brussels police headquarters pushed the investigation in every geographical direction. The typed notes were painstakingly analysed. Rumours of links of several political entities to the FFYF circulated. Journalists looked into Soetendrop's past for clues. Leads emerged but led nowhere.

Natalie Soetendrop announced on TV her willingness to pay a ransom, no matter the amount. It was rumoured that an undisclosed sum made available by the government would be given to the captors to secure the actor's safe return. The Justice Minister quickly issued a disclaimer: "Belgium doesn't fall prey to ruffians. If the Soetendrop family is willing to pay, it is free to act as it wishes." Soon after, another typed note arrived at Rabbi Frydman's address. It claimed the kidnappers weren't interested in a ransom. Theirs was an ideological struggle "to cleanse the country of rubbish."

Then, on Wednesday, December 21st, behind a curtain of snow flurries, a shivering, dishevelled, ostensibly bruised Maarten Soetendrop, noticeably thinner, his hands tied behind his back, faeces on his hair, blood on his face, abdomen, and sweater, was discovered by a passerby in a dead-end street near the Groeninge Exhibition Centre in the city of Bruges. "I was abducted by hatred," he was quoted as saying.

The reporter for *De Telegraf*, called Erik Eddelbuettel (who authored the obituary Yosse sent along), was the first on the scene. He was followed by the police, an ambulance, and the forensic squad. It was Eddelbuettel who found a typed note stuck to Soetendrop's sweater. It appeared to be Spanish: "*Judeos de mierda. ¡Furia!*"

"Do you recall the day?" Yosee wonders. "The news was wired all around the globe, including the United States. You sent me a comment on a piece you read in *The New York Times*."

I was indeed shocked when I read the piece. The memories of the prominent Flemish actor on stage in Brussels came back to me like a comet. His safe return pleased me

306

and I was angry at the publicity the neo-Nazis were receiving at Soetendrop's expense. I saved the clipping thinking it substantiated my friend Yosee Strigler's belief that, after the creation of the state of Israel, life in the Diaspora was no longer justifiable. I was curious as to Soetendrop's whereabouts during his absence. What type of torture had he been subjected to? Would he be able to overcome the prolonged periods of depression associated with incidents of this nature?

Needless to say, I couldn't have envisioned the twisted knots behind the affair. A day after his re-emergence, Soetendrop, in better shape but still in the hospital, described being seized at a bar by a single man "about my size, perhaps a bit shorter, and certainly slimmer." They pushed him into a car where he was bound and blindfolded. They ripped off the star of David he wore around his neck. Later he found himself in a sewer tunnel, daubed with faeces, and with a swastika dyed on his chest. He remembered being hit in the stomach, losing consciousness. The humiliation reached a climax when, aware of his surroundings, he was asked to kiss a small photograph of Adolf Hitler.

Natalie Soetendrop rushed to her husband's side. Actors, politicians, and religious leaders paraded through the hospital. Hermann Musaph was interviewed on TV. "Musaph is a Treblinka survivor," Yosee states. "He told viewers that, with the exception of Poland, more Jews were killed during World War II in Belgium and Holland than anywhere else."

Yosee sent Soetendrop a greeting card the next day. He never got a response. He later found out the actor received close to three thousand just on his first day at the hospital.

On January 6th, a month and three days after Soetendrop's ordeal began, Soetendrop confessed to his own kidnapping. At two-hundred-thirty-five pounds, he was extraordinarily elastic. He had come up with the whole thing: his own injuries, the neo-Nazi commando, the typed

307

notes, including the one in flawed Spanish. Collective sympathy soon became unimpeded animosity. The public was furious: it had trusted its actor, but the play itself turned out to be a lie. New demonstrations plastered the streets. There was talk of retribution. The police department sent Soetendrop a bill. (It was dutifully paid.) There were swastikas painted in bus stops and a cemetery was desecrated. In Brussels, the synagogue in the Anderlecht district where Soetendrop had found his faith during a Yom Kippur service was set on fire by a Molotov cocktail. "Is it a surprise that the actor and his wife failed to respond, retreating to their Deventer residence?" Yosee wonders. "Maarten was ashamed of his deeds — but he never found the right words to articulate his emotions. It isn't surprising. When it comes to guilt, are Belgians — even Belgian Jews — capable of those words?"

To describe the rationale behind Maarten Soetendrop's misguided self-flagellation is to ratify — if proof were needed — that reality invariably outdoes the most baroque of dramaturges. My alibi is that nothing in this story is invented. Eddelbuettel, in the obituary, argues that the actor had been involved in a series of Jewish efforts to block an anti-Semitic play by Reiner Werner Fassbinder, *Garbage, the City, and Death*, its debut scheduled in Brussels for 1986. It is about a prostitute, Roma, whose fortunes turn around after her encounter with a Frankfurt speculator for the municipal government called The Rich Jew. Frank, a pimp and Roma's husband, leaves her. Roma then asks her lover to kill her. As a result of his connections, The Rich Jew isn't accused of the crime; instead, Frank is. The play was originally written in 1975. Its anti-Semitism forced officials to block it in Germany. A hurricane of op-ed pieces, letters to the editor, and radio broadcasts decried the blockage as a "suspension of freedom of speech in Belgium." Political pundits talked of the tentacles of a Jewish lobby controlling the government. It was printed by the *Frankfurter Allgemeine Zeitung*. Suhrkamp Press released it in book form. The publisher withdrew it and would not release it until Fassbinder changed the name of The Rich Jew. The director steadfastly refused. In 1984, a couple of years after Fassbinder's death, the Old Opera in Frankfurt attempted to stage it once more. It was again stopped. (In the interim, the Yoram Loewenberg acting school in Israel performed it.) Another company tried to stage it in Belgium soon after without success. An anti-Fassbinder protest led by Rabbi Frydman, and supported by Maarten Soetendrop took hold. There was more censorship. A publisher in Antwerp released it in Dutch translation. In mid 1987 it was read on Belgian public radio. Still, no theatre agreed to produce Fassbinder's play.

"What are the uses of hatred?" Yosee asks in his letter. "Maarten's intentions were good. His ploy might have forced a referendum in the Netherlands, the land of Baruch Spinoza and Anne Frank, but not in Belgium, where 'the mendacious amnesia' — the phrase was used by Soëten — accumulated over decades remains unexposed. Instead, he ended up being confronted by a tribunal of his own device, one staged in a theatre as big as the world entire. He wanted to understand the power of silence. But in this area, he was short of talent."

At the time of the confession, Soetendrop's lawyer, Luuk Hammer, described his client as being "in a state of panic." But he wasted no time in exculpating him: "Is our illustrious theatre star guiltier than the rest of us are? Maarten Soetendrop may have lost his boundaries. He is an expert in theatre but not an expert in crime."

The actor's sole response came after the Justice Minister requested an "official" apology. Soetendrop went on camera with an epigrammatic — and, in Yosee's eyes, suspicious — statement read on Thursday, May 10th, 1988. "If in any way I've offended the Belgian people in particular, and the Low Countries in general, I deeply regret it. My life has been a pandemonium since I was five."

In the obituary in *De Telegraf*, Eddelbuettel claims Soetendrop was in the Charleroi sewer system for only three days. Disguised in a woman's clothes (wig, lavender dress, heavy winter coat), he stayed in a homeless shelter until after Christmas Day, then moved to a place on Rue Émile Vandervelde until January 2nd. Surreptitiously, he broke into his dressing room at the theatre at midnight the next day, took make-up equipment, a curtain rope, a knife, and some paint. A night guard reported hearing odd noises but didn't spot him. Less than forty-eight hours later, he was already in his thespian apparel in Bruges.

Did Soetendrop truly repent? Not in Yosee's eyes. "Even when he apologised to the Justice Minister, I'm convinced Maarten was still acting. In fact, he acted all the way to the grave."

In his letter, my friend offers convincing evidence. It is an indictment of journalistic practices. "Reporters only scratch the surface. They are impatient. Their next deadline is a distraction. Had they bothered to look up the actor's past meticulously," he writes, "they would have come across unsettling data. Did he really devise his own disappearance? He was an intelligent man. But he was haunted. Becoming an actor was a way to alleviate his inner doubts. It allowed him an opportunity to take a regular vacation from himself."

Yosee listed valuable information about Soetendrop's father, mother, and brother. After a career in the regional stage, his father retired in the seventies and died of an aneurism in 1981. He and his eldest son seldom spoke to each other. The link between Soetendrop and his mother was even more tenuous. Ostensibly, she, along with one of her grandchildren, visited him after a performance of *Platonov* in Louvain and tried to reintroduce herself. Believing she was a stalker, Soetendrop avoided her. His mother subsequently attempted another reunion. Although by then the actor knew well who she was, he refused to see her. She died in 1994 while on a trip to Greece.

"The bond with Hugo Soetendrop is more convoluted," Yosee adds. In *"Wertewelt des Judentums,"* the sections

310

dedicated to him are called "Pandemonium." They are surveys of their tense relationship, describing Hugo as "a loving brother who learned to loathe." But they conceal more than they reveal. For instance, Soetendrop stressed, at total of nineteen times, that since he left for the farm near Leeuwarden, he and Hugo never saw each other again. "Why over-emphasise the point?"

After Yosee read the autobiographical essay, he sent Soetendrop a congratulatory note. In it he asked him about his brother. Again, Soetendrop failed to respond. Yosee was intrigued, though. He looked for the name "Hugo Soetendrop" in the national birth registry; he found it. Then he searched telephone records; this time he was empty-handed. A reference in a school yearbook in Kortrijle led him to one François Soëten; it was a dead-end. Another one in Roeselare talked about a Sutendorp brewing company. He then searched for Soetendrop's stepfather, Siegbert Himmelstrup. An entire dossier became available. He identified Himmelstrup as a metal worker in Antwerp, a sixty-seven-year-old devout Catholic, married with four children: Heinrich, Julian, Ute, and Elfriede. A series of archived photographs gave Yosee the certitude he wanted: Hugo Soetendrop had been re-baptised — and reeducated — as Julian Himmelstrup. He had been a member of the Nazi Youth League. After the war, he studied engineering in Bielefeld, in Westphalia and eventually returned to Brussels. For a short while in the eighties he lived in Madrid, where he signed up for a four-week course on the Spanish Civil War. "I was rewarded with a nemesis," Yosee writes. "Hugo lived in Bruges, where he was a part-time employee at the Federal Department of the Environment. He was divorced by then and I know little about his first wife. He tried to have a child with a second wife, but it took its toll and after three miscarriages, she left him. Estranged from everyone, Hugo lived in a rented room near Rue Émile Vandervelde. Like his stepfather, whom he adored, his support for Nazism didn't diminish after the war. Indeed, until the end he believed Hitler's overall mission to racially improve Europe would one day be accomplished *in toto*."

Hugo followed his brother's career with a mix of wonder and resentment. He kept a distance: Soetendrop's renewed faith in Judaism disgusted him. His reluctance to interact changed in the aftermath of the anti-Fassbinder protests. In Hugo's view, Belgium made an irreversible pact with the devil when *Garbage, the City, and Death* was cancelled.

Knowing Soetendrop was scheduled to be part of a rally organised by Rabbi Frydman, Hugo hid amidst the crowd. Did Soetendrop spot him, too? Hugo heard his brother give a speech about the perils of amnesia. "It was then that he plotted Maarten's kidnapping," Yosee writes. "Or is it the other way around? I confess to be on shaky ground in this area of my search. But that doesn't make it less believable. I've discovered, for instance, that Hugo — *aka* Julian Himmelstrup — gave final notice to the Federal Department of the Environment on December 27th, 1987. The room he rented was vacated the day before. 'An old woman took everything with her,' the owner told me. She said Monsieur Himmelstrup was indisposed. As long as she gave me the last monthly pay, I didn't care to ask for specifics." The Olivetti used for typing the notes purportedly written by the Flemish Fascist Youth Front was found."

That cold afternoon in Charleroi on December 3rd, Hugo caught up with his sibling, his tipsy older — and odder — self, at a bar on the way to the theatre. "Did Maarten recognise him? There is no way to know. Julian Himmelstrup was, unlike his brother, thin, pale, and with teeth even the British would abhor. He was a nobody. That afternoon he was wearing a fedora. Probably neither of them thought the encounter would last long. I've tried to imagine the dialogue they engaged in, but it isn't easy in a generation taught not to use words. They walked a few blocks together and then they disappeared. I don't think *De verdwijning* was a *fait*

312

accompli in the mind of either of them, as the media led us to believe. Things were improvised, the way they often are when madness sets in. But this kind of madness was more coherent, more intelligible. One of them — was it Maarten? — let his pathos run wild. Ah, the media! Is there a less trust-worthy theatre? Are we all fooled more often by any other device? I don't trust the interviews granted by Natalie Soetendrop, Luuk Hammer, anyone… To me it looks as if they, I, and everyone had been fortuitously invited to a performance in the biggest theatre imaginable. Harry Mulisch, who won the Prijs van de Nederlandse Letteren in 1995, published a novella-cum-play (he calls it "a contradiction') made of a pair of monologues and an intermezzo. It is narrated at Soetendrop's funeral. Maarten becomes Herbert Althans and Natalie Magda. But it distorts the intricacy of events. This is because literature is always a game. Why distort what has already been misrepresented?"

Yosee bluntly visualises the scene in which the siblings have reached the Charleroi sewer system. "The city was built in 1666, the year in which the pseudo-messiah Sabbetai Zevi, who eventually became an apostate by converting to Islam, expected the world to come to an end. At the time Spain ruled the Low Countries. The idea was to build a fortification in order to stop the imperial troops of Louis XIV. The sewer system is a macabre web made of symmetrical dungeons. Maarten and Hugo walked the maze until they found a large, dank chamber where the air was fetid. There was only a slimmer of light. The memory of the Hanukah "bacchanal" I spent with Maarten and Natalie lies in sharp contrast in my mind. For hours they stared at each other's shadows. Had they done anything else in life?" Then Maarten probably said: "I thought I killed you inside me a long time ago. But when I saw your face in the crowd, I realised I was wrong. After we expiate the guilt we've been forced to inherit — what the Germans call *Schuld* — only one of us is likely to emerge from this darkness."

313

The final paragraph of Yosee's letter is the most eloquent. "So there you have it: another retelling of Cain and Abel. Before his death in a hotel in Charleroi, on Rue de la Providence, Maarten was dangerously overweight — close to three hundred pounds, according to Eddelbuettel. In the last few years the public recognised him mostly for his soap endorsements on TV. And I know little else except that on the High Holidays he and Natalie prayed at Brussels' elegant Sephardic synagogue on Rue du Pavillon and that he donated money to the Belgian Jewish Museum to buy back art stolen by the Nazis. And, of course, Maarten remained an assiduous patron of the most refined French restaurants. Did he sin through the mouth to compensate for the lack of words? These questions have no answer. When did Maarten come up with the FFYF? Who typed the notes sent to his wife, Rabbi Frydman, and others? It doesn't matter. The fact is, Hugo was never seen again. I've checked hospices, morgues, crime logs. He seems to have vanished into smoke. In our debates, Ilan, I always took the stand that Israel would finally solve the dilemmas of the Diaspora. It would make the Jew beautiful, a bronze man, a warrior. Our ancient sense of inferiority — the metaphorical hunchback we've carried with us for generations and generations — would be disposed once and for all: no more apologies, no more inferiority complexes. As you know, I tried to live up to my opinions by making *aliyah*. It didn't work. I became a lawyer who specialises in Holocaust reparation cases. I wanted to do some good after the pervasiveness of evil. But evil is an essential component of Nature, the opposite of good. One can't exist without the other. All things considered, I'm a diasporic creature like you, one comfortable looking at things as an outsider. For centuries Jews kept the prohibition against idolatry. Among other things, this meant that acting was forbidden. To be someone else, even for a short while, is to compete with the Almighty's creation. The prohibition back-fired: at heart, all Jews are actors. The art of impostures is encoded in our DNA. How

314

else could we exist with the contradictions that inhabit in us? In what other way would we pretend to live a happy life among strangers and still dwell in our unique unhappiness? Maarten's odyssey frightens me. He put a serious face in front of millions while pretending to have been kidnapped. People believed him. But who ended up losing?"

Yosee Strigler's letter was postmarked in Israel.

George Szirtes

Solferino Violet: Blood Guilt

Once he had opened his violin-case
that inner plush overwhelmed me. I know
there is a question here, an innuendo
I don't intend to answer to your face,
like synaesthesia, or something to do
with sexuality, mother, or the bowels,
that there is a power within us which howls
at the moon. And then the old man drew
the bow across and the strings vibrated sad
and dusty answers back at me. The room
was responding to him in its turn.
This reciprocity was all we had
between us and it had begun to bloom
Judaic flowers: Oistrakh, Heifetz, Stern.

Get real, I said. These are the grandfathers
you never knew and felt no strong desire
ever to meet. Old schlocks gone to the fire
with their doilies and candles; infrequent bathers
in the Protestant sun, solemn upholders
of precedent, given to self abuse
and cancer, eternal bearers of bad news.
I was an unwilling fly on their shoulders.
I believed my own propaganda like
anyone might. I didn't want them, wished
them gone. With the floor vibrating under
my feet, I was waiting for the music to strike
some respect into me so I should feel ravished
by its omnipotent *yes* of squeal and thunder.

When thunder came I let the violet seep
into my bloodstream along with all that
ravishment. I was in a shallow sleep
where dreams move in insidious flat
planes under the watchful eye of a mind
left unattended. And then cherries! A wood
full of cherries appeared somewhere on my blind
side, disorientating, the colour of blood.
A memory of rolling down the hill
gorged with black cherries, my mother looking on
then rolling with me. And so everything
kept rolling. I could imagine being ill
with too much sweetness, finding myself alone
with a stretch of wire, a single metal string.

Resin along horsehair. My brother stood
in front of the open window, tightening strings.
A G-Plan coffee table, more glass than wood,
supported an ashtray and some tea things.
The suburbs were singing. He wore a quiff,
Cliff Richard style. Felix Bartholdy
waited on the stand. There was something stiff
about the day, stiff and melancholy
as the furniture. Slowly I was waking
from nightmare to a kind of lovely music.
My brother played. He really was good at it.
I accompanied him, my fingers aching
with tension and all the summer air thick
with the sound of the colour violet.

Rousing those violets, the old man ran
a couple of scales through his withered hands.
Light from the stained glass window threw bands
of colour across his fingers. He began
some other piece whose name I now forget.
I felt like leaving. I didn't want to be
wound into this, not here, in Kingsbury,
North London, staring at that violet
plush in the open case. I felt, as they say,
strangely moved. It was a long time ago.
Some thirty years. Even now the faint buzz
of the lower strings can give me away.
It's nice to think of a colour called Solferino.
Of course, I didn't then know what it was.

Gina Waldman

Souvenir from Libya

I was nineteen years old, working my first summer job at a British engineering company in Tripoli, Libya. One very warm day in the office, as the air conditioner hummed monotonously and I typed some technical documents on my Olivetti typewriter, Mohammed, the company driver, suddenly barged into my office, his eyes full of rage. Banging his fist on my desk, determination in his voice, he barked menacingly, "Don't expect me to take you home today!" Afraid to ask him why, I simply watched the anger seep through his narrowed eyes.

Mohammed turned to leave my office, and one of the company's engineers came in, proclaiming, "Israel is at war with Egypt. It's just come over the radio, haven't you heard? The Israeli army is already in the Sinai desert and is advancing. Pretty soon we shall have to switch to Israeli currency!"

It was June 5, 1967, the beginning of the Six-Day War between Israel and its Arab neighbours. Egypt and four other Arab countries had amassed 100,000 troops, thousands of tanks, and hundreds of jet bombers on Israel's borders. Egypt had closed the international waters of the Straits of Tiran to Israeli ships and kicked out all UN peacekeeping forces in the Sinai. Israel was forced to launch a pre-emptive strike.

For days before the war broke out, we had heard broadcasts from mosques and the Egyptian radio station, inciting fellow Muslims to join the jihad, the so-called holy war, and "drive the Jews into the sea." Just a week earlier, I had been visiting at my aunt Rina's home, when we heard shouts outside: *"Ya biladi Falistin! Falistin!* (My country, Palestine! Palestine!)"

Thousands of people had taken to the streets, carrying huge anti-Israel banners. My aunt took my cousins and me into her bedroom, closed all the shades, turned off the lights, and asked us to be very quiet. The crowd marched toward the centre of Tripoli for an anti-Israel rally, which ended with the blood-curdling cry, "Death to the Jews!"

Aunt Rina had lived through the 1945 Mara'ot — a pogrom in Tripoli where rioting mobs murdered about 150 Jews, attacked and wounded scores more, destroying five synagogues, and looted nearly all the rest. During the Mora'ot my mother had jumped from the rooftop of her home to escape, eventually hiding in the home of a Christian neighbour.

This time, while the demonstrators raged on outside, Aunt Rina sat on the bed and prayed in Hebrew, asking G-d to spare us. When the crowd finally dispersed I was able to go home.

I was alone in my office, surrounded by strangers — Europeans, mostly British Christians, who could neither comprehend nor understand my fears. Part of me was elated that Israel might win the war, and the other part was apprehensive about the repercussions my family and I would suffer at the hands of the Libyan government and the masses. Jews in Libya were barely tolerated, living in constant fear even under ordinary circumstances. All this even though Jews had lived in Libya for over 2,500 years, prior to the Arab Muslim conquest that began in the seventh century. In 1492 Spanish and Portuguese Jews fled to Libya, escaping the Spanish Inquisition, and the two separate communities lived together for close to five centuries.

Though Libyan Jews were a vibrant part of society, and despite the fact that we contributed a great deal to the country, Libya persisted in its refusal to grant us citizenship. The Libyan government, moreover, was single-minded in the way it persecuted us: arbitrary arrests were common, we were stripped of basic human rights and we were divided from the rest of the Libyan population. I knew a war with Israel would further inflame anti-Jewish sentiment and resentment, giving mobs carte blanche to indulge their worst instincts.

The sharp ring of the telephone broke the heavy silence that had fallen in my office. It was my mother, her voice quivering. "Don't come home! Mobs are rioting in the streets. They have burned your father's warehouse to the ground, and now they have come to burn our house down too. Whatever you do, don't come home, and be careful!" She was crying, panicked.

My eyes clouded with tears, I instinctively ran into my boss's office. "I can't go home, Mr Hubert. Can you help me?" I pleaded, my voice trembling. A tall, imposing man in his fifties, Mr Hubert raised his bushy eyebrows and said with impeccable British calm, "Sit down, my dear. Tell me all about it, will you?" I tried to muffle my sobs, putting my hand in front of my mouth. My voice cracked. I paused and calmed my breathing.

"Mr Hubert, Jewish properties are being plundered and burned everywhere. My mother just called me to tell me that a group of demonstrators poured gasoline around the perimeter of our apartment building and prepared to set it ablaze. Our Egyptian neighbour convinced the rioting mob that my family had already left the country and that no Jews were in the building. He said he was the only person living there and cautioned the mob not to burn the home of a Muslim brother."

The demonstrators started to argue with each other, my mother had told me. Since they could not decide whether or not they should burn the building, they agreed to leave a watchman outside, to make sure my family truly had left.

"My returning home is bound to give my family away," I continued. "I must find a place to hide!" Silence followed; the now-now-dear-let's-see-what-we-can-do kind of silence. I felt churning in the pit of my stomach. Mr Hubert looked at me with compassion, nodding pensively. I registered with relief that he felt my anguish. He smiled at me encouragingly. "I will see what I can do." I went back to my office to wait. I was swept away by sadness, yearning to be with my family.

Brian, one of the British engineers in the firm, agreed to take me home to stay with him and his wife. As we left, I could see a cloud of smoke coming from the warehouse district where fire was fiercely consuming my father's warehouse, like a wild beast consuming its prey. Thousands of surplus military blankets, tents, boots and bales of clothing which my father sold to oil companies throughout Libya, curled up into a dark, black cloud. The building was licked by savage flames that left behind a desolate landscape of charred ruins.

Instead of fighting the flames, firemen stood on top of their engines, raising clenched fists and shaking hands with the excited crowd, like members of a soccer team congratulating one another after a good game. The authorities did not pursue the rioters, because they themselves condoned the violence.

Only after several days of rampage and destruction did the authorities finally bring some order and impose a curfew. That is, when the fires spread to Muslim property, the government responded. According to the news that trickled through some foreign broadcasts, reporters who came to Tripoli to cover the riots were sent back, without ever being allowed to leave the airport.

For over three weeks, Brian and his wife Deirdre gave me a safe place to live. They took me to work with them and tried their best to make life as normal as possible for me. In the evenings, however, our silence was laced with anxiety. Time stood still.

Each night, I lay in my small bed in their home. Nothing in the room looked familiar, and I felt disoriented. The only things I recognised were my turquoise dress and the sandals I had worn the day I went into hiding.

The prospect of never seeing my family again kept me awake, frightening me more than the drunken violence outside. Shadows gathered in my room in the stillness of the warm night. I dreamt of leaving Libya with my family.

My dream filled me with hope, but I never allowed myself to collude with the conspiracy of my dream; I was afraid it might shatter. Pre-dawn light finally caressed me to sleep and every morning I awoke to the smell of scrambled eggs and buttered white bread.

Brian and Deidre barely knew me and had never met my family, yet they opened their home to me at their own personal risk. People helping or hiding Jews were often threatened and harassed. I felt a heavy responsibility for having placed Brian and Deirdre in possible danger.

I often wondered why they helped me. I guess they did it for the same reason my Muslim neighbour saved my family's life. Despite the evil surrounding us — the murder of innocents, the torching and looting of properties — there was still goodness in some people.

During one of our phone conversations my mother told me that a school friend of mine had been raped and murdered, and that her family, including eight brothers and sisters had been shot to death. Deborah had been a shy nineteen-year-old, with a mass of brown curls and a slender figure that moved with the grace of a dancer. As I hid in Brian and Deirdre's home Libyan soldiers had come to Deborah's home, claiming they were going to escort the family to a refugee camp. The soldiers claimed it was for the family's own protection, since it was becoming increasingly dangerous for Jews to stay in their own homes. Deborah's family packed a few belongings, then disappeared forever.

My anxiety grew into profound fear. I shared my feelings with Brian and Deirdre and they began to make plans to secure my family's escape. At a meeting with trusted friends they discussed plans to smuggle my family and me to safety. A company in England regularly shipped heavy machinery to our engineering company, using very large wooden crates. My family and I would hide in these crates, with a built-in air passage, and clandestinely be shipped out of the country.

Yet during my sleepless nights I saw my mother suffocating within the walls of a wooden crate. My fear turned into panic. I became consumed with nightmares about being found by the authorities, thrown in jail, and raped by my jailers, or dying a stifling death inside a box. Was this the beginning of the end for us?

As my depression increased, I resolved that I would not be catapulted into a state of utter despair. Instead, I would cope with the tumultuous events around me by developing a strategy to leave the country through legal means.

Like most Jews, my parents were not allowed to have a phone, so they had to go upstairs to our Egyptian neighbour to call me. Brian and Deirdre did not have a phone either, which made communication with my parents difficult and infrequent. Sometimes Brian would walk me to his English neighbour's house, so I could call my parents — very risky after curfew.

Every day, very early in the morning, Brian and Deirdre took me to the office with them, so as not to leave me alone in the house. I had to bend down in the back seat of the car, to avoid being seen by his neighbours and the young Arab kids roaming the streets. Still, one day, as we drove past a group of young boys, they started throwing stones at Brian's car. Luckily we got away safely.

Toward the end of June, three weeks after I had gone into hiding, I received a call at the office from my cousin Moris. His voice full of excitement, he informed me that the Libyan government was allowing all the Jews to leave the country. The government was freezing all of our assets — properties, lands, homes, and bank accounts — and they would permit us only to take a few suitcases and a little bit of money, but we would be free to go.

At first, I was elated by the prospect of leaving. Soon, however, my happiness clouded over with apprehension of economic uncertainty, and I became angry. Yes, we would be free, but we would have no resources. We would have to emigrate to some country where we would not know anyone, not own anything, and not have any money. We would end up in some country where my family had never been and where the language would be foreign to us. I did not even know where we would end up — England? France? Italy?

The most important thing, I began repeating to myself like a mantra, was that we were going to be free. Free! I had not seen my family for almost a month. Finally we would be reunited.

A few evenings later, I walked into my home. I was greeted by mustiness, mingled with the lavish scent of my father's pipe tobacco. The shades were drawn, the house was dark. My father sat mute on the edge of his bed, smoking his pipe, his face haggard and unshaven. His eyes looked at me blankly. The family's tower of strength now sat silent, beaten and powerless, a wounded tiger in retreat. I wanted to say something to him, but my voice broke. I tried to swallow the sob in my throat.

My mother greeted me warmly, but her voice was grave, and her eyes welled with tears. Her dark hair was pulled tightly into a bun on the back of her head. "We can't open the windows," she cautioned me, "or in any way show that we live in the house. The man the mob left is still outside, watching us. You must walk and talk very quietly during the day. At night, the watchman is gone, and it's alright to make noise."

Nonno, my grandfather, put his shaking hand on my head, his voice breaking. As he sobbed, he blessed me by reciting a Hebrew prayer: "*Baruch atah adonai eloheinu melech ha'olam..*" This ritual, a symbol of his religious observance, reconnected me with my Jewish heritage.

Over the few days that followed, the family sat together around the table, but we did not touch the food. We walked noiselessly around the house. We did not speak much about our future. Stillness filled the warm stuffy air. At times, the silence was so strong, I could hear it — the silence of fear. It slowly crept into my soul.

I spent many hours alone in my room, immersed in my thoughts. I felt as though my youth had been snatched away from me, ripped out of my hands and broken like fragile glass, shattering into pieces all around me. I wanted to scream with anger, but my screams never escaped the dark spot in my soul.

As much as my family and I wanted to leave the oppressive environment surrounding us, we recognised that our perpetrators would dictate the terms of our departure. We would be given no time to plan or make provision for the future, a reality that caused in me a strange mix of feelings, from a sense of deprivation to one of relief.

A few days after my return home, a firm knock on the door broke the never-ending silence. Fearful, we didn't open it. Minutes later, however, we heard our neighbour's voice, "Open up, it's me." I opened the door.

Our neighbour was accompanied by a uniformed officer — a man in his forties, tall and broad-shouldered. He had olive skin, a thick-trimmed moustache and jet-black hair that was greased with brilliantine. He wore a starched military khaki uniform and shiny, black leather boots, adding weight to his already-imposing figure. The colourful stripes adorning his lapel signalled his authority.

I glanced at the officer, taking in his stiffness, but when his expressionless eyes met my gaze, I lowered mine. He asked for my father. I stepped back, allowing him to enter our dark, musty living room. The officer told my family that if we wanted to leave the country, we needed to give him our travel documents. He would procure our exit visas for us and return the documents in a few days.

My father went to the safe to get our travel documents. Jews were not allowed to have passports, because we were not recognised as citizens. Without proper passports, we were severely restricted from travelling outside Libya. My father returned, holding the documents in his hand, a worried look on his face. He hesitated. *Didn't Deborah's family also surrender their identification papers to the police? Didn't the police tell them they were going to take the whole family to a military camp, for their own safety?*

As my father stood holding the documents in his hand, nobody spoke. After a few minutes, he handed over the documents and whispered to the officer, "Please follow

326

me. I want to speak with you privately." The officer followed him to the living room, and my father closed the door behind them. Later on, my father told me about the conversation.

"I can make out a cheque for you," my father had said. "You can cash it today, in exchange for providing my family and me a police escort, to see us safely to the airport." The officer became excited. "Sure, sure," he replied, "you can count on me!" He left with the cheque in his hand.

A few days later, the officer returned with our visas. A month had passed since the Six-Day War and Radio Cairo had reported Egypt's victory over Israel. Occasionally, my father was able to tune in to the BBC. The government jammed it constantly, but we were able to hear that Israel, in fact, had won the war and taken Jerusalem. We did not know what to believe.

In the midst of this confusion, we found out that the few planes leaving Tripoli were full, as a result of the panic the riots had created. Brian and Deirdre came to the rescue, calling on their friendship with the British Airlines director. By taking off seven British passengers, the director was able to secure seven seats for my family. Destination: Malta, a small island in the British protectorate off the North African coast. We were finally leaving.

The night prior to our departure, I could not sleep, and I doubt anyone else could either. Pacing the floor, I could not make up my mind about what I wanted to pack. I was allowed only one bag. Should I just take clothes? What about my school diplomas and other mementoes, which were so much part of my life? And the photographs! I picked up my photo album and slid my fingers over its black lacquered cover. It was hand painted with the image of Tripoli's castle in pale pink, a gray-blue mosque next to it, and a calm turquoise seascape with white surf hitting against the sea walls. "Souvenir of Libya" was painted in gold letters at the bottom. This serene cover was such an ironic contradiction to the political turbulence plaguing my country.

Leafing through my album, I saw photos of myself at boarding school in Switzerland, with my closest and dearest friends, and I saw photos of myself posing with my cousins at Giorginpopli Beach. The black-and-white photos brought back the summer days I had spent swimming in the warm water, eating yummy *panini be-tonno u felfel* — tuna sandwiches with hot peppers — that Nonna, my grandma, used to pack for me.

These photos were my memories, and I knew I had to take them with me. I walked toward my bag, took out my only winter sweater and replaced it with the photo album. Shortly after, my mother walked into the room and said, "Make sure you take some warm clothes with you." I nodded. I knew my friends and cousins would keep me warm.

At 5.00 a.m. the next morning, the doorbell rang. Two soldiers wearing fatigues and army boots stood at the door, with machine guns strapped around their shoulders. In a monotonous tone, one of them said, "We are taking you to the airport. We are the escort you asked for. *Yella*. Let's go." The soldiers ran downstairs to wait for us, their boots making a staccato sound as they moved with agility down the tiled stairs.

A military truck with another two soldiers waited outside our home. These soldiers greeted us with hostile silence and penetrating stares, and I was struck by the extent to which they were consumed by hatred. Were they really driving us to the airport, or were they driving us to our death?

The military truck drove only a few blocks, leaving us outside a hotel on the outskirts of town. The officer my father had bribed was waiting there. My father approached him. "Why are your soldiers not escorting us all the way to the airport?" my father asked, "Remember, you and I had a deal." The officer's face turned red, and his veins swelled at the temples. In a rage, he shouted, "Do you think that we have nothing better to do than to protect Jews? You want to go to the airport, take the bus!"

The officer boarded the military truck, where all the soldiers laughed and jeered at us, leaving us stranded on the street with our suitcases. Shortly after, an airport bus pulled up. As my family boarded, I noticed that the driver and the conductor were the only other people on the bus.

As soon as the bus set off, the conductor asked to see our passports and airline tickets. As his fingers slid across the pages of our documents, I whispered to my mother, "It's unusual for a bus conductor to check passports, don't you think?" She nodded. Something was not right and I felt frightened.

I leaned my head against the cool glass window. In the airless heat, my throat felt dry; my head ached; and my hands were feverish. It was about six in the morning and dawn was breaking, lighting up the sky. There were a few palm trees scattered along the arid landscape, and the silhouettes of a few laden donkeys appeared in the distance. The rooftops of scattered huts shimmered in the warm morning light as the town moved away from us.

Engrossed in the stillness of the landscape, I pondered the unpredictability of our future. From a distance, I heard the Muslim call to prayer, *Allah Akbar*! (G_d is great!) Suddenly, without warning, the bus stopped. I shot up out of my seat and walked to the front of the bus. "What's going on? Why did you stop?" I asked the conductor.

"There is something wrong with the engine," he answered. "I will have to go and call a taxi for you." He got off the bus and squatted down, looking under the engine. Drops of perspiration trickled down his nose. When I called down to ask if he knew what was wrong with the bus, he waved his arms around his head but remained silent.

The conductor returned to his seat, muttering, "There is something wrong, can't you see? There is something wrong." I turned to look at the rest of my family, Nonna Regina, my grandmother who was always in control, appeared anguished and fragile. Nonno, my grandfather, gave me a thin, bitter smile and continued to pray. My mother was pale, tears streaming down her cheeks. My father stared stonily out of the window, as though to blot out any danger that might confront us. I felt my heart aching.

I approached the conductor. "If you get us to the airport I will get my father to compensate you well," I said with a trembling voice. "We can make a deal."

"You Jewish whore!" he spat accusingly. "You are killing our brothers in Palestine!" His face was red, eyes intense with rage. He dismissed me by raising his arm toward me, then got off the bus and disappeared into the distance.

A knot grew in my throat. Where was he going? I turned to my mother and told her I was going to get help. I looked around furtively and then darted off the bus. As I ran, my stomach burned and my legs quivered. My face and neck dripped with sweat. My fury kept me going.

From a distance, about half a mile away, I discerned a square, concrete building with men standing outside. I was passing by a *kahwa,* a roadside café, where men congregated, drank coffee and smoked water pipes. Women were not permitted entry, as Muslim tradition strictly forbade them from being in the same room as men who were not close members of the family.

When I got close I heard loud, excited voices fused with the Libyan national anthem, the "Jamahiriya" on a blaring radio. The men in the café stood to attention, bellowing, "*Ya biladi, Ya biladi…*" with passion and fervour. Suddenly the singing stopped. The announcer introduced General Gamal Abdel Nasser, Egypt's president. As Nasser spoke the excitement and anger surged, a fire fused with hatred. "We must free our brothers in Palestine…"

What if these men noticed me, a woman walking alone in a semi-deserted area at 6.00am? I could easily be killed or worse still, raped. Perspiration soaked through my dress. My legs stiffened with fear, but the voices battling inside me slowly subsided. My courage was rekindled by the thought that my actions could affect the outcome of a whole lifetime for my family and myself.

I began walking gingerly, as though stepping on flowers, past the *kahwa*, looking straight ahead. I approached a gas station, and the pungent smell of gasoline invaded my nostrils. I asked the attendant if I could use the phone. He looked at me with curious eyes, then pointed to a small cabin. When I entered, I thought my heart would stop. The bus conductor was inside the cabin, using the phone. "Yes," I heard him say, "everything is under control." As he faced the small entrance, he saw me, and his face turned ashen. He hung up but kept his hand on the receiver.

"I need to use the phone," I said. Narrowing his eyebrows, the conductor gave me a stern look and kept his hand on the receiver. The room was small, dusty and silent. A naked bulb hung on an old electric cord, gleaming a dim light.

I stood motionless, facing the conductor. I had no desire to look at his cold questioning eyes. I simply wanted him to go away, to leave us alone. I prayed that he would not physically assault me, for I knew I would fight back, even if I had to pay with my life. My throat was tight, my eyes itchy, my head pounding.

I thought of the past few weeks, image after image burning in my mind. Our only way out was through a phone call. *I must seize that phone!*

I snatched the receiver from the conductor's hand, turned toward the wall to avoid his gaze, and dialled, calling Brian's English neighbour. "We are in danger," I said, speaking in English as fast as I could, for fear the conductor would understand what I was saying and sabotage my only escape plan. "We are on the road to the airport, about a kilometre away from the first gas station as you leave town. You must tell Brian. You must come quickly. We are in danger! We are in danger!" As soon as I heard, "We'll be there," I hung up.

I turned toward the door to leave, but three men blocked the exit — the conductor, the gas station attendant and a third man. The conductor was in the middle. He stared at me. The air was thick, suffocating. There was a moment of stillness.

Freedom was on the other side of that doorway.

With a burst of energy, I pushed my way through the men and ran, noticing the expression of surprise and bewilderment as I passed. I ran and ran and ran. Although it took me about twenty minutes, it seemed as though I were running for hours. By the time I reached the bus, I was completely out of breath.

As I approached, the first thing I noticed was the driver standing near the bus. Trotting closer, I saw a pool of liquid beneath the vehicle — gasoline that the driver had discharged from the tank! I realised the plan was to set the bus on fire and my heart hammered. My family was still inside, still silent.

The driver was holding something tightly — a box of matches. Fixing my eyes on the matchbox, I followed every move of the driver's hands. I looked back quickly to see how far away the fast-approaching conductor was.

The conductor caught up with me at the bus, and he and the driver both stood facing me, staring, saying nothing. Peasants on donkeys and people on their way to work began congregating around, whispering to one another. One young boy pointed at the bus and shouted "*Yehuda*! (Jews!)" As my gaze travelled from the matches in the conductor's hands to the road behind the bus, where I scoured the landscape for Brian's jeep, everything seemed to move very slowly.

Suddenly a jeep appeared on the horizon, followed by another jeep, and I began to sob. Brian and his friend raced up to the bus, saw the pool of gasoline, and motioned to me to get my family off immediately. Brian looked at the driver and said, "I am a mechanical engineer. Would you like me to look at the engine and tell you what is wrong?" The driver said, "No, no, we have called for help, thank you." Neither the driver nor the conductor tried to stop us. They just stared in disbelief, as my family quickly crammed into the two jeeps and sped off.

When we arrived at the airport, a young man asked to see our passports. He looked at our documents and exclaimed in disbelief, "Bubil family? You are not supposed to be here!" If we had any doubts about a plot to kill us, they were promptly dispelled.

Customs officials handed us sheets and sheets of forms to fill out. My hands trembled, and I had such difficulty holding the pen; filling out the paperwork seemed to take forever.

Next, the porters refused to load our luggage onto the plane, because we were Jews and we therefore had to load our own bags. The officer in charge of passport control additionally commanded my father, "Hand over the keys to your car and tell me where it is parked. I have a big family, I need a big car." My father did as he was told.

Finally, we all boarded the plane. As the steward closed the plane door, I counted the members of my family. My uncle was missing. "Stop!" I yelled. I ran back to passport control, where my uncle was standing in the centre of the room, encircled by porters and airport workers. They were spitting at him and waving their fists, laughing cruelly.

"We will kill you and cut you into pieces!" I heard someone shout. I grabbed my uncle's hand, cold with fear, and said, "Let's go! The plane is leaving!"

Forty-five minutes later, we landed in Malta. Forty-five minutes from oppression to freedom.

Nurses, doctors and stretchers greeted us. The crew did not know what had happened to us before boarding the plane, but just by looking at our faces, they decided to radio in for an ambulance. Struggling through sobs, we tried to express our gratitude to the nurses and the plane crew. "Do you need help?" they asked. "What happened to you?"

"There are still Jews in Libya," my father cautioned us in Arabic. "We can't say anything, or there may be retaliation." We all looked at each other and cried uncontrollably. My mouth felt dry. When I tried to ask the nurse for water, words would not come out; I felt as though I were being choked.

In Malta, we boarded a plane to Rome. After a short flight, we landed in the Italian capital. We saw a large, friendly crowd waiting for their relatives. They were waving their arms, talking and laughing. A handsome young man winked at me and with a dashing smile said, "*Ciao!*" Then I looked up and saw the most beautiful sight — a sign which said *Benvenuti a Roma!*

Shelley Weiner

The Vote

There was once a poor young maid who found work in a great house in Johannesburg. The maid's name was Martha and her employer's name was Juliette, and each of them thought how very lucky she was to have come upon the other. Juliette, a renowned hostess who was married to one of the city's leading financiers, had been searching far and wide for a malleable, presentable servant whom she could train for the eventual position of cook-general in her Lower Houghton home. And Martha had been seeking stability. She'd been looking for a live-in position with good prospects so that a regular sum of money could be sent to the black township where her children were growing up. Despite her apparent youth and innocence, Martha had already produced two off-spring — thanks to a feckless lad called Jim, who'd kept wooing and impregnating her. But, she assured Juliette, she was finished with all that now.

"That's over, madam," she declared. "I tell you, madam, I've had it with men."

"And who looks after the children for you?" Juliette had had bitter experience of maids with dependents. They tended to let one down.

"My sister," said Martha. "She's very reliable."

"Ah," said Juliette. She knew all about sisters. And so-called cousins and aunts. They usually turned out to be professional childminders who lacked long-term commitment and eventually dumped their charges on their natural mama. Or worse. Anyway, one couldn't cater for all eventualities, and Martha seemed keen and unspoilt and reasonably intelligent. She decided to take her on.

"Thank you, madam," said Martha, with effusive gratitude. "You won't be sorry, madam — you'll see."

"I hope not," Juliette said — not in quite the right sort of tone for an artistic soul with liberal inclinations. So she added a few pretty phrases about Martha's future happiness and the excellence of the staff quarters in the Keller home and the mutual benefits that would result from their working relationship.

"If you're fair to me, Martha, I'll be fair to you. I see you have an excellent reference from that Mrs…"

"Mrs Swart, madam. I was there three years but the family had to move to Krugersdorp and it was difficult for me, with the children here in Soweto…"

"I understand. Now let me show you round the house and explain the sort of thing I'll expect you to do. As you can see, we have many valuable things around here and, if there's one thing I can't stand, it's a clumsy girl…"

Martha started work the following Monday. The day before, she had arrived with a single small suitcase and taken occupation of her room. Juliette had introduced her to the facilities. Everything, she'd pointed out, was of the very best.

"Here's your toilet and basin," she'd said. "And very soon you'll be getting your very own bath. Mr Keller and I have always believed that servants should be treated properly — we're not like some people."

"Yes, madam. I can see that." She could indeed. At the Swarts, she'd had to drag buckets of water from the kitchen to her room at night and there had been no prospect of a basin — let alone a proper working bath. It seemed that she'd been lucky with this job. Very lucky.

"I'll leave you to settle in now, Martha," Juliette had said. "At six o'clock I want you to come to the kitchen to meet Mr Keller — he should be back from golf by then. Our daughter, Joanne, will also be here I expect. She's at university, studying dentistry — God knows why a girl like her would want to do something like that. We tried to put her off, but she's stubborn. No-one's ever been able to tell Joanne what to do…"

Martha had arranged her possessions and tried on the

uniform which was provided with the job. A nice one, too. Pink overalls with a frilly white cap and apron. Mrs Swart had never stretched to anything like that. And as for Mr Swart — he'd hardly acknowledged that Martha existed except when the food was overcooked or his shirt not properly ironed. Mr Keller, though, struck her as a gentleman. A proper gentleman.

"How do you do, Martha?" he'd said. "We hope you'll be happy with us."

"Yes, master."

She was absolutely sure she would, for the job offered more than any girl could reasonably expect.

Meanwhile Juliette, in her turn, was equally certain that she would derive long-term satisfaction from her new employee. "I think we've got a winner here, Stanley," she confided to her husband at the end of Martha's first week. "I have a feeling that she's exactly right for us."

It was a perfect match. Juliette was convinced — and she never had reason to change her mind — that Martha was heaven-sent. It amused her to think that God must have set aside a moment from his interminable sorting of man and wife to allocate this maid to her madam.

As the years passed Martha became an integral part of the Keller home, renowned for her loyalty, her sobriety, her celibacy and — most of all — her excellent Duck à l'Orange. Her cooking, generally, had blossomed under Juliette's guidance and she had soon become capable of producing lavish dinners for up to twenty without additional help. She was never clumsy and invariably cheerful and, all in all, an asset whom Juliette prized even more than her three-carat diamond engagement ring. She always made sure that Martha's salary was well above the market rate.

And Martha, whose appreciation of her good fortune in finding a position with the Kellers never dimmed, repaid her madam with a steadfast fidelity.

"You can count on me, madam," she avowed, when Juliette expressed apprehension about a forthcoming dinner party or a houseful of guests or when Mr Keller (who worked exceedingly hard to support their Lower Houghton life-style) was taken to hospital with a heart attack. He recovered, but Juliette's confidence in his reliability had been shaken. The fixed point in her life had become Martha. Martha, who turned up each day in the kitchen, rain or shine.

Joanne, meanwhile, had graduated as a dentist and married another dentist called Geoffrey and — in her strong-headed way — had announced to her parents that she and her husband had decided to emigrate to England. The future looked more promising there.

"I can't tell you how upset I am," Juliette confided to Martha. She had started confiding in her maid more and more as the years went by. "Not that we've seen very much of her recently — once a week if we've been lucky. Still — England's so far away. You know how one worries about them…"

"I know, madam. Children can be such a worry."

Martha's two were growing up under the tutelage of a series of sisters and cousins and aunts. Their mother saw them regularly and was proud that — thanks to the Kellers — she could afford to have them well educated. But Jason, her son, had started running with a wild crowd, a political crowd, and was in danger of getting into deep trouble with the police. And Angel, her fourteen-year-old daughter, was pregnant.

"Children," sighed Martha. "You're lucky, madam, that you only have the one." She didn't share with Juliette her anxieties about Jason and Angel for that was not the way things worked. And Juliette, who also knew the rules, rarely asked.

Instead, she kept Martha closely informed about Joanne's preparations for life abroad and wept profusely on her shoulder when the day of her daughter's departure finally came.

"Don't cry, madam," Martha said. "I'm here. I'm not going anywhere."

"Thank goodness for that," said Juliette, meaning it with all her heart. And she said it again — even more

338

fervently, if possible — on the awful day of Mr Keller's second coronary. This time he died.

So Juliette was the sole occupant of the vast master bedroom with its "his and hers" dressing-rooms and spacious en-suite bathroom, while Martha still resided in the same little room she'd been allocated sixteen years before. The bath that had been installed soon after her employment had commenced was cracked and discoloured.

But Martha didn't complain. On the contrary, she still believed implicitly in her good fortune and, with her madam, bemoaned the upsurge of violence in the country and the fact that Lower Houghton was not longer a safe place in which to live. By now, many of Juliette's friends had left South Africa and, despite all the measures she had taken to secure her home, Juliette confessed that she was often frightened at night.

"You mustn't worry, madam," said Martha with her usual show of conviction. She didn't let on that she'd heard Jason and his friends threatening to plunder the suburbs, to kill the whites, to reclaim their rights. They were wrong. She'd tried to tell them they were wrong. But it seemed they were talking a different language. How strange it was that she could understand her madam's fear better than her children's anger. How much more effective she felt consoling her madam than trying to calm all that bitter young wrath.

So she spent more and more time in Lower Houghton, even on her once-weekly day off. A panic-button was installed to link Juliette's suite with that of her servant and, as a show of appreciation for Martha's devotion, the maid's room was enlarged and a new improved bath (with shower unit) was installed. Martha was delighted.

Her delight was somewhat dampened, however, when — a few months later — Juliette announced that, despite all the security measures and the staunchness of her servant, she had decided she couldn't continue living in South Africa any longer. Her nerves were at breaking point.

"I'm a reasonable person, Martha," she declared. "You know how reasonable I am. And it's not as though I don't believe that things could be shared more equally — that the blacks don't have any rights."

"Of course, madam," said Martha, who had long stopped associating herself with the blacks. She'd stopped thinking of herself as anything but Juliette's maid. That was all.

"It's just the way things are being handled," Juliette continued. "The violence. The chaos. Now that Mandela's been let out of prison, I don't know where it will all end..."

"Who knows, madam? Who knows..."

That was when Juliette made her proposition.

"Joanne and Geoffrey have found me a flat in London," she said. "It's a very comfortable place, I believe, in a smart part of London called St John's Wood."

"I see," said Martha.

"And I was thinking that if you wanted to come with me — there's a place for you there as well."

"For me?"

"Well, we've been together a long time, you and me, and I was hoping..."

"Me in London, madam?"

"Why not, Martha? I'd take care of you — you know that."

"I know that, madam, it's just..."

"You'd be much better off with me in London than with all the trouble about to break out over here. Think about it. I'd never force you, of course, but I believe it would be best. For both of us."

Martha thought about it. She pondered for days. So distracted was she that she broke an antique vase and forgot to add seasoning to the meatballs and finally, one morning, arrived in the kitchen more than half-an-hour late for work.

"You're not getting careless, are you?" asked Juliette, who had begun voicing her concern about Martha's latter-day absent-mindedness across various bridge tables in

Lower Houghton. "It's not like you, Martha. Is something the matter?"

"It's…"

"What? Tell me."

"This London business, madam, I can't decide."

"Well, time is getting short. You're leaving it very late. The packers are due in three weeks."

"I know, madam. I know." She paused, frowning and rumpled her apron uneasily. "Maybe if madam can give me the weekend off, I can go and speak to the children…?"

This was not a convenient request, for it required the postponement of a dinner party. The urgency of the situation, however, called for adaptability, so Juliette — who saw herself as infinitely flexible — agreed.

Martha went to Soweto, feeling alien and rather frightened on the crowded train. She wasn't accustomed to it any more — the crush, the smells, the noise. Her life had become so tranquil, so orderly, while her people, it seemed, had grown wild. The children had turned into crazy, drunken creatures. There was madness in their eyes. "Change is coming," they exalted to Martha. "Black South Africa. Can you imagine it? South Africa for all."

She tried to talk to them, to discuss her predicament with them — but instead of listening, they jeered at her. "Madam," they taunted, laughing hysterically. "Madam. Just wait. One of these days she'll be calling you madam."

"Sshhh," said Martha warningly, but they continued to tease. And finally she left them, she made her way home. Home to her room and her bath, which she filled with steaming water and the jasmine-scented grains Juliette had given her for Christmas. "Ahh," she luxuriated, lying back. "That's better."

The next day she told Juliette that she had decided to accompany her to London.

"Good," said Juliette briskly, successfully hiding her immense relief lest Martha should imagine that she was irreplaceable. That never worked, with servants. "We'll

341

have to get ourselves organised. Tomorrow I'll start making lists."

It was a brilliant campaign, orchestrated by Juliette with Martha, tireless Martha, carrying out the duties of a medium-sized regiment. Within weeks, the contents of the flat had been sorted, listed, pruned, packed and despatched for shipping in two vast containers. Juliette's personal possessions had been deposited into seven suitcases, five of which were being sent ahead as unaccompanied luggage.

"There," said Juliette with satisfaction when the final item had been packed. Martha was released to see to her own belongings which, fortunately, were not copious. The bulk fitted into a spare suitcase inherited from the late Mr Keller and the excess was taped into a large cardboard box.

All that remained was for the madam and her maid to be transported to the airport and for Juliette to be installed in her first class seat on South African Airways and for Martha to be squeezed into the economy accommodation at the rear.

It was unbelievable, she thought, holding her breath while the air hostess fastened her seat belt. Astonishing. She couldn't believe her luck. A girl from Soweto, to be travelling so far, in such style? If only her friends could see her — her aunts, her sisters, her children.

But no-one saw her. No-one noticed her much at all. Undeterred, she kept marvelling to herself as the aircraft climbed to its cruising altitude and dinner was served — served! To her! And the lights dimmed and she dozed and was woken for breakfast — again! Served again! Oh, how clever she'd been to have found such a job, to have kept such a job, to be flying here high above the clouds into a new world. Clever and lucky.

The new world, though, turned out to be remarkably similar to the old. With its towering apartment blocks, St John's Wood seemed to Martha much like Lower Houghton, and the flat in London almost replicated Juliette's Johannesburg abode. Much smaller, of course — but Juliette appeared delighted with it.

"It's gorgeous — don't you think so, Martha?" she gushed over her shoulder, as Joanne and Geoffrey led the way inside.

"Yes, very lovely, madam," Martha panted, following with the suitcases.

"Madam?" echoed Joanne, disbelievingly. "Surely, mother! You can't have her calling you that here."

"No, no. Of course not." Juliette patted her daughter placatingly, remembering the withering force of Joanne's scorn. "Martha, I forgot to tell you — you'd better call me Mrs Keller from now on. It's not — er — done in England to use the word madam. Things are different here."

"Yes, ma… Mrs Keller."

But things didn't turn out very different at all. Not really. Almost immediately, Martha slipped into the familiar routine. The laundry on Mondays, the kitchen on Tuesdays, the silver on Wednesdays, and so on. The only real change was that Juliette took to referring to her as "the domestic" rather than "my maid" — but that was only when other people were present. Alone, they remained on the same easy terms. "Don't worry, madam," said Martha, when Juliette grew tearful over the hurts inflicted on her by Joanne. "You mustn't take these things to heart. Children will be children."

Children. Martha couldn't prevent her own heart constricting when her mind dwelt on her own. Despite her huge efforts to keep her attention focused on her job and kind madam and great good fortune, she was lonely sometimes. She missed the sound of her language and the fellowship of other servants and the African light and the sun. But still — who was she to complain?

"So — aren't you glad you decided to come to London?" Juliette asked her after a few months. She had purchased new curtains for Martha's room and presented her with a portable black and white television set which Joanne and Geoffrey had discarded. Martha had thanked her effusively.

"Of course, madam. Of course I am."

343

"I tell you — South Africa's a good place to be out of at the moment. Everyone says so. With that election coming up, who knows what will happen. It's an explosive situation."

Juliette had read that in the papers. She'd always considered herself an apolitical person. Much more the creative type, she'd always said. But now, in London, everyone seemed to think she had to have an opinion on South Africa. More than an opinion — a passionate desire for equality, for justice, for peace. Which of course she had — in a theoretical way. At any rate, she wished the country well. It would be churlish not to, after all the material advantages it had lavished on her. And although she was happy to be in London, at odd moments she was beset by a tight knot of longing, an indefinable sense of loss.

"An explosive situation?" repeated Martha, alarmed. "Does madam really think it's going to be bad there? Mandela was on the television last night and he seemed calm, madam. He was talking about peace, forgiveness. Maybe it will be all right?"

"Oh, Mandela," Juliette said dismissively, leaving the room. How she wished she could stop thinking, talking, hearing about bloody South Africa. She had left it. Her life was here, in London. Surely a person was entitled to start afresh. Nelson Mandela, Nelson Mandela. Honestly — everyone singing his praises. What did they know? How could anyone who hadn't lived there begin to understand the complexities? Every day, in almost every news bulletin, there he was with his saintly face. And Juliette watched him and sometimes, despite herself, found she was believing, hoping, wishing, longing to be there, to be part of it. Then she caught herself, remembering how very fortunate she was to have got away.

And now they were saying she ought to vote.

"You are voting, aren't you Juliette?" everyone asked her.

"Naturally," she said, wishing they'd mind their own business.

"It must be such a privilege to be able to take part in something historic."

"Oh, it is, it is."

"And your housekeeper — what's-her-name…?"

"Martha."

"Yes, Martha. She must be excited. Is she going to vote?"

"I'm not sure. We haven't really discussed it."

"You really should."

"I suppose so," said Juliette.

So they did.

"Martha," she began that evening as the supper plates were being cleared. "Martha, I was wondering — about the elections, you know."

"Madam?"

"The elections in South Africa next week. For the new government. Apparently South Africans living abroad can vote too. People like me and…" She paused momentarily. "And you."

Martha didn't appear to notice the hesitation. She continued to clear the plates.

"Martha?"

"Madam?"

"Martha, are you going to vote? Do you want to vote?"

"Is madam going to vote?"

"Of course," said Juliette quickly. "Joanne and Geoffrey have offered me a lift. I'm sure you could come along too."

Martha carried on clearing in ponderous silence.

"Or else," Juliette continued, suddenly desperate to elicit a proper response from this woman who had — damn it, she had just about shared the best years of her life with her. Surely she, out of everyone, understood the conflict, the belonging, the not-belonging? "Or else — if you'd prefer it — we could go by taxi, me and you. We could go and vote together."

Martha stood still. She turned to Juliette and met her gaze. "Let's do that, madam. The two of us can go and vote together."

They sat alongside one another in the taxi. Only a few miles separated St John's Wood from Trafalgar Square, but the journey seemed longer and even more momentous than the flight from Johannesburg. At last they reached the South African embassy and joined the queue. An excited, jostling queue.

"All right, madam?" asked Martha, noticing for the first time that her employer was growing old. She seemed frail and uncertain in the boisterous crowd. Martha took her arm. Juliette didn't resist.

"I'm fine, Martha," she said, as they walked in step, side by side. "And you? How about you?"

Bart Wolffe

"Tonight, when the shadows return, so do the ghosts"

Eight o'clock in the morning and the sound of the milk cart. Two in the afternoon and the sound of the coca-cola vendor rattling his wares. No time has passed, however, because it's just one music, two beats. The milk pints have a slightly higher pitch than the litre bottles of coke. I bought the milk.

I said no time has passed. The witchdoctor's son is old now; he sits outside the window and curses, a cold phlegm through his tongue. He too came to the city and left his father's bones behind. Now, the sun is shining, a cool blaze in the light winter sky. Tonight, when the shadows return, so do the ghosts.

As the darkness deepens over the city the occasional streetlamp goes on the blink. It leaves deeper holes of shadow for not only the prostitutes but other creatures to hide. Holes for the subconscious, the primitive mind. Oh, but we don't like that word — primitive — though. We are busy building a city and it grows like new clothes over our naked skin, the skin of Africa, the dust. We will plant parks with foreign trees and the tourists will come with pennies from heaven, to purchase the masks we hide behind and to take photographs.

Tonight there will be no moon to speak of. And the stars will hide their spear tips behind the orange curtain of streetlights. It will be cold for the unemployed, the squatters, the beggars under yesterday's newspapers. The temperature will have dropped nearly twenty degrees from now. I will go out, for I have work to perform.

That is why I can sit here now, listening to the coca-cola man peddling his syrup even as he makes his way onto the avenue to the next block of flats.

Let me smoke a cigarette. For a moment, I feel today is a good day to give up smoking. It could be any day, but it isn't. Today is the second day of the month of August and the rent has not yet been paid. I am told it is the second of August the same way I am told my birthday was on such and such a day. The problem is that I can't remember being born. I have to take someone's word for it; my mother's. And she has no birth certificate to prove it.)

Perhaps that is the reason for wanting to sleep today. To get back and dream of that first soft shaping place where the blankets become my body the way a warm bath does, fitting me like a second skin, until I can't feel my legs anymore, where they begin and the blankets end. I lie here and watch the hills and valleys folding amongst the blankets and pillow while the radio is playing on the table and feel an itch begin. Rubbing my toes on my right foot against the toes on my left, my eyeballs roll in ecstasy.

The newscaster is mumbling on about ESAP — the economic structure adjustment programme, how we should all tighten our belts for the hard times ahead and how half a loaf is better than none, The government line again. As I am not strictly unemployed, it does not worry or disturb my peace. What does interrupt my pleasure is the sound of two neighbours.

Their voices crescendo in an argument next door. The walls of modern apartments are thin. It is not like home in my village. There, there is distance between our houses, even though they are made out of mud and cow-dung plastering. And there never were the noises of the city, the sirens of the President's cavalcade, or the fighting of strangers. Yes, there were no strangers in our village when I was a boy. Just the uncles that visited, bringing with them gifts of sweet things, blankets and new clothes from the city where they worked.

All my brothers and I knew we had to cross that bridge of history and burn it behind us. We were the educated, the lucky ones, who had a place at the mission school and

348

could read magazines. And we wanted those sweet things and the dollars that would buy them for us.

And how the girls from the city smelled so sweet and the beer came in bottles! But there was no work for me or my brothers. In the city, the glass is tearless, the windows do not cry. SALE flames out dryly in reds and yellows. NEW is a dirty word for last year's fashions. Thirst in the street where nothing grows. In offices, papers accumulate dead leaves like dust. Each word has a price but does not circulate. And so inflation grows and even milk costs more than a few weeks ago however many cows there are. It is the time of the drought years. The cows are all going to slaughter anyhow. The abattoirs are full and there will be meat upon the tables somewhere in Europe. Harare — the capital; its water supply stands at a muddy twenty percent of normal capacity. In a few months, it will be finished unless the rains come early this year. If the rains come at all this year, that is. So son, mother, cow, brother, all are waiting. Waiting for the rain... This is the only story. So many people become bitter in the midday heat. And still they wonder why there is no rain. No rain for the man who was once a boy and danced naked with his brother in the park fountain on his first visit to the city, when the moonlight played upon the silver coins falling from heaven. Then, Mwari — God — was a revelry in every breath. Then, all that was did sparkle. My brother Joe, he was the eldest of the four of us. He specialised in Mazdas and Datsuns and could remove any model from under its owner's eyes if the owner turned round for no longer than you could hold your breath. He died in the rain with the silver pieces of the broken windscreen falling all about him. But two thousand dollars, no questions asked, was more than enough to pay the family rent. It's easier than how Rose, my neighbour, must make her living. You can hear the pain of her stilettos on the pavement at night, crisp as frost and know that no short skirt can keep her warm, however many bodies lie beside her. Already, she is sick and does not find the customers so easily. She has two small children of her own. She, too, must pay the rent.

My brother Joe gave me the first watch I ever owned. We used to sell them on the street corners, as little as ten dollars, battery included, until every street-wise citizen had one. When I heard it tick away inside my head at night, I knew it was a bomb. A time bomb. Three o'clock now, three hours to go before I go to work.

I unload a cigarette from the hand-snug pack. Flick it out and up and light, inhale, feel the bite of smoke curl round and catch, breathe out, am ready now... Ready for nothing which is exactly what happens next...Ready for whatever must follow; dreamtime, time to think of time unchained. Time to talk, to lock up in an instant all of life for that's how long it took for the eye to say YES, to pick up a page and read. (And I've spent so much time inside this body which is the bomb, defusing time, that I'd forgotten how to say hello to life.) And now will there be time enough not to grow old, will there be time enough to re-live all the loves I've never had the chance to know? Other totems than my own simply remain as strangers. Uncried, these words of Africa, my page unheard by history's tribes numberlessly roaming, herds giddy, gourds empty, spilt goods and wrecked gods that roam the echoes of a drought wind's tongue...

"Go..."
"Come..."
"Go..."
"Come..."

Gone. Gone are the days of history. I can imagine, a moment, that I could go back across the river. To that place where my young bones were not yet stripped of childhood. Where the land was an open invitation to my stride, from far horizon to far horizon, with no rent waiting to be paid. But no, gone are the days when I would have walked a good half-mile through the summer screen of my own sweet sweat and having reached the little bridge by the side of the track that lead to the dam, followed a watercourse of privacy; my own private,

350

independent path. In my mind, I see myself there yesterday, amidst the downstream rocks and undergrowth, where I won't observe another face but for the green-headed lizard that runs the ramparts of his bouldered fortress, checking for intruders; those little insects that he quickly despatches with a soft, flick-eyed tongue. It seems that I am still a young stone which still can be rung, dripping moisture and sweating juice. The paint is not yet dry in my eyes, I gaze with wonder at the wind's warm rhythm that bends the reeds before me, while a beetle whispers in the leaf mulch underfoot.

In these few feet of stumbling rock and watery imprint, there is promise that my thoughts are the first to travel with me. No other man Friday has been. Let me travel on down this land of my memories.

Back in the bush do I track between a puff-adder and a paw-paw tree, and there is me. Home. Growing up like a gangle of branches, all bity and berried, bright with ideas and never a boring moment. I have listened to the Mbira, instrument of Africa made from the gut of a gourd, speak in my hand. It speaks the wind's voice, rattling in the reeds of a far-hung vlei. I have seen the slow river wind, serene, round rock and bend. And I have heard the sun whisper in tongue of honey in the hollow tree. And summer's come. Feet, true with perspiration, stamp down on dusty ground to proclaim in the way of ancestors the coming of the rain. For the rain is the only rent we need. Without it, there is no food to keep us in our grass huts in the bush of no-man's land. We pray to the ancestors for its coming. We dance the rain dances. Even in the church, we ask the Christian God for rain.

The mission church bells rings. It rings a welcome across the dusty day. Cotton bells nod in a rusty field and brown, frost-bitten banana leaves crackle their wooden tune in the still air where the sleeping breeze is sweet in the sugar cane. In my uncle, Babamagaru, the teacher's house, he has African masks on the walls and home-woven wicker chairs round as a pot in the middle of the room.

And the door on wire hinges that refuses to stay closed and the smell of woodsmoke from the village fires and not to forget the nip of ants on the bare, earth floor as feet make the impossible journey to the adjoining outhouse for a shit into the long-drop.

Overhead, old man of the sea, the moon, hangs full over the valley of Mutoko nestling in the granite hills near the farms. Bats swoop and dive in abandonment of joy. It's hello again to old feelings of home. Of country roads and freedom and laughter from the dancers down the road.

Walk the path to the edge of the huts to witness the dance. The masked figures are Zvinyau; water spirits who pray for the coming of the storm.

From the tideless pool of faith, the great lake in the North, these dancers come. They have put on their loins the skins of animals. They emerge from banana and mango grove rustling and restless to the beat of the drum. It is a rhythm of throbbing hearts, gyrating and undulating, an adulation to the blood inside. The drumskins of buck and cow are taut, tightened over wooden hollows hard with promise like the selected maidens who wait in tension to tamp the dust their spirit fathers trod in tears and rain.

The circle weaves as now frenetic the drumbeat increases, pounding to the whistles and the chant of simple faith which is unworded, of all who watch the dust and sky like the grandmothers of so many seasons. Their cackles match the scuffing of the angled chickens pecking in the dirt and the old rooster's cocked crow that is Zimbabwe's dawn, entering the arena to win his cock-eyed mate. And now the whistles and the drum are more frenzied than before as the rag-flag pole ripples, shudders, in the breath of muscle-mounting climax, one lead dancer calling all the others to join in the ever-living coil of bodies tightening to the drum. But just as the final beat crescendoes, crashing all dancers to the ground, so the play is over, the images flicker, fade and fall. I close the book of dreams, old clothes replaced in the cupboard of the past. They say that at day's end, something dies in each one of us. So I stub out my cigarette. Take off my watch, remove my national ID from inside my jacket's right-hand pocket, as if I were putting all my dreams to one side. I insert wire and keys in their place.

It is time to go to work. The dance is over, the honeymoon gone. Streetlamps come on. The darkness deepens.

There will be those who are warm and safe tonight behind locked doors. Car owners and lovers, the well-fed, the rich. Let them sleep well tonight; yes, I hope they are busy dreaming in front of videos and TVs, even while my keys are in my hand. The temperature is dropping fast now. A knock on the door. It is Rose... We share the same timing, the same collective mind which belongs to the darkness that is our inheritance.

"Time, my friend..."

"Yes, time to go to work, Rose. I hope you rested today?"

"Tendai, my daughter, was sick. I couldn't sleep."

"Well, perhaps tomorrow will be better."

"I hope so..."

"Have a good night, Rose. And watch out for those in uniform."

"You too, my friend, you too."

I remind myself that good neighbours are hard to come by these days, as I double-lock the door behind me and step into the shadows that match my skin.

Nessim Zohar

Blue Thunder

"You were set up, Mister Leon!"

Leon Alfandari sat by his usual table at the Shatbey casino counting the amber prayer beads in his hand, with the detached and measured movements of an automaton.

"You were set up, Mister Leon!" repeated Gaafar el Gaza'ar, debt collector and muscle man, expert in matters that are beyond the realm of civilised negotiations.

"Let's order dinner first."

"I'll have Sayadeya fish"

"Great." Leon clapped his hands, summoning Ali the headwaiter,

"Two Sayadeya fish casseroles, Ali."

They pursued their business meeting only after the kitchen-boy cleared the table and Ali set before them two glowing water pipes.

"Cheers!" called Leon Alfandari and kissed his prayer beads, as Gaafar belched loudly, then according to etiquette, retorted with an even deeper belch, the sonority of which would not have shamed Tito Gobi.

"Cheers!" congratulated the patrons sitting close by.

The two men drew at their hookahs, exhaling towards the ceiling a thin and continuous jet of richly scented smoke, and Leon returned to his prayer beads.

Ali approached with two glasses of sweet dark tea.

"Thank you, Ali."

"At your service, master Alfandari."

A gentle breeze caressed Leon Alfandari's thinning hair as he turned towards the sea to enjoy the cool of the salty evening air. Enchanted by the movement of the waves and the lullaby played by the bubbling surf Leon gazed at the water allowing a soft smile to soften his stony features.

"The tea is very good," he said, giving Gaafar the cue to

continue his report. Gaafar held the scalding tea-glass between his thumb and his third finger, making contact only with the tepid rim and thick insulated bottom, and then carefully raised the hot beverage to his lips. He took a quick noisy sip drawing a rush of fresh air together with the tea so as to lower the temperature of the liquid as it travelled from the glass to his palate.

"We were set up Mister Leon!" said the muscle man, including himself among the cheated as a token of loyalty and in order to avoid unnecessary suspicion.

"Excellent tea," he added taking another noisy sip,

"Yes sir, we were set up!"

"I believe you've said that already. I want to know who, and how."

"Well sir, I got hold of the stable boy and shoved hot Shata peppers up his ass; he started singing at once! You know, I peel the skin of the peppers so that the vitriolic meat of the pepper is in direct contact..."

"Please stick to what you found out."

"Sure," said Gaafar, disappointed by the lack of interest manifested by his employer towards his methods of extracting information.

"Blue Thunder was drugged. They gave him a powerful laxative. All night long he was shitting his guts out — excuse the language. The stable boy was bribed to clean the stall so as not to arouse suspicion."

"What else?"

"I got hold of the stable master at Smouha racecourse; I shoved hot Shata peppers up his... sorry. Anyway he admitted mixing a full bottle of 'Agarol' in Blue Thunder's oats. I once had a spoon of 'Agarol', after eating too many prickly figs. It had a creamy pleasant taste, so I swallowed a second spoon. Allah help the Armenian pharmacist! I almost died sitting on the toilet seat. Can you imagine what a whole bottle can do?"

Leon Alfandari, bookmaker and racehorse expert did not have to use his imagination. He was in his box at the stands when the eight horses shot across the start line of the weekly mile sweepstake. Blue Thunder was a born miler galloping all the way at a fast steady pace. Desert Prince was a slow starter with a notorious finish. They both held the central lanes and a hundred yards into the race were already a full length ahead of the pack. Three hundred yards into the race and Leon did not need his binoculars to see something was wrong; the two horses were still galloping neck to neck. Blue Thunder should have been half a length ahead by now.

Five hundred yards into the race, Desert Prince was leading by a full length and the racecourse crowd was on its feet: Blue Thunder never lost a race! Leon slowly picked up his binoculars. The horses were now approaching the stretch closest to the stands. Leon saw no sign of dark sweat on Blue Thunder's flanks or under the saddle. He concentrated on the horse's head and distinguished a slight wobble. Blue Thunder's eyes were popping out of their sockets and his muzzle was dry apart from chalky white foam around the nostrils, Leon put down his binoculars. Blue Thunder was dehydrated!

Eight hundred yards and Blue Thunder crashed head over heels into the turf sending his jockey over the fence. The crowd was quiet, training their binoculars from the horse to Leon and back again.

"Did you find out who was behind it?"

"Sure I did! I got hold of the betting controller and shoved..."

"Gaafar..."

"Yes, of course. Anyway Nabil Shoukri is behind it. Lots of betters all over town, mostly riffraff, ten to one against Blue Thunder. Small bets so as not to arouse suspicion."

"Nabil Shoukri?"

"Sure. Mister Leon. He funded the whole thing."

"Nabil Shoukri could not have funded his own funeral!" said Leon in disdain.

"Well, I heard El Kenawi is the master-mind..." whispered Gaafar,

"He picked the sweepstake so no-one could trace the

winnings, and of course because of the Sabbath, you being a pious man..."

"Angelo sent a carriage to pick me up from the synagogue," explained Leon, uneasy of the fact that he was at the racetrack on a Saturday,

"Did you find out who mugged him?"

"That was definitely Nabil Shoukri himself! I got it from the stable master. Why did he have to beat up Angelo? That is what l do not understand!"

"Angelo would have refused to ride if he had seen Blue Thunder!"

"So Shoukri mugged him and put one of the freelancers in the saddle!"

"Yes."

"So Angelo sent for you Mister Leon, in order to save Blue Thunder?"

"Yes, but I got there just in time to see the horses shoot out of the gates!"

"Criminals I say," grumbled Gaafar displaying his discontent by spitting on the floor,

"Criminals! What with the Sabbath and all..."

Leon toyed with his prayer beads and kept his silence for a long moment.

"Would you like me to get hold of Shoukri, Mister Leon?" Being a man of action, Gaafar could not understand his employer's reflective mood.

"Patience is a gift from Allah, Gaafar," replied Leon philosophically.

The information extracted by Gaafar's hot Shata peppers only reinforced that which Leon already knew. Long before Blue Thunder failed to make it to the finishing line, Leon Alfandari knew he was a marked man.

"Zionist's intestines!"

"What?"

"Zionist's intestines sir, only a piaster sir. Zionist's intestines!"

A young barefoot peddler, not more than twelve, stood in front of Leon holding a bunch of thin, twisted rosy balloons.

"Zionist's intestines indeed!" grumbled Leon, stacking red-hot cinders on the tobacco of his smoke, using the small brass tongs especially designed for this purpose. There were days when Leon would have clouted that little ignorant lout! But times had changed. The war in Palestine has turned the Jews into aliens and now Leon Alfandari has become an easy target.

Gaafar waved the boy away and turned uncomfortably towards Leon, who busied himself with the burning coals on the crown of his water pipe.

"His fault is on my head, Mister Leon," said Gaafar, atoning for the peddler's insensitive blunder.

"It's the prayer beads," said Leon. "He saw me holding the prayer beads and mistook me for a Muslim."

"That is not the point, Mister Leon," retorted Gaafar,

"These disgusting balloons are an insult to any Egyptian! What has become of us? Have we no manners, no education?"

Leon laid back the miniscule brass tongs on the platter of the water pipe and nodded at Gaafar, acknowledging his friendly gesture. He then took an envelope out of his pocket and slid it across the table towards Gaafar who opened it and hurriedly put it back as though bitten by a snake.

The envelope contained at least a hundred pounds in crisp new one-pound notes!

"This is the kind of money someone pays for elimination and disposal," said Gaafar pushing back the envelope towards Leon, "Sorry mister Alfandari, I do not do that sort of thing!"

"You do not have to do anything. It's your fee for a job well done!"

"One hundred pounds? It doesn't make sense. Ten would have been very generous — a hundred? What is it, toy-money you give to children?"

Leon leaned forward indicating to Gaafar to do the same.

"You are almost right Gaafar. But it is not toy-money it

is counterfeit money!" he whispered. "And there is no way to detect the forgery!"

The stem of the hookah hit the floor with a dull thud as Gaafar opened both his hands in astonishment.

"See for yourself," continued Leon before his listener could regain his breath. "Check any number of notes anywhere you like! Go to the police, go to the bank... check the money!"

Gaafar picked up the smoke rod of the hookah, wiped the mouthpiece on the sleeve of his striped *ghalabia* and drew an enormous amount of smoke, making the water boil madly in the glass container of the water-pipe.

A hundred pounds is indeed a lot of money. One could live for half a year on a hundred pounds! With one hundred pounds one could cure the trachoma plaguing the eyes of one's daughter. With one hundred pounds...

Gaafar sat motionless for a long moment, during which Leon, honouring his friend's silence, turned his gaze towards the sea. Glittering light was dancing upon the crest of the shallow waves while on the horizon across the eastern harbour the tall minaret of the "new mosque" appeared to be piercing the golden disc of the setting sun. How on earth would he ever be able to leave Alexandria was beyond his imagination. Suddenly Gaafar pocketed the envelope, stood up and left without bidding Leon goodbye. On his way he caught the balloon peddler by the ear and dragged him screaming out of the casino.

"Bless your soul, Gaafar" smiled Leon to himself. "Alexandrians are still honourable men!"

At the Anfoushi police station Gaafar submitted a complaint for fraud and handed over two one-pound notes for a confirmation of authenticity.

"The money is good," said the police expert, handing back only one of the notes. "The second pound note was ruined by the testing procedure," he added sheepishly as Gaafar left the station.

"I told you it was a perfect forgery!" laughed Leon. "Here take another fifty!"

"I don't understand, Mister Leon, if the forgery is so good why doesn't the counterfeiter use the money himself? He could become a millionaire!"

"Tell me, Gaafar," replied Leon in a fatherly manner "does a peasant grow tomatoes to eat them himself or to sell them in the market-place?"

Gaafar smiled at the propounded proposition and was about to pose the next question when Leon stopped him.

"The less said the better..."

Gaafar was pleased of the confidence given to him, yet Leon knew Gaafar would spill the beans and the news about the incredible counterfeit notes would spread like fire.

That was exactly what he aimed at.

That same night the telephone started ringing as some of Leon's acquaintances, sniffling for a deal, started calling. Leon evaded the issue, blaming the caller to be a tasteless practical joker or that the whole matter was a malicious rumour spread by his enemies. It took two days before the caller he prayed for was on the other end of the line.

"How are you Mister Leon?"

He recognised the caller at once. "The fish has spotted the bait," he smiled enjoying the pleasant warmth generated by this revelation.

"I shall be honest with you, dear Shoukri: times are hard. The unexpected fiasco with Blue Thunder put me in a very delicate position."

"In our line of business you have honey one day, onions the other. You should have spread your risks."

"That would have been a death blow to my reputation, dear Nabil."

Both men where accessing each other's position with the expected small talk.

"Rumour has it Blue Thunder's crash cost you five thousand pounds!"

360

"Money comes and money goes, dear friend," answered Leon giving no foothold to his adversary. If Nabil wants part of the action, he would have to spring the question directly.

"I hear you have come by some interesting merchandise."

"Interesting only to he who is curious, dear Nabil."

"I was under the impression you never deal with these sorts of goods. After all, your people are commanded not to defile their souls."

"One has to make a living, honourable Shoukri." Leon swallowed the insult. It was not the time for crossing swords.

"Are the goods available for inspection?"

"Only in Cairo, Mister Shoukri. The stock is in Cairo. They sell in units of ten thousand pieces. The price — two to one!"

"That's madness Leon! No one will buy at that price! It's pure madness!"

"Not for this merchandise master Shoukri, not for this merchandise. You double your investment with every turnover!"

"I have to check with my investors, five thousand is unheard of..."

Feeling the rush of a blush on his stony face, Leon hung up. If the fish will swallow the bait he will surely call back.

A week later Leon Alfandari and Gaafar el Gaza'ar rang the bell of a small apartment in the centre of Cairo. Gaafar carried a brown leather valise. Nabil Shoukri opened the door.

"Ten thousand in one pound denominations," announced Leon once the door was securely shut behind him. "As agreed, Gaafar is the trustee. He holds the money until the final execution of the deal. He will render for inspection any number of bills you require. I'll wait for you here."

Nabil Shoukri hurriedly left the flat accompanied by Gaafar carrying the brown leather valise. In the early

361

hours of the afternoon they both returned from their proofing trip among the banks, exchangers and forgers of Cairo.

"Unbelievable master Alfandari!" exclaimed Nabil Shoukri to the impassive Leon who noted that excited Shoukri now addressed him by his last name.

"Incredible! I took the money to Giorgi Salimidis, he must have checked half of the bills. 'The money is true' he says. 'Forged,' I tell him. 'True,' he bellows. 'Forged,' I shout. He almost hit me!"

"Salimidis is a small time counterfeiter; he is not in the same class with my suppliers."

"I called my partners in Alex; they may want to increase the order."

"Ten thousand a month, not a piaster more. My suppliers are very cautious."

"Now why on earth do they say that Jewish people are greedy?" exclaimed Shoukri in mocked astonishment.

"Nothing is what it seems to be, dear Nabil," answered Leon seriously.

"I was just joking Mr. Leon, no offence meant."

"None taken, Shoukri. Still it is a fact of life — nothing is what it seems to be!"

Nabil Shoukri opened his shirt and, as is the custom of rural folk, produced from a wide linen belt that girdled his belly the five thousand pounds, price for counterfeit money. In an act of total confidence Leon took the money without counting the bills. Gaafar handed over the brown leather valise to Nabil Shoukri and all three men left for the central train station.

"Gaafar and me will be getting off at Tanta," said Leon. "It would not be wise for us to arrive in Alexandria together."

At Tanta station l.eon and Gaafar disembarked, bidding Nabil a successful completion of the journey.

"Now to the stationmaster!" announced Leon the minute the train left the station.

"Why the stationmaster Mister Leon?"

Leon only smiled back and entered the office, leaving bewildered Gaafar on the platform.

"What can I do for you, your Highness?" asked the stationmaster, accosting Leon with excessive warmth and pomp, in anticipation of a large tip.

"I forgot a piece of luggage on the train that just left for Alexandria," informed Leon and gave a full description of the brown leather valise.

"Does Your Excellency by any chance also remember the seat number?"

"Of course," replied Leon, handing over the tickets together with a ten-pound note to cover "any unexpected expense." The station master took vigorous and immediate action.

At Damanhor six uniformed policemen boarded the train heading directly towards the coach where Nabil Shoukri and the brown valise were situated. Four of them blocked the entrances while the remaining two, leaving nothing to chance, checked every single piece of luggage along their way. By the time they stopped by the brown valise Nabil Shoukri was on the verge of hysteria. The possibility of spending ten years in one of His Majesty's prisons for dealing in counterfeit currency wore his nerves to a thread and cold perspiration trickled down his spine.

"Is that yours?" asked the policemen in a stern tone, as is the wont of policemen.

"No!" shrieked Shoukri, "I have no luggage. This valise belongs to a passenger who disembarked in Tanta. He wore a white suit. Looked Jewish to me... very fishy..." The policemen took the brown leather valise and disembarked from the train, paying no attention to Nabil's nervous chatter.

"Ayoooo!" Bellowed Gaafar, "you have cleaned Nabil of five thousand pounds! He will be looking for you."

"Why should he be looking for me?" wondered Leon innocently, "I kept my end of the deal!"

"Sure, but the police returned the suitcase with the

363

money to you!"

"That is something only you and I are aware of!"

"And the police. Nabil will try to find out; he'll go to the Damanhor police!"

"Tell me, Gaafar, would you have gone to the police to ask about a brown valise containing ten thousand pounds in counterfeit money?"

Gaafar pondered over the question for a moment then burst into a fit of uncontrolled laughter.

"You have nerves of steel, Mister Alfandari," he said in admiration when he finally regained his breath. "The police could have opened the suitcase, asked questions and would have soon found out the money is forged!"

"The money is true! It's not counterfeit. It's my money — clean!"

"Your money?"

"I have a withdrawal receipt."

"Clean money, not forged?"

"Nothing in life is what it seems to be, Gaafar! That was clean honest money!"

"Ayoooo!" Shrieked Gaafar. "You are a genius, Mister Leon! Ayoooo! Nabil raised the five thousand from the El Kanawi gang! They will sure be shoving hot Shata peppers up his ass!"

"That is your cut," said Leon handing to Gaafar a roll of ten pound notes.

"I can't take it, Mister Alfandari, it's your own money!"

"This is Nabil's money and ten percent is your cut, you earned it."

"I feel it is farewell money, Mister Leon."

"As you said Gaafar, they will be looking for me!"

Gaafar was right. Within a couple of days all Alexandria had heard about the sting and Nabil Shoukri together with Abdulla el Kanawi started looking for Leon Alfandari.

"Let them look!" shouted Leon, from the deck of the Esperia sailing to Naples. It was midnight and the Esperia was passing by the eastern harbour lighthouse on its way

364

to the open sea. For the first time in his life Leon Alfandari was leaving the shores of his beloved city. Leaving never to return.

The skyline of Alexandria melted into the darkness and Leon Alfandari unconsciously opened his hand allowing the prayer beads to slip out of his grip. The Esperia blew its horn, drowning the feeble splash of the prayer beads.

Biographies

André Aciman is the author of *Out of Egypt: A Memoir* (Farrar, Straus & Giroux/Riverhead), *False Papers: Essays on Exile and Memory* (FSG/Picador), and the co-author and editor of *The Proust Project* (FSG) and of *Letters of Transit* (New Press). He was born in Alexandria and lived in Egypt, Italy and France. Educated at Harvard, he has taught at Princeton and Bard College and teaches Comparative Literature at The CUNY Graduate Centre. He is the recipient of a Whiting Writers' Award, a Guggenheim Fellowship as well as a fellowship from The New York Public Library's Centre for Scholars and Writers. He has written for *The New York Times*, *The New Yorker, The New Republic, The New York Review of Books* and *Commentary*. He is currently working on a novel.

Avraham Adgah was born in a small Jewish village in Ethiopia in 1965 and at the age of thirteen moved to another town for his junior and high school studies. He started his journey to Israel when he was seventeen. This entailed travelling about 350 miles on foot day and night through the jungle and the desert until he arrived in Sudan where he stayed in refugee camps for about a year. In 1984 he emigrated to Israel where he learned Hebrew and studied civil engineering. He currently works as a building project supervisor for the Haifa Technion and also lectures at schools, colleges, study groups and other platforms on the history of his ethnic group and the experience of the epic journey. He is a volunteer worker for educational veterans and newcomers. He has published two books about his journey and the absorption and is currently working on a novel.

David Albahari, born 1948, is a writer and translator from the former Yugoslavia. He has published eight novels and eight collections of short stories in Serbian. His novel

Bait won the NIN award for the best novel published in Serbia in 1996. His books have been translated into fourteen languages; translations into English include *Bait* (Northwestern University Press), *Gotz and Meyer* (Harvill) and *Snow Man* (Douglas & McIntyre). He has also edited a number of anthologies of short stories, published in Belgrade and has translated into Serbian many books including novels by V. Nabokov, S. Bellow, T. Pynchon, J. Updike and M. Atwood. In 1994 he moved to Canada and lives in Calgary with his wife and two children.

Eli Amir, born in 1937 in Baghdad, Iraq, arrived in Israel with his family in 1950 and was sent to study at a kibbutz. Amir is well-known in Israel for his lectures, articles, radio and television programmes and especially for his book, *Scapegoat*, a semi-autobiographical novel that depicts the integration of an Iraqi-Jewish youth in an Israeli transit camp soon after the establishment of the state. This and other novels by Amir are included in the secondary school syllabus. His books published in Hebrew are *Scapegoat* (novel), Am Oved, 1984 [Tarnegol Kaparot], *Farewell, Baghdad* (novel), Am Oved, 1992 [Mafriah Ha-Yonim] and *Saul's Love* (novel), Am Oved, 1998 [Ahavat Shaul]. Amir began his career as a messenger boy in the Prime Minister's Office and worked his way up to Arab Affairs Adviser to the Prime Minister. Amir has concentrated on the social problems of new immigrants and was appointed deputy director-general of the Ministry of Immigrant Absorption. Today he is the director-general of the youth immigration division of the Jewish Agency. He won the Yigal Alon prize for outstanding pioneering service to Israeli society.

Shimon Ballas was born in Baghdad in 1930 and emigrated to Israel in 1951. A major novelist, Ballas has published fifteen works of fiction, several important studies on contemporary Arabic literature and numerous translations from Arabic. Although he began his career in

367

Arabic, Ballas changed to Hebrew in the mid 1960s. Since then Ballas has opened a window onto the political and psychological life of the contemporary Arab world, both at home and in exile. His first novel *The Transit Camp* (1964) was the first Israeli novel to depict life among the Arab Jewish immigrants of the 1950s, *A Locked Room* (1980) portrays a Palestinian architect returning home for a visit after years in Europe, *Last Winter* (1984) depicts a community of Middle Eastern political exiles in Paris and *Outcast* (1991) the ruminations of a Jewish historian converted to Islam in the Baghdad of the 1980s. Other books include *Facing the Wall* (1969), *Essay from Baghdad* (1970), *Clarification* (1972), *Downtown* (1979), *The Heir* (1987), *Not in Her Place* (1994), *Solo* (1998), and *Tel Aviv East* (1998). His important study, *Arab Literature Under the Shadow of War*, appeared in 1978. He continues to write critical works in Arabic, the most recent of which, *Secular Trends in Arabic Literature*, was published by the Iraqi exile publishing house al-Kamel Verlag, in Cologne, Germany. Ballas retired from the Department of Arabic Literature at Haifa University and now spends part of the year in Paris, where he does most of his writing.

Marion Baraitser was born in Johannesburg, South Africa and left in 1972. She now lives in Britain. She is an award-winning published playwright and short story writer. Her play *The Story of an African Farm*, was co-produced with The Young Vic Studio, 2000 (Oberon Books), and was broadcast on BBC Radio 4, 2000. *The Crystal Den* was commissioned and produced at the New End Theatre, 2002 (Oberon Books). Her play Mafeking/ *Mafikeng*, about the Black South African ANC leader Sol Plaatje, was produced in London in 2006. Among other works, she has edited *Theatre of Animation: Contemporary Adult Puppet Plays in Context* (1999). Her graphic novel for teenagers, *Home Number One,* set in the transit camp of Theresienstadt, was published in 2006. Marion Baraitser founded Loki Books in 1996, a small press specialising in literature by women writers. She has an MA in English Literature and tutored for Birkbeck's Diploma in Literature for several years and for London Metropolitan University postgraduate script-writing course.

Ruth Behar was born in Havana, Cuba and grew up in New York City to where she and her parents fled in 1961 in the wake of the Cuban Revolution. She has worked as an ethnographer in Spain, Mexico, and Cuba and is Professor of Anthropology at the University of Michigan. Her books include *The Presence of the Past in a Spanish Village*, *Translated Woman: Crossing the Border with Esperanza's Story*, and *The Vulnerable Observer: Anthropology That Breaks Your Heart*. Behar is co-editor of *Women Writing Culture* and editor of *Bridges to Cuba*. Behar is also known for her essays, poetry, fiction, and work as a filmmaker. Her classic essay, "Juban América" appeared in *King David's Harp: Autobiographical Essays by Jewish Latin American Writers* and her short story, "La Cortada", was included in *Telling Stories: An Anthology for Writers*. Behar's poems have been published in *Burnt Sugar/Caña Quemada: Contemporary Cuban Poetry in English and Spanish, Sephardic American Voices: Two Hundred Years of a Literary Legacy, Little Havana Blues: A Cuban-American Literature Anthology*, and *The Prairie Schooner Anthology of Jewish-American Writers*. Her collection of prose poems, *Everything I Kept/Todo lo que guardé*, was published in 2001 in Matanzas, Cuba. Behar wrote, directed and produced "Adio Kerida/Goodbye Dear Love: A Cuban Sephardic Journey", a documentary based on the life stories of Sephardic Cuban Jews living in Cuba, Miami and New York. Her forthcoming book is *In Search of the Jews of Cuba: Stories and Photographs*.

Mois Benarroch was born in Morocco and lives in Israel. He writes in three languages: Hebrew, Spanish and English, and his poetry has been published in numerous magazines and anthologies worldwide. He was featured poet in the international Austin poetry festival, 1999, in poetrymagazine.com (July 2000) and has read his poetry in Israel, Spain and the US. He has published books of poetry, prose and novels in Hebrew, Spanish and English. Benarroch has published two collections of poetry in English: *Horses and Other Doubts* and *You walk on the land until one day the land walks on you.*

Erez Bitton, poet and writer, is of Moroccan origin but was born in Oran, Algeria in 1942 and since 1948 has lived in Israel. For ten years he was a journalist for the daily newspaper *Maariv* and has also chaired the Association of Israeli Poets. He is currently editor of the Israeli literary journal *Apirion* which focuses on Mediterranean and Middle Eastern culture and he chairs the international Mediterranean Centre in Israel. He was seriously injured at eleven years of age by a grenade explosion which blinded him.

Benjamin Black (a pseudonym), born in Scotland, emigrated to Israel in the mid-1990s. However, he fled from Israel into exile after his refusal to be conscripted on pacifist grounds. He is author of *Breaking Ranks*, (2001). Despite efforts to trace the author we have been unsuccessful and we would be pleased to hear from him.

Roohieh Darakhshani was born in Hamadan, Iran and whilst a child moved to Tehran. For many years she worked as a secretary for an Abadan oil company and was also a radio presenter for the company radio station, writer for children's programmes, presenter on local television and a part-time correspondent for a Tehran weekly magazine. A book of her stories, *Sahereh*, was published during this time. Roohieh came to the UK some thirty years ago and now lives in Newcastle. Her books include *Life in the Sea Graves, Mad,* and *Life and Love — Unfulfilled* (in Persian). Roohieh is now a Bahai.

Ariel Dorfman the Chilean American author of numerous works of fiction, plays, poems, essays and films in both Spanish and English, holds the Walter Hines Page Chair of Literature and Latin American Studies at Duke University. His books have been translated into more than thirty languages and have received many prizes. Dorfman's works include the novels *Mascara, Hard Rain, Konfidenz, Widows, The Nanny and the Iceberg* and *Blake's Therapy;* a bilingual book of poetry, *In Case of Fire in a Foreign Land* and his memoir *Heading South, Looking North*. He has also written a book for children, *The Rabbits' Rebellion*. Among his plays — performed in more than one hundred countries — are "Death and the Maiden" (which won England's Olivier Award for Best Play and was produced on Broadway and made into a feature film directed by Roman Polanski), "Reader," and "Widows," both of which have won Kennedy Centre awards.

His most recent works are *Exorcising Terror: The Incredible Ongoing Trial of General Augusto Pinochet*, a book of his essays, *Other Septembers, Many Americas: Selected Provocations, 1980-2004* and a travel memoir, *Desert Memories: Journeys through the Chilean North*, for which he won the Lowell Thomas Silver Award. A recent novel co-written with his younger son, Joaquin Dorfman, is *Burning City*. A new play, "The Other Side," had its New York premiere in December 2005 and was opened on London's West End in 2006 with Sir Peter Hall directing.

An expatriate from Chile since the military coup in 1973, he has been active in the defence of human rights for many decades, having addressed the General Assembly of the United Nations. His play "Speak Truth to Power: Voices from Beyond the Dark," has been performed around the world. The play was published by Seven Stories Press as *Manifesto for Another World: Voices from Beyond the Dark*.

(Musa) **Moris Farhi**, born in Ankara, Turkey, 1935. He is the author of the novels *The Pleasure of Your Death* (1972); *The Last of Days* (1983); *Journey Through the Wilderness*

(1989); *Children of the Rainbow* (1999). His poems have appeared in many British, US and international publications and in the anthology of 20th Century Jewish Poets, *Voices Within the Ark* (Avon). For many years he has been an active campaigner on behalf of persecuted writers through English PEN and served as Chair of International PEN's Writers in Prison Committee during 1997-2000. He is a Vice President of International PEN and a Fellow of both the Royal Society of Literature and the Royal Geographical Society. In 2001 he was appointed an MBE for "services to literature". His novel, *Children of the Rainbow*, has received two prizes: the "Amico Rom" from the Associazione Them Romano of Italy (2002); and the "Special" prize from the Roma Academy of Culture and Sciences in Germany (2003).

His latest novel, *Young Turk*, (Saqi, 2004) has been published in the US, Turkey, Greece, Holland, France, Italy and is due to appear in Poland soon. The French edition of *Young Turk* (*Jeunes Turcs*) received the 2007 Alberto Benveniste Prize for Literature. He is working on a new novel.

Predrag Finci was born in Sarajevo in 1946. He is in exile in London. He completed Gymnasium, Drama Studio and Philosophy at the University of Sarajevo, and a two year Counselling Course in London. He also studied at the University of Paris X (under Mikele Dufrenne) and in Freiburg (under Werner Marx). He completed his MA in 1977 and PhD in Philosophy in 1981. Before finishing his studies in Philosophy he pursued an acting career, after which he was involved in academic work. Finci lectured at the Department of Philosophy and Sociology (University of Sarajevo) and gained his Professorship in Aesthetics. He is a founder-member of Bosnian PEN. He has published nine books in Bosnia and Croatia and numerous texts in English. He works as a freelance writer and research fellow at UCL.

Juan Gelman, the distinguished Argentinian poet born in Buenos Aires in 1930, is in exile in Mexico. His many books of poetry include *Violin and other Questions* 1956, *The Game in which We Walked* 1959, *Gotan* 1962, *Under Other People's Rain* 1980, *Towards the South* 1982, *Dibaxu* 1994, *Ni el flaco perdón de Dios/ Hijos de desaparecidos* 1997 and *Tantear la noche* 2000. In 1997 he received the Argentine National Award for poetry. The themes of his poetry relate to his Jewish heritage, family, Argentina and The Tango. Much of his work reflects his personal, painful experience with the politics of his country. His son and pregnant daughter-in-law were among "the disappeared" in Buenos Aires in 1976 and he fled into exile. His daughter-in-law and son were taken to Montevideo, Uruguay by members of the Uruguayan military and after his daughter-in-law had given birth to a daughter she was murdered, as was Gelman's son. The daughter was given to an infertile couple from the Montevideo police and only in 2000, twenty-three years later, was she found.

Farideh Goldin, born in Iran, is in exile in the US. She is author of *Wedding Song: Memoirs of an Iranian Jewish Woman* (2003). She was born in 1953 in Shiraz to a family of *dayanim*, the judges and leaders of the Jewish community. Farideh's family moved out of the *mahaleh*, the Jewish ghetto, to a Muslim neighbourhood when she was eight years old. Later, attending an American-style university, she was torn between her loyalty to her family, who obeyed strict social, cultural and religious mores, and her Western education, that promoted individualism and self-reliance. *Wedding Song* reveals Farideh's struggle in balancing her two worlds. In her later essays she confronts issues of identity as she searches for a place in American society as an Iranian immigrant. She is a Master of Fine Arts in Creative Writing and in Humanities from Old Dominion University and also studied at Shiraz University, Iran. Her work appears in several anthologies including *The Flying Camel: and Other Stories of Identity* *by North African and Middle Eastern Jewish Women* 2004. Her essays on Iranian and Iranian Jewish women appear in a range of journals. She was a finalist at the National Association of Sephardic Artists, Writers, Intellectuals Literary contest in 1998.

Ladislav Grosman was born in Humenne, Slovakia in 1921. After completing high school he spent most of the year in hiding, as the Slovak state began deporting Jews to concentration camps. Most of his family perished in the war. He moved to Prague immediately after the war where he completed a PhD in Philosophy and began to write and publish fiction. In 1965, he wrote the script for the film "The Shop on Main Street" based on his novella. The film was awarded the Academy Award for Best Foreign Picture. Following the Soviet occupation of Czechoslovakia, Grosman, his wife and son left for Israel. He continued to write and publish there while also teaching Slavic literature at Bar Ilan University and screenplay writing at Tel Aviv University. His books were published in the United States by Doubleday and translated into many languages. Ladislav Grosman died of a heart attack in Tel Aviv in 1981, just before his 60th birthday. His widow, Edith and son George live in Israel and in Toronto, Canada.

Henryk Grynberg was born in Warsaw, Poland in 1936 and is in exile in the United States. He was brought up in the hamlet of Radoszyna in eastern Mazovia where the family lived until autumn 1942 when virtually all the local Jews were sent to their deaths in Treblinka. He and his mother survived the war partly in hiding and partly on "Aryan" papers. Between 1954 and 1958 he studied in the Department of Journalism at the University of Warsaw. In 1956 he was caught up in the political enthusiasm engendered by the "Polish October" and shared in the subsequent disillusionment when Gomulka placed severe restrictions on further political evolution in the direction of a pluralistic and democratic society. In 1959 Grynberg became an actor in the State Jewish Theatre and began to publish short stories and poems. At the end of 1967 he went with the theatre to the USA and remained there in protest against what he considered was an anti-Jewish campaign and censorship in Poland. He has a Master's degree in Russian Literature from the University of California and since the end of communist rule in 1989 has been a visiting professor at the University of Warsaw. Most of Grynberg's novels and stories are thinly fictionalised versions of his own life. They include *Zydowska wojna*, 1965 (*Child of the Shadows*, 1969*), Zwyciestwo, 1969 (The Victory, 1993), Zycie ideologiczne, 1975, (Ideological Life), Zycie osobiste*, 1979 (*Personal Life*), *Ojczyzna*, 1970-71, (*Fatherland*), and *Kadisz*, 1987 (*Kaddish*). Grynberg has also published a collection of short stories — *Ekipa Antygona*, 1963 (*The Antigone Ensemble*) as well as seven volumes of poetry including *Rysuje w pamieci*, 1995 (*I Draw in Memory*). His recent book *Drohobycz*, 1997 comprises a series of documentary stories. His latest work is *Memorbuch*, 2000. (Information from: *Contemporary Jewish Writing in Poland*, edited by Antony Polonsky and Monika Adamczyk-Garbowska, University of Nebraska Press, 2001).

Roya Hakakian was born in Tehran, Iran and is now in exile in the US. She is the author of two acclaimed collections of poetry, the first of which, *For the Sake of Water*, received honourable mention in the *Oxford Encyclopedia of the Modern Islamic World* and was nominated as the poetry book of the year by *Iran News* in 1993. Her memoir of growing up a Jewish teenager in post-revolutionary Iran, *Journey from the Land of No* was *Elle Magazine's* Best Non-fiction Book of 2004. She writes for numerous publications, including the *Washington Post*, and the weekly *Forward*, and is a contributor to NPR's *Weekend Edition*. Hakakian was the recipient of a MacDowell Fellowship and the 2003 Dewitt/Wallace Reader's Digest Fellowship in writing. She is a founding member of the

Iran Human Rights Documentation Centre. She has collaborated on over a dozen hours of programming for some of the most prestigious journalism units on network television. Commissioned by UNICEF, Roya's most recent film, *Armed and Innocent*, on the subject of the involvement of underage children in wars around the world, has been selected among best short documentaries at several festivals.

Vesna Domany Hardy was born in Zagreb, Croatia in 1941 in a progressive Jewish family of which only her mother (Eva Garlic, see her book *Memories*, ed. Durieux, 1998) and she survived the Holocaust, her mother by joining the resistance movement and Vesna as a hidden child with a gentile family in Zagreb. At the end of World War Two her mother re-married but they were soon separated again when her mother and stepfather Danko Garlic were made political prisoners by Tito's regime and sent to an island prison camp. It was during those difficult post-war years in a children's home that Vesna was made aware of being a Jew, without any knowledge of the implications, and ostracised for her parents' "political guilt". Her mother and stepfather had returned by 1953 and, despite many difficulties, they managed to build a modest but dignified existence for the family. Later her brother graduated in film studies in Prague while Vesna studied at Zagreb University, after which she worked as a teacher of English and literature. In 1974 she left Yugoslavia to marry her present husband, whose career was in the British Council. She lived in Pakistan until 1977, in France until 1981, in Italy until 1991 and since 1991 in the UK.

She is now a freelance writer, researcher, translator and interpreter, and her writings on cultural themes and humanitarian issues, book reviews and poetry translations have been published in periodicals or weekly papers such as: *Stone Soup*, London, *Context*, Canterbury; *Young Mind*, London; *Refugee Network*, Oxford; *Social Work in Europe*,

Brussels; *The Jewish Chronicle*, London; *Mak*, Novi Pazar; *Bridge*, Mostar; *SaLon,* London; *Prolog,* Zagreb; *BBC,* Croatian Section; *Radio Free Europe*, Prague; *Radio Zagreb, Vjenac,* Zagreb; *Zarez,* Zagreb; *Kruh i Ruze,* Zagreb; *Ha Kol,* Zagreb; *Novi Omanut,* Zagreb; *Voice,* Zagreb. For her story "Sharon And Set" she received an award for a story on a Jewish theme at Beyahad 2001 in Croatia.

Naim Kattan was born in 1928 in Baghdad, Iraq. He studied at the University of Baghdad and at the Sorbonne before moving to Montreal in 1954. A prodigious writer, Kattan has produced books of essays, novels, including the autobiographical *Adieu Babylone* (1975; *Farewell Babylon*, 1976) and *Les Fruits arrachés* (1977; *Paris Interlude*, 1979); and several collections of short stories — *Dans le désert* (1974), *La Traversée* (1976), *Le Rivage* (1979) and *Le Sable de l'ile* (1981), *The Neighbour and Other Stories* (1982). He is head of the Canada Council's literary section in Ottawa.

Albert Memmi, professor of sociology, novelist and essayist in French, was born in the Jewish ghetto of Tunis. During the German occupation of Tunisia he was interned in a labour camp from which he later escaped. After the war he completed his education in France before returning to Tunis where he taught philosophy, worked as a journalist, and practised as a psychologist. When Tunisia gained independence in 1956 he resettled in France where he continues to reside. He has written numerous novels, essays and analytical works. His auto-biographical first novel, *La Statue de Sel* (1953; *The Pillar of Salt*, 1955), was followed by *Agar* (1955; *Strangers*, 1960), established his early reputation as a provocative and controversial author. *Portrait du colonisé* (1957; *The Coloniser and the Colonised*, 1965), focused on the destructive elements of oppression. A study of the Jewish condition, *Portrait d'un juif* (1962; *Portrait of a Jew*, 1962), was followed by *La Libération* *du juif* (1966; *The Liberation of the Jew*, 1966). After the publication of *L'Homme dominé* (1968; *Dominated Man*, 1968), he returned to fiction with *Le Scorpion* (1969; *The Scorpion*, 1971). His controversial study *Juifs et arabes* (1974; *Jews and Arabs*, 1975), was followed by *Le Désert* (1977). Two further studies, *La Dépendance* (1979; *Dependence*, 1984) and *Le Racisme* (1982), were followed by *Le Pharaon* (1988), *Le Nomade Immobile* (2000) and *Teresa et Autres Femmes* (2004).

Sami Michael, born in Baghdad, Iraq in 1926, is one of the leading Israeli novelists. During World War II he became involved in underground leftist activity against the oppressive regime in Iraq and in 1948 escaped arrest by the Iraqi regime by fleeing to Iran. Eventually he made his way to Israel in 1949 to avoid extradition to Iraq. After serving in the army he joined the editorial staff of an Arabic weekly. For twenty-five years he was a field worker for the Ministry of Agriculture. He studied Arabic Literature and Psychology at Haifa University and was awarded an Honorary Doctorate by the Hebrew University. He began to write at an early age, first in Arabic and later in Hebrew. The themes of his novels are Middle Eastern relationships in Baghdad or Israel. His best-selling novel, *Victoria* (1993), an expansive family saga set in Baghdad, has been translated into several languages, including Arabic. Gershon Shaked wrote about him, "Sami Michael is one of the most powerful naturalists in modern Hebrew literature, one of the very few who understands the mentality of the fighting parties in the Middle East." His books are: *All Men Are Equal, But Some Are More So* (novel), 1974, *Storm Among the Palms* (youth), 1975, *Refuge* (novel), 1977, *A Handful of Fog* (novel), 1979, *Tin Shacks and Dreams* (youth), 1979, *These Are the Tribes of Israel* (non-fiction), 1984, *A Trumpet in the Wadi* (novel), 1987, *Love Among the Palms* (youth), 1990 *Victoria* (novel), 1993, *Brown Devils* (youth), 1993, *Water Kissing Water*, 2001, *Pigeons at Trafalgar Square* (novel), 2005.

Gina Nahai was born in Iran which she left for the USA when she was sixteen, expecting to return. She now lives in Los Angeles. As an Iranian Jew, Gina Nahai was often referred to as "non-Iranian" and as a Jew with a French Catholic grandmother she was told in her own home that the Jews killed Christ. After attending boarding school in Switzerland, Nahai received her bachelors and masters degrees in International Relations from the University of California. Nahai's first novel, *Cry of the Peacock* (1992) told the three thousand year story of the Jewish people of Iran and won the Los Angeles Arts Council Award for Fiction. Her second novel, *Moonlight on the Avenue of Faith* (1999), is about the Iranian exile population in the United States and was a finalist for the Orange Prize and the IMPAC award in Dublin. Her third novel, *Sunday's Silence*, is the tale of a Kurdish Iranian Jewess living among Christian fundamentalists in the United States. Her novel *Caspian Rain* was published in 2007. Nahai's novels have been translated into twenty-six languages, and are taught at a number of universities in the US and abroad.

Samir Naqqash (1938-2005), the Iraqi Jewish Arabic novelist, columnist, and translator, was born in Baghdad in 1938 to a well-to-do family. The political turmoil in Iraq during the 1940s and the early 1950s anti-Jewish events forced his family to emigrate to Israel when he was thirteen years old, forging the experiences for Naqqash's writings. He is adept at creating stories full of Iraqi folklore, fantasy, philosophy and social realism. Traces of Western writers, like James Joyce, Kafka, Sartre and Camus, whose output Naqqash read in Arabic translation, are apparent in several of his books, as he employs surrealism and absurdity. Naqqash was the only Iraqi Jewish writer in Israel who wrote solely in Arabic and explored different Iraqi dialects, including the Jewish dialect with its rich imagery and complex style. Aware of the frustration that some Iraqis as well as non-Iraqis might feel because of the extensive use of local dialects, Naqqash provided glossaries in the standard Arabic of those dialects. Naqqash's literary output includes thirteen books (five collections of short stories, three plays, and five novels) and is more known in the Arab world and Europe than in Israel. His first collection of short stories was published in 1971 and his last novel in 2004. Naqqash struggled greatly to leave Israel to settle in another country, to the extent that he crossed the border to Lebanon, hoping to travel from there to London. The effort proved futile and after spending a few months in a Lebanese jail he was returned to Israel. In the sixties he spent several years in Iran, Turkey, and India. Eventually, he settled in Manchester, England in 2002 only to return to Israel again when the newspaper *al-Mu'tamar* for whom he worked, moved to Iraq two years after the invasion in 2003.

Alicia Partnoy was born in Bahia Blanca, Argentina in 1955 and was banished to the United States in 1979. Partnoy was a member of a political party opposed to the military dictatorship that ousted Peron. One of Argentina's 30,000 "disappeared", in 1977 she was abducted from her home by secret police and taken to a concentration camp where she was tortured. Her writings were smuggled out of prison and published anonymously in human rights journals. *The Little School* (1985) is Alicia Partnoy's memoir of her disappearance and imprisonment in Argentina in the 1970s. She has testified before the United Nations, the Organisation of American States, Amnesty International, and the Argentine Human Rights Commission. She is a poet as well as an academic, human rights activist and translator. Her collections of poetry include *Revenge of the Apple* (1992) and *Little Low Flying* (2005) and she is editor of *You Can't Drown the Fire: Latin American Women Writing in Exile* (1988).

Mauricio Rosencof, born in 1933, lives in Montevideo and is a distinguished Uruguayan playwright, political activist and former leader of the urban guerrilla movement MLN — Tupamaros. He spent thirteen years as a political prisoner of the Uruguayan military, eleven and a half of which were in solitary confinement. To date he has written seventeen plays and published seven books comprising poetry and novels including *Las Cartas que no Llegaron* (The Letters that Never Came), an autobiographical novel, *The Horses*, *The Battle in the Stable*, *The Frogs*, *The Return of the Great Tuleque* (play), The *Rebellion of the Cañeros*, *Brave Hairband* (novel), *Memories of the Jail* (in collaboration with Eleuterio Fernandez Huidobro), *Conversations with the Canvas Shoe* (poetry) and *The Bataraz* (novel).

Matyas Sarkozi was born in Budapest. His father changed his religion as a teenager and, although of Jewish origin, he became a well-known Catholic poet. This did not save him from being taken away and he died in the Nazi labour camp of Balf during the spring of 1945. Matyas Sarkozi lived through the Holocaust as a child, taken in by a peasant family in a remote village. He was a trainee journalist when, in 1956, he escaped to the West. Settling in London he studied book illustration at St Martin's School of Art and later literature and linguistics at London University. From 1966 until his retirement he worked in the BBC World Service's Hungarian section. Since then he has been London correspondent of the Hungarian daily *Magyar Hirlap* and of *InfoRadio* Budapest. Sarkozi is the co-author of the *Xenophobe's Guide to the Hungarians* and wrote a biography of his dramatist grandfather Ferenc Molnar. However, he publishes prose predominantly in Hungarian. "And Now in Amsterdam" first appeared in a Hungarian collection and is based on a true story.

Max Sawdayee, from an old established Iraqi Jewish family, is from Baghdad, Iraq where he was a businessman. He escaped with his family in 1970, eventually settling in the UK. His diary, *All Waiting to be Hanged,* was self-published in 1974.

Bracha Serri was born in San'aa, Yemen, and lives in Berkeley and Jerusalem. Her activities over the years have been quite diverse; from being a teacher and a principal, researching Yemenite dialects, protesting against injustice as a peace activist, to helping people by counselling and energy healing. Her overtly political and feminist poetry also draws heavily on the linguistic and metaphoric tradition of the great Yemenite religious poets such as Shalom Shabazi. Serri has never shied away from bringing the full weight of judgment and traditional morality into the context of radical politics. Her books include *Tfilot V'Shtikot (2002), Nurit (2001), Kidushin (*1999*), Sacred Cow* (1991), *Red Heifer* (1990) and *Seventy Wondering Poems* (1983).

Ruth Knafo Setton is the author of the novel, *The Road to Fez* (Counterpoint Press). Born in Safi, Morocco, the descendant of martyrs, mystics and musicians, she often writes about her Sephardic heritage. The recipient of literary fellowships from the National Endowment of the Arts, Pennsylvania Council on the Arts, and PEN among others, her fiction, poetry and creative nonfiction have appeared in many journals and anthologies, including *Best Contemporary Jewish Writing, Wrestling with Zion, The Flying Camel, Nothing Makes You Free, The North American Review, Nimrod, Tikkun, The Jewish Quarterly, Another Chicago Magazine, Lilith, With Signs And Wonders: An International Anthology of Jewish Fabulist Fiction,* and *Sephardic-American Voices: Two Hundred Years of a Literary Legacy.* She is the Writer-in-Residence for the Berman Centre for Jewish Studies at Lehigh University, a visiting faculty member of the MFA programme at Georgia College & State University and the Fiction Editor of *Arts & Letters: A Journal of Contemporary Culture.*

Gillian Slovo, born in South Africa**,** has lived in England since 1964, working as a writer, journalist and film producer. Her first novel, *Morbid Symptoms* (1984), began a series of crime fiction featuring female detective Kate Baeier. Other novels in the series include *Death by Analysis* (1986), *Death Comes Staccato* (1987), *Catnap* (1994) and *Close Call* (1995). Her other novels include *Ties of Blood* (1989), *The Betrayal* (1991) and *Red Dust* (2000), a court-room drama set in contemporary South Africa, which explores the effects of the Truth and Reconciliation Commission. *Red Dust* won the RFI Temoin du Monde prize in France and has been made into a film starring Hilary Swank and Chiwetel Ejiofor. *Every Secret Thing: My Family, My Country* (1997) is a moving account of her child-hood in South Africa and her relationship with her parents, both heavily involved in the anti-apartheid movement. *Ice Road* (2004), set in Leningrad in 1933, was shortlisted for the Orange Prize for Fiction. She is also co-author of the play *Guantanamo — Honour Bound to Defend Freedom* produced in London, New York, Chicago, Washington and Stockholm.

Ronny Someck was born in Baghdad in 1951 and went to Israel as a young child. He has worked with street gangs, taught literature, and currently leads creative writ-ing workshops. He has published eight volumes of poetry, the last entitled *Revolution Drummer* and a book for chil-dren with his daughter Shirly ("The Laughter Button"). He has been translated into thirty-three languages. Two selections of his poems have appeared in Arabic transla-tion, one in French (with the exiled Iraqi poet, A.K. El-Janabi), Catalan, Albanian, Italian and English. He has recorded three discs with the musician Elliott Sharp, enti-tled *Revenge of the Stuttering Child, Poverty Line* and *Short History of Vodka*. In 1998 he mounted an exhibition at the Israel Museum with Beny Efrat entitled *Nature's Factory, Winter 2046*.

Ilan Stavans (Mexico, 1961) is Lewis-Sebring Professor in Latin America and Latino Culture and Five College-40th Anniversary Professor at Amherst College. His books include *The Hispanic Condition* (HarperCollins, 1995), *Latino USA: A Cartoon History* (Basic Books, 2000, with Lalo Alcaraz), *On Borrowed Words* (Viking, 2001), *Spanglish* (HarperCollins, 2003), *Dictionary Days* (Graywolf, 2005), *The Disappearance* (Northwestern, 2006), and *Love and Language* (Yale, 2007, with Verónica Albin). He edited The *Oxford Book of Jewish Stories* (Oxford University Press, 1998), *The Scroll and the Cross* (Routledge, 2001), *The Poetry of Pablo Neruda* (Farrar, Straus and Giroux, 2003), the 3-volume *Isaac Bashevis Singer: Collected Stories* (Library of America, 2004), *Rubén Darío: Selected Writings* (Penguin, 2005), the four-volume *Encyclopedia Latina* (Scholastic, 2005), and *Cesar Chavez: An Organizer's Tale* (Penguin, 2008). Routledge published *The Essential Ilan Stavans* in 2000 and the University of Wisconsin Press released *Ilan Stavans: Eight Conversations*, by Neal Sokol, in 2004. The recipient of numerous awards and honors, including a Guggenheim Fellowship, Chile's Presidential Medal, the Rubén Darío Distinction and the National Jewish Book Award, he hosted the syndicated PBS series *Conversations with Ilan Stavans*. His work has been translated into a dozen languages. His story "Morirse está en hebreo" is the inspiration of the movie *My Mexican Shivah* (2007), produced by John Sayles.

George Szirtes was eight years old when his family arrived in England from Hungary as refugees following the revolution in 1956. He was educated in London and trained as an artist. He writes in English. His poems began to appear in the press in the mid-seventies and since then he has produced a dozen books of poetry from Faber, Secker, OUP and Bloodaxe and roughly an equal number of books of translation from Hungarian, including poetry, fiction and drama. He has won various major literary prizes and been shortlisted for others. He was the 2004 winner of the T.S. Eliot Prize for Poetry for *Reel*. He has also written plays, books for children and edited a number of anthologies. He is one of

384

Victor Határ's translators. His most recent books are: *The Budapest File* (Bloodaxe, 2000), *An English Apocalypse* (Bloodaxe, 2001), *Reel* (Bloodaxe 2004).

Regina Waldman was born in Libya and is now in exile in the US. She is a contributor to the anthology *The Flying Camel: Essays on Identity by Women of North African and Middle Eastern Jewish Heritage* (2003). As director of the Bay Area Council for Soviet Jewry, Waldman was instrumental in winning freedom for many Soviet Jews. Regina worked closely with various Russian dissidents, including Nobel Peace Prize winner and human rights champion, Andrei Sakharov. She has fought human rights abuses in Argentina and Chile, during Augusto Pinochet's regime, and has also worked to resettle Muslim refugees from Bosnia in the San Francisco Bay Area. Together with Joseph Abdel Wahed, Waldman founded JIMENA (Jews Indigenous to the Middle East and North Africa) to bear witness to the suffering of other Jewish refugees from Arab lands.

Shelley Weiner was born in Port Elizabeth, South Africa where she trained and worked as a newspaper reporter. After her move to London in 1977 she was employed as a journalist, PR writer and editor in a publishing house before turning to fiction. Her first novel, *A Sisters' Tale*, was published in 1991. Three others followed: *The Last Honeymoon*, *The Joker* and *Arnost*. Her short stories have appeared in anthologies including *Winter's Tales*, *The Slow Mirror*, *Valentine's Day, Mordecai's First Brush With Love* and on BBC Radio 4. Shelley is a Fellow of the Royal Literary Fund with a placement at Middlesex University for the 2004/5 and 2005/6 academic years and, currently, at Westminster University in London. She is co-founder and head of training for Words at Work, which provides workshops on good written English to the private and public sectors. Shelley has served on the Editorial Board of the *Jewish Quarterly* and chaired the judging panel for the *Jewish Quarterly* literary prizes. She has lectured on the creative writing programme at Birkbeck College and, among other institutions, taught for the Open University, the Taliesin Trust, the British Council in Israel, and Durham University Summer School. Scores of new fiction writers have emerged from her "First Novel" workshops held in Camden Town, Wales and in her Highgate kitchen. Shelley continues to write reviews and features while working on a new novel set in South Africa in 1948.

Bart Wolffe was born in Harare, Zimbabwe in 1952 and in 2002 left for exile in Germany via London. He is one of Zimbabwe's leading playwrights with work performed in nine countries. His fourteen plays include *The Sisyphus Road* (2002), *The Art of Accidental Stains* (2002) and *Killing Rats* (2001). He worked extensively, not only in Zimbabwe, but throughout the countries of Southern Africa as well as in Edinburgh running theatre and play writing workshops and touring shows and performing. He has several published books, mostly poetry, including *of coffee cups and cigarettes* (1991) and *Changing Skins*. His work has been included in numerous anthologies such as *New Accents,* a joint anthololgy of five African poets and his collection of short stories is entitled *A Twist of Tales* (1989). His novel *Eye of the Witness* (1995) is unpublished for fear of political repercussions. He was a freelance journalist working in film, television, print and radio. His theatre columns commented on the use of stage as a social platform where government control had not altogether taken over the artists' voices. However, the banning of all independent newspapers and the jamming of radio stations curtailed his freedom to continue to make a living as a writer and free thinker. The lack of freedom of expression meant that continuing as an artist in Zimbabwe became impossible.

Nessim Zohar, actor and playwright, was born in Egypt in 1937 and emigrated to Israel in 1950. He started his acting career with the Haifa repertory company. Upon receiving a grant as most promising young actor, he lived for some years in New York where he attended the HB Professional acting workshop and studied film-making at NYU. During his long career, he has written and translated plays for the theatre and cinema. The story in the anthology is from his first collection of short stories *Aubergines and Okra* (2000).

Jennifer Langer is the founding director of Exiled Writers Ink and is joint editor of the literary/cultural magazine *Exiled Ink*! She edited *The Bend in the Road: Refugees Writing* (1999), *Crossing the Border: Voices of Refugee and Exiled Women Writers* (2002) and *The Silver Throat of the Moon: Writing in Exile* (2005), all published by Five Leaves. She has an MA in Cultural Memory from the School of Advanced Study, University of London. Her own poetry focuses on her identity as the daughter of German Jewish refugees and on political and human rights issues. She previously ran refugee education programmes in the Further Education sector in London.

Acknowledgements

I would like to express my thanks to the following individuals and organisations:

Judy Lown, with whom I had interesting discussions and who regularly produced fascinating articles from her bag!

Miriam Frank who kindly translated Juan Gelman's poems from the Spanish to the English.

Haya Hoffman and Hadar Makov-Hasson of The Institute for the Translation of Hebrew Literature, Israel.

Antony Polonsky for his kind assistance on exiled Polish Jewish writers. He is joint editor of the anthology, *Contemporary Jewish Writing in Poland,* edited by A. Polansky and M. Adamczyk-Garbowska (University of Nebraska Press, 2001).

George Grosman for granting permission to include his father's work.

Ilana Bakal with whom I had discussions about Mizrahi writers and who introduced me to the writer Samir Naqqash.

Sadok Masliyah, Samir Naqqash's friend, translator and advocate of his work posthumously.

Loolwa Khazzoom, editor of *The Flying Camel: Essays on Identity by Women of North African and Middle Eastern Jewish Heritage*, Seal Press (2003)

Max Sawdayee and his wife who welcomed me into their home.

Lawrence Joffe who provided me with information on South African Jewish exiled writers.

Lloica Czakis and Stella Maris who led me in the right direction regarding Latin American Jewish writers in exile.

Pam Lewis of Jewish Book Week.

Debra Kelly, University of Westminster.

Predrag Finci.

Branko Danon of La Benevolencija, London.

Sephardi Library, Lauderdale Road, London whose staff were extremely helpful.

Eveleen and Aldo Habib who gave me access to Aldo's testimony about Libya.

Maurice and Pat Maleh and Ted Nahmias of the Association of Jews from Egypt (UK) who kindly welcomed me to an evening of memory entitled "Our Time to Speak."

Soheila Ghodstinat who led me to Roya Hakakian.

Ziba Karbassi for introducing me to Ruhi Darakhshani.

Albert Memmi for granting me the privilege of translating his poetry into English for the first time.

Eugenia Farin Levy, President of the Jewish Community of Santiago de Cuba.

Previously published work, with gratitude to the authors and publishers

Farewell Baghdad by Eli Amir from *Farewell Baghdad*, *Mafriach Hayomim*, Am Oved, 1992 (published in Hebrew; previously unpublished and untranslated into English).

Imaginary Childhood by Shimon Ballas from *Down Town*, a collection of short stories, publ. 1979, translated by Ammiel Alcalay.

Poems by Mois Benarroch first appeared in *Take Me to the Sea*, ZePublished, 2002.

Poems by Erez Bitton and "Jerusalem and San'a", "I am the Daughter of Lot" and "Dish" by Bracha Serri first appeared in *Keys to the Garden: New Israeli Writing* by Ammiel Alcalay, City Lights Books, 1996.

Wedding Song by Farideh Goldin, Brandeis University Press, 2003.

Journey from the Land of No by Roya Hakakian, Three Rivers Press, 2004.

Moonlight on the Avenue of Faith by Gina Nahai, Scribner, 1999.

Diary extracts from *All Waiting to be Hanged* by Max Sawdayee, self-published.

Every Secret Thing by Gillian Slovo, Little, Brown, 1997

'Souvenir from Libya" by Gina Waldman first published in *The Flying Camel: Essays on Identity by Women of North African and Middle Eastern Jewish Heritage, edited by* Loolwa Khazzoom, Seal Press, 2003.

The Letters that Never Came by Mauricio Rosencof translated from Spanish by Louise B. Popkin, University of New Mexico Press, 2000.

Young Turk by Moris Farhi, Saqi, 2004.

'The Vote" by Shelley Weiner, from *The Slow Mirror and Other Stories*, ed. S. Lyndon & S. Paskin, Five Leaves, 1996.

Breaking Ranks by Ben Black, Lonely Planet Publications, 2001.

Delirium by Roohieh Darakhshani first appeared in *Mad*, Nazgol Publications.

Le Mirliton du Ciel by Albert Memmi, Juillard, Paris, 1990.